FORGETTING AND THE FORGOTTEN

Shawnee Books

FORGETTING
AND THE FORGOTTEN

A THOUSAND YEARS OF CONTESTED
HISTORIES IN THE HEARTLAND

MICHAEL C. BATINSKI

Southern Illinois University Press
Carbondale

Southern Illinois University Press
www.siupress.com

24 23 22 21   4 3 2 1

Cover illustration: Picketing Carter's Café. Courtesy of General Photograph Collection, Special Collections Research Center, Morris Library, Southern Illinois University Carbondale (cropped and colorized).

Library of Congress Cataloging-in-Publication Data

Names: Batinski, Michael C., 1943- author.
Title: Forgetting and the forgotten : a thousand years of contested histories
    in the heartland / Michael C. Batinski.
Description: Carbondale : Southern Illinois University Press, [2021] |
    Series: Shawnee books | Includes bibliographical references and index.
Identifiers: LCCN 2021018953 (print) | LCCN 2021018954 (ebook) |
    ISBN 9780809338375 (paperback) | ISBN 9780809338382 (ebook)
Subjects: LCSH: Minorities—Illinois—Jackson County—Historiography. |
    Social classes—Illinois—Jackson County—Historiography. | Marginality,
    Social—Illinois—Jackson County—Historiography. | Local history. |
    Jackson County (Ill.)—History. | Jackson County (Ill.)—Historiography. |
    Jackson County (Ill.)—Race relations—Historiography.
Classification: LCC F547.J2 B38 2021 (print) | LCC F547.J2 (ebook) |
    DDC 977.3/994—dc23
LC record available at https://lccn.loc.gov/2021018953
LC ebook record available at https://lccn.loc.gov/2021018954

For Ginny

CONTENTS

ILLUSTRATIONS

ABBREVIATIONS

JCHS	Jackson County Historical Society, Murphysboro, Illinois
LM	John A. Logan Museum, Murphysboro, Illinois
LPL	Abraham Lincoln Presidential Library, Springfield, Illinois
ML	Special Collections, Morris Library, Southern Illinois University Carbondale

PREFACE

ONE TIME WHILE standing on the bank of the Mississippi River at Grand Tower, I was asked the question: why wasn't I writing a history of this place? I remember that moment, meditating before the powerful waters pushing south. I do not remember my reply. I do remember fumbling for words and feeling discomfort. But I could not forget the question.

Slowly, often unawares, I began to address the question. As I listened to neighbors express deep, even passionate, interest in their local history, and as I pored through piles of local histories for my research on early America, I became fascinated with the people who recorded their local pasts, be they New Englanders or Midwesterners. I was beginning to answer the question but in a way I had not first imagined. What fascinated me was not what really happened but the people who cared enough to keep their local pasts and how they arranged their stories—in short something called historical consciousness.

But I had not yet returned to that riverbank. Instead, for personal reasons, I began this project with the keepers of the past in a small New England town. As I explored the ways that people in Deerfield, Massachusetts, had kept their past, I was learning two lessons. First, beneath the habits of remembering lay persistent habits of forgetting. That subject—forgetting—became the focus of this second project. Second, I came to understand that the sense of rootedness that inspired the people of this New England town had been stirring my imagination as well. Born in a nearby town, I had spent important portions of my formative years exploring that local past with my parents. And so I returned to the Mississippi riverbank in Jackson County, Illinois, where I had made my home for nearly half my life.

While satisfied with my inner motives, I moved forward always mindful of my method. I had once considered a comparison of four communities, but I realized that forgetting by its very nature led me to the hidden, the marginal experiences and muted voices at the edge of community and thereby dictated tight focus on a single place. At the same time, I had read enough local histories throughout the Midwest and the rest of the country to discern common cultural patterns embedded in those works.

As I explored, I continued to learn from a dear friend from graduate school. For decades Peter Carroll and I have been investigating the hidden niches in this land: the river towns on the Mississippi from Minneapolis to Natchez, small black communities in eastern Oklahoma, the rural world of the Dakotas and later Nebraska and Kansas, Pine Ridge and Medicine Wheel. While Peter lives the life of a poet and I remain a historian, I have learned from our talks and am satisfied that this story of forgetting is repeated throughout the Midwest and beyond.

ACKNOWLEDGMENTS

MORRIS LIBRARY AT Southern Illinois University Carbondale has been my home for decades. The staff has generously assisted me with my countless questions. I am grateful to the staff at Special Collections, whose knowledge of the manuscript treasures and of southern Illinois history became indispensable. David Koch guided me through the initial stages of research, pointing me to collections I may have otherwise overlooked. He will be missed. Aaron Lisec understood the project from the historian's perspective and, as he became acquainted with the collections, offered indispensable assistance and advice. Dona Bachman and Eric Jones at the university museum shared important material related to twentieth-century public history.

The Jackson County Historical Society contains a wealth of material. I thank the volunteer staff: Kenneth Cochran, Mike Brush, and Robert Morefield opened mountains of material and patiently indulged me as I asked questions they alone could answer. Across the street is the General John A. Logan Museum. Mike Jones is a model example of the public historian who has done so much to promote awareness of the local past among his neighbors. He and Laura A. Varner pointed me to a wealth of materials. The staff at the Carbondale branch of the Illinois Regional Archive Depository assisted my searches through numerous collections. I also thank the librarians at the Carbondale Public Library and Murphysboro's Sallie Logan Public Library. Lucia Kelso provided school records at the office of the Carbondale Community High School District 165.

In Springfield I relied on Glenna Schroeder-Lein at the Abraham Lincoln Presidential Library. Also at that library I regularly turned to Kathryn Harris, a Carbondale native, for advice not only on collections but also on life in her hometown. David Joens at the Illinois State Archives assisted at critical points in my research, as did Terrance Martin and Angela Goebel-Baine at the Illinois State Museum.

As always, the staff at the Newberry Library in Chicago have generously provided invaluable assistance and advice. Also helpful were the librarians at the manuscript division of the Library of Congress.

I was fortunate to find assistance from Darrel Dexter, whose expertise in the region's history is legend. Several friends shared important and essential details: Mary Sasse, Kathryn Harris, Joseph Brown, Coreen McDaniel, Shirley Portwood, Brad Skelcher, Paul Welch, and Brian Butler. Pepper Holder, Franklin Hamilton, Marilyn James, Helen Mataya Graves, Paul Hendrickson, and Melvin LeRoy Green MacKlin also shared details essential to this story. In the course of this research I came to appreciate Mark Wagner at the Center for Archaeological Studies at Southern Illinois University Carbondale.

Early drafts and versions of this project were read by Howard Allen, Ellen Nore, Kay Carr, and Shirley Portwood. I am thankful.

Two friends enlightened and encouraged me. Peter Carroll and I explored distant places in this country where together we discovered the complicated fabric of this society's history and culture. I learned much about friendship that has endured for half a century. Ginny Hoffman and I have been together in Jackson County for over three decades. We have watched the hawks nest, the sun set over the lake, the grasses turn brown in the autumn light. Here in Jackson County we have raised a family together. Ginny has encouraged me to stay true to myself. Each day I awaken to her trust and love. I continue to learn and be thankful.

FORGETTING AND THE FORGOTTEN

INTRODUCTION

FORGETTING LIES NEAR the heart of community life by sustaining a shared sense of identity. It is the silent and indispensable partner of remembering. By connecting their present to the past—by remembering—neighbors fix themselves in place and time, affirm who they are, and thereby create for themselves a usable past. In doing so they keep what they deem significant—useful—and sweep aside other portions of the past as irrelevant. But by forgetting, they make themselves vulnerable to experience and to dissenting voices on the edge. The process demands work and is forever meeting resistance. This is a story of the varieties of historical consciousness as they slide past and grate against one another in one Illinois county on the Mississippi River. But the story might be about any community in the Midwest.[1]

In short, this book pursues three themes: first, how beliefs of neighbors guide the creation of a dominant narrative; second, how the habits of forgetting lie embedded within this process; and third, how the dominant narrative and those lurking at the margins interact.

In the nineteenth century, no sooner had Jackson County been planted than storytellers and writers began to create a local history that became a dominant synthesis by the century's end and continued well into the next. Part one discusses that development. While dominant, this narrative remained fragile, always undermined not only by experience but also by weaknesses internal to the story. Thus vulnerable, the story rested on stubborn imagination. The story line began with origins—settlement, the domestication of wilderness—and developed with civilization's steady improvements. Implicit in that telling was whiteness—of white settlement even while native

1

and black voices could be heard telling their own and contradictory stories (chapters 1 and 2). Haunted by the native, the pastkeepers' narrative was susceptible to translation into an account of dispossession. Thus, their history required the erasure of eight hundred years. So, too, the whiteness of the story required concerted efforts to push the experience of black people to the edge. The story of settlement that carried the domestication of the wilderness could easily be turned into a tale of violence. The storytellers themselves carried family memories of bloodshedding that stretched continuously over generations from the Appalachian frontier, into the Illinois territory, and forward into the trans-Mississippi west. While settlement carried connotations of rootedness, experience suggested that this county was instead a waystation. Transient workers, farmers who tried their luck and disappeared, were integral to the county's life. The pastkeepers themselves knew; they could not suppress this wanderlust (chapter 3). The Civil War affected life in ways that did not comport with the prevailing historical consciousness (chapter 4). While the war provoked violent civil conflict within the county, forced whites to reconsider the whiteness of their community, and left veterans physically and emotionally scarred, the pastkeepers stubbornly perpetuated their narrative of whiteness and domesticity and thereby erased both a growing black presence and pervasive personal trauma. In the Gilded Age, this narrative achieved synthesis powerful enough to forget continuing violence in the form of labor and racial conflict (chapter 5).

These habits of forgetting were so deeply embedded in historical consciousness that the dominant pastkeepers were able to look at, even document, the dissonances without troubling themselves to reflect on their significance. Part two examines two themes in local historiography that illustrate the crippling effects on imaginations from the nineteenth century and well into the twentieth. These two themes, class (chapter 6) and race (chapter 7), were issues hiding in plain sight throughout. Even while historians sought to gloss over these subjects, they could not erase them. Laborers and capitalist investors, black people and American Indians appear momentarily, as if asides. Yet, even while espousing the ideal of a democratic history that included the commons, their imaginations froze. By comparison with race and labor, environmental degradation and gender remained tucked far below the surface, rarely troubling imaginations even momentarily. Neither subject posed a continuous challenge to historical imaginations until the late twentieth century and after the events depicted in this book. That class and race lay so near the surface, persistently challenging the dominant historical narrative, documents most clearly the efforts to forget.

This is the story of historical imaginations grating against one another, of power and its limits. The purpose of its telling is not to correct or to replace one rendering of the past, though such revision is implicit, but to recount the ways that competing historical perspectives, no matter their veracity, occupied the same space. The struggle for a usable past and community identity turns on beliefs and ideas. Whatever their limitations, they remain essential for understanding community life.

This project focuses on a small niche in the landscape and is informed by attending to the larger scene. A single place seemed appropriate to a study of these habits of forgetting. By its nature, what is forgotten is tucked away in dark corners and can be discovered by rooting through piles of obscure sources. While the interplay between habits of forgetting and remembering can best be understood by careful attention to one place, what transpired in Jackson County was repeated in countless locations throughout the region, indeed the nation. But for specific detail, other local histories mirror the narrative structure found in this county's historical awareness. Moreover, these histories of small places do bear a relationship to the dominant national narrative. On first glance, they include little of relevance to the national histories: they appear to be histories of places where nothing seemed to happen. Yet closer attention reveals an organization shared by both historiographies. Jackson County's white settler narrative served as corroboration of a spread-eagle national story. In recent years, Americans have come to question that story, and they peer into the dark corners of the past to discover the forgotten. That process of self-examination informs this work as well.

PART ONE

FORGETTING HABITS

Nineteenth-century Americans felt the itch to uproot themselves. Neighbors bade farewell to neighbors. While they rushed forward into the future, they looked backward wistfully. The image of the young man, standing with knapsack in hand, bidding farewell to mother, knowing that he would never cross the threshold again, haunted imaginations. Uprooted and rooted alike felt inspired to write histories of their communities.

Perhaps New England's local historians responded to the departures. But the uprooted ones felt the need to keep the past of places where they had recently planted themselves. Unlike their New England counterparts who proceeded with assurance that their past was deep, indeed embedded in the landscape, these aspiring historians gazed at the surveyors' maps with gridwork stamped on what seemed empty spaces. These possessors of the land, themselves newcomers, themselves rootless, sought to fill in the squares on the grid, to create a local past. Perhaps they too yearned for what they had left behind.

The surveyors' grid carried historical meaning. The squares turned the land into property, thereby establishing the foundation for planting settlements, for beginning civilization's flowering. Relying principally on experience and the testimony of neighbors, guided by a pervasive American historical consciousness, historians filled the spaces with a story that excluded—forgot—eight centuries. By the Gilded Age local historians had created a synthesis that rested on habits of forgetting voices of dissent, incongruent experiences, and disquieting subjects that was, in turn, reproduced with slight variation throughout the region.

CHAPTER ONE

DISPOSSESSING: LAND AND PAST

THE FIRST PEOPLE had been forgotten when the white settlers planted in Jackson County. The words they used to name themselves as well as the places that had been their villages and the burial grounds of their ancestors—these words had not been spoken for generations, even centuries. Tales of wonder that once grasped toward the mysteries of the cosmos and gave meaning to their lives were lost. Yet these people had not vanished from the land. Settlers were plowing up arrowheads, pieces of pottery, sometimes a skeleton as they farmed. They wondered. In the decade after the Civil War, the puzzles served as a starting point for Robert Allyn, the president of Southern Illinois Normal University, who chose to begin the county history with "the aborigines."[1] He may have chosen otherwise had he followed the example of neighboring county histories that opened with European arrivals.[2] Dillingers, Hensons, Kimmels, and Boons had written their names on the property deeds, census lists, and court orders and had recorded their genealogies in family bibles. Parents recited for their grandchildren the stories of their pioneer forebears and sang the songs they learned at the fireside. Educated opinion dictated history began with the European.

Yet these nameless ones haunted imaginations. Allyn acknowledged their presence and, though the evidence was scant, ventured to write them into the history. He had been listening to colleagues as they wondered over unearthed relics, sometimes a tablet with strange figures seemingly dancing, their faces raised to the heavens, or a stone pipe shaped in human form. There were the mounds west of Carbondale beyond Murphysboro and below the bluffs overlooking the Mississippi River; farmer Henry Vogel counted a cluster of eleven on his land with one rising twelve feet high and covering an area 190 by 130 feet. South of Carbondale, along the railroad track and just east of the Makanda depot, farmers and teachers gathered to ponder the meaning of a cluster of stones arranged methodically to make a wall three feet high and nearly three hundred feet long.[3] Some, believing treasure lay waiting to be found, tore the mounds apart. Others simply collected curiosities recovered from the earth. Whatever their reasons, they wondered at these relics of a vanished, nameless people and of a deep, elusive past.[4]

Allyn had recruited two young teachers, Cyrus Thomas and George French, who were drawn to the ancient relics. Though both were entomologists, they attended to the farmers' stories and took notes. French submitted preliminary reports to the Smithsonian Institute, one on the mounds and the results of preliminary excavations and another on the stone wall. Meanwhile, Professor Thomas had moved to Washington, DC, where he directed the Smithsonian's survey of mounds and artifacts in the eastern United States. For the Jackson County inventory he commissioned James Middleton to report on the Vogel mounds as well as two other earthen clusters. The summary catalog of "prehistoric works" included seventeen sites in Jackson County.[5]

Drawing of dancing figures on copper plate found south of Jackson County. "Report on the Mound Explorations of the Bureau of Ethnology," in *Twelfth Annual Report of the Bureau of Ethnology to the Secretary of the Smithsonian Institution* (Washington DC: Government Printing Office, 1894), 161.

Crouching warrior effigy pipe found in Jackson County. Courtesy of the Illinois State Archaeological Survey, University of Illinois, Urbana-Champaign.

Abundant and mute, these relics stoked scientific curiosity. Since the beginning of the nineteenth century, scientists had been discovering the imprint of the mound builders along the Ohio River Valley and had been speculating on their origins. At once aware of this scholarship and of the local discoveries, Allyn felt somehow that the story insisted to be told. Yet he ventured onto ground that shook with both intellectual and moral uncertainty. His section on the "aborigines" served as preface to the arrival of the American settlers that promised to give readers shining illustration of republican fulfillment. By convention, that story rested on deeply engrained belief in human progress. But those who told that story also heard an alternative and grating account that turned on bloodletting, removal, and dispossession. Jackson County was named to honor a president and famous Indian fighter who vowed to sweep large portions of the eastern tribes from their lands; residents of the county told that story of the dispossessed who had been herded across southern Illinois, had encamped for a winter just miles south of Carbondale, and had then been ferried across the Mississippi in the spring. The cries of protest registered by reformers like William Lloyd Garrison and Lydia Maria Child pricked consciences and challenged the conventions of history writing. When Allyn wrote, memory of expulsion and dispossession was revived with the mounting concerns over government

9

aggression against the plains Indians and the construction of a reservation policy. Soon Helen Hunt Jackson's *Century of Dishonor* and her novel *Rowena* would remind readers that removal and eradication of indigenous populations melded into a continuous national narrative.[6]

By attending to his "aborigines" and to his settler neighbors who had taken possession of this land, Allyn grappled with a pervasive moral dissonance. On the one hand, the vocabulary of progress, moral and scientific, came to him instinctively. He spoke as a New Englander who believed that the words of Ralph Waldo Emerson and John Greenleaf Whittier inspired the national character and that the example of abolitionist reformer Wendell Phillips served as a model of progressive leadership.[7] On the other hand, he had attended to the troubled and grating voices of antislavery leaders who also pressed the republic to realize that removal of the eastern Indian tribes compromised the nation's virtue. And so a history that might be written in a self-congratulatory manner and celebrated the memory of pioneer forebears collided with the ancient relics and nagging questions. Allyn addressed the issue when he reminded his neighbors that "those who occupy a land" had good reason to ask themselves, "Who were the first men on the ground?" Certainly, this people was deserving of "remembrance." The question became especially troubling "when the living nation has driven away the aborigines" even while recognizing them as the "objects of sympathy."[8]

Consciously, Allyn stepped onto troubled ground as he brought competing national narratives, one bright and one dark, together in Jackson County. He might instead have sidestepped this territory, as evasions were readily available to him. The sources were so few, he confessed to the reader, that "to describe" these people became near "impossible." "To write their history would be to set forth 'the baseless fabric of a vision.'" Though he had reason to set the story aside as lost forever, he did not. And so with no names, no events, none of the materials that made for written history, and only pieces of chipped stone and broken pottery and mounds of earth, he proceeded.

Allyn and his colleagues had joined a long-standing scholarly inquiry. Since the beginning of the century, scientists who struggled to understand the mounds wrestled with questions that cut to the core of their republican culture.[9] As they looked at the mute reminders of past civilizations, they might have wondered about the process of dispossession. Was it possible that the people who recently had been herded from their woodland homes on the eastern side of the Mississippi to the western prairies were the descendants of these people? Did that possibility turn the newly created republican identity into a sham? And what about deeply engrained faith in progress? What if the builders of these sites were the ancestors of present-day American Indians? If so, the differences in technological skills pointed to a process of degeneration. Such evidence then undermined confidence in history's direction.

The scholarly community provided reassuring answers.[10] The mound builders, wrote Ephraim Squier, were not the same people who occupied the continent when Europeans arrived. This ancient and gifted race, which had built a thriving civilization in the Mississippi and Ohio Valleys, had been driven out by warlike savages and fled to Central America where they built the Mayan civilization. Allyn's forbears had then encountered the descendants of the primitive hordes. The difference between the ancient people and the contemporary Indians of North America was so great that Squier argued for a separate creation. Others who measured cranial size as a means to differentiate race came to supporting conclusions. Although some experts like Henry Schoolcraft dissented, Squier's argument prevailed. Allyn need only have consulted William McAdams, who was beginning his research on the mound builders and would become president of the Illinois Natural History Society. The evidence, though murky, confirmed that this ancient, highly intelligent race "fell prey to neighboring barbarians."[11]

Guided by learned opinion, Allyn introduced his readers to this deep past. Evidence abounded that an ancient people once flourished on the lands now owned by farming families such as the Vogels and the Schlimparts. While the mounds and earthworks along the Mississippi Bottoms and the Big Muddy River, Crab Orchard and Cedar Creeks, the stone implements, the "idols of religious worship," and a "few personal articles of luxury" yielded insufficient information for telling their story, the labor demanded for moving such vast quantities of earth demonstrated that this was a "numerous population" directed by "well ordered customs" and thus capable of "acting in concert." These people were of a higher order than the shiftless "Red Men" who drove them out. Perhaps, he speculated, they fled south to build the Aztec civilization. "But no ingenuity has thus far obtained any key to this riddle."[12]

When Cyrus Thomas left Southern Illinois Normal University, he embarked on a career to confirm this explanation. In his years at the Smithsonian, remains of this deep past continued to be unearthed throughout the county— at Crab Orchard and Piney Creeks, at the Korando family farm, and at

Fountain Bluff overlooking the Mississippi River. Pictures of strange birdlike figures, serpentine creatures, and crosses in circles were found carved or painted on rock walls. To the north stood the mound clusters at St. Louis, and across the river the great mound at Cahokia. A short distance north, the people of Alton told stories of a great bird—a Piasa—carved in the bluffs overlooking the river. The first French explorers had gawked at the monstrous creature.

All was shrouded in conjecture and myth. Professor McAdams, while poring through the evidence, turned to oral traditions. His research demonstrated to his satisfaction that the stories told about the Piasa bird that once preyed upon the ancient peoples of the area were modern-day concoctions bearing no relationship to the beliefs of the original inhabitants. If ancient stories were found, he dismissed them summarily. Like "Mother Goose's stories" that revealed nothing about the "unwritten history of Europeans," the "myths" of the American Indian contained nothing of a verifiable past.[13]

* * *

THE SCHOLARS COULD not imagine using Mother Goose as a window into a specific historical era. That the answer to "Who did kill Cock Robbin?" echoed popular response to the fall of Sir Robert Walpole's government could not be considered any more than that the Jack and Jill rhyme might apply to Tudor court politics.[14] If they had listened more carefully, perhaps these scholars might have encountered the people who remembered that their ancestors had come from southern Illinois and who saw meaning in the ancient signs and carvings. To the west, across the Mississippi River, Osage keepers of tradition recounted that their ancestors had lived in the place where the Mississippi and the Ohio Rivers came together. To the north, the Winnebago elders told similar stories. These peoples had lived in this place nearly a millennium before it was called Jackson County. They had migrated before the French explorers wrote down the descriptions of the people they encountered. If the descendants had returned and stood before the art on rock walls depicting a birdlike human and serpents, they would discern significance. If they had walked along the rock overhangs where once their ancestors took shelter and had looked upon the springs that still seeped through the rock faces, they might have sensed the same sacred presence that their forebears had once revered.[15]

Perhaps, if the archaeologists studying the mounds and rock art had attended to their associates who were sitting with Osage and Winnebago memory keepers and were recording their stories, they might have recognized the connections. Cyrus Thomas's report on the mounds, with his speculations on their meaning, appeared in the same annual reports of the Smithsonian's Bureau of Ethnology that contained the work of these ethnographers. But the archaeologists were so entrapped in the debate over racial origins, were so fixed on verifying or rejecting Mayan connections to the south, or were so dismissive of oral tradition and its veracity that they did not pause to consider what lay before them. In the villages people were telling stories that echoed those once told around the rock carvings of Jackson County. James Dorsey transcribed and translated the words of Red Corn of the Osage. To illustrate his recounting of the Osage genesis, Red Corn showed him the map of the cosmos that was tattooed on his chest. In turn, Dorsey was allowed to sketch the map so that he might compare it with similar tattoos of other tradition keepers.[16]

The stories kept by Red Corn had changed over the generations since his ancestors had departed from the lands that became Jackson County. Tradition had been uprooted, transplanted, and modified to match the prairie world. While the memory keepers pointed to a distant region of origin, they did not remember the specific places at Fountain Bluff, the caves at Piney Creek. They had not followed the course of the Big Muddy River as it twisted slowly through the hills. When the ancestors migrated across the Mississippi River toward the western prairies, they reshaped their stories to fit their new environment and experiences. And as they listened to the European newcomers, they sometimes adapted and even incorporated elements of the strangers' explanation of the divine into their worldview. But essences echoed over generations. While one Winnebago discussed his traditions, he cautioned the ethnographer not to fret about forgotten pieces: "[W]hat is lost are the parts that are unimportant; those that are of real value have come down to us."[17]

Connections between past and present had become frayed. Certainly, the Osage and Winnebago memory keepers had not hunted the white-tailed deer on the ridge overlooking the Mississippi River or picked shellfish from the streambeds. Nor had their immediate forebears entered the cave overlooking the river where their ancestors had carved images of the birdman on the wall. They had forgotten how their ancestors had lived in the Mississippi Valley's forests and bottomlands. So, too, the scholars who puzzled over the bits of unearthed pottery and surveyed the mounds had only the vaguest inklings of the society that once flourished on these lands. When England's nobles forced King John to sign the Magna Carta, people had been thriving in communities along the streams that meandered sluggishly through the hills toward the Mississippi River, in the verdant marshy bottomlands, and on the banks of the great river. In this borderland where the vast prairie stretching from the far north gave way to forest, the people hunted deer, sometimes elk, and a variety of small animals such as squirrel, opossum, rabbit, and raccoon. Hunters returned to villages with an assortment of fowl—turkey, geese, ducks. Along the waterways they caught muskrat, beaver, and otter. They supplemented their diet with mussels and various fish, including carp, bass, and catfish. And the diet was enriched with varied nuts and wild plants.

The people gathered in settlements near the streams that laced the landscape. Along Crab Orchard Creek, which enters the county just east of Carbondale, small settlements abounded. Families hoed the earth and planted corn, beans, and squash and dug large pits for storing crops and nuts collected from the forests. Along Cedar Creek, which flows toward the Big Muddy, the people gathered for shelter beneath rocky overhangs. Families devised ways to erect shelters, first by planting single posts from which they constructed a roof and later by setting rows of posts for walls that they daubed with mud and thatch. In time, some sites became permanent. Generations of families became accustomed to burying their dead in common grounds; some were shaping the earth into mounds for burial. Some settlements grew into villages and, in turn, became focal points for outlying settlements.

Villages near the rich Mississippi bottomlands prospered and emerged as trading hubs linking the region to an extended exchange network. Chert quarried in nearby Union County provided the materials for local toolmakers and was exchanged with neighboring communities along a riverine network that extended to the Great Lakes. New leaders emerged by gathering the symbols of religious authority into their hands. Priests or shamans marked out centers that were used for religious purposes. They designated a cave tucked away amid the rocky bluffs overlooking the Mississippi Bottoms. In this dark place they carved representations of monstrous birdlike creatures and some birdlike humans, serpents with antlers, human hands, and

14

encircled crosses. As leaders acquired power, they mustered workers to build platform mounds—like those at the Vogel site—that they employed for ceremonial purposes.[18] Over generations, as these people buried their dead in the mounds and as they returned to the sacred places, they were creating meanings in the landscape. The dark crevices in the earth and the caves secreted away in the ridges over the river were designated as sites of awe, as entryways into mysterious worlds. Spring water seeping from rock surfaces evoked awareness of unseen sacred mysteries beneath. Over generations the elders returned with their young and recounted the stories. With each return they added the pictures of the birdlike humans and the ominous serpents. Out of custom and in ritual performance they carved signs, like the cross in circle and the bilobed arrows, into the rock walls. And these people designated certain special places by piling rocks together in long rows, as if demarcating locations for ritual. They carved their signs in trees as well. Through the carvings, wooden and rock, at Piney Creek, Peters Cave, and Fountain Bluff, they turned the landscape into a richly textured representation of the mysteries of the cosmos.

The villages with their outlying satellite settlements were connected to a network stretching north and south along the Mississippi River and up the Ohio. Their descendants would call the Mississippi the Ni-u to-ga, and they called themselves the people between rivers. The people at the Vogel mounds lived midway between two large urban complexes, one to the north at Cahokia and the other to the south at the confluence of the Mississippi and Ohio Rivers. In each, chiefs and priests consolidated the authority to build huge mounds and lesser works and to level the earth into large plazas. Together the large mounds and central plazas were laid out to align with astronomical sightings and thereby to represent the cosmic order. Woodhenge posts were set in the earth to align with celestial calculations. Atop the taller mounds were constructed large imposing buildings that served as temples or gathering places for the elite and that, in turn, worked to awe those who lived below. As this urban complex grew, the leaders directed the construction of large palisades encircling and protecting the community.

These peoples at Cahokia, Vogel, and Twenhafel, while not united in a single political system, were part of a large, diffuse cultural world that extended down the river to the Gulf and eastward into Alabama. Whether or not they could speak with one another, they recognized the same signs, be they encircled crosses or the birdlike humans, and understood similar

15

transcendent meanings. While traders moving through this riverine network brought practical commodities such as chert from southern Illinois to the Great Lakes region and returned with metals extracted from the far north, they also carried art objects laden with significances recognized by these scattered peoples.

And then these people left. Two centuries before the first Europeans arrived, they abandoned Cahokia. Yet their presence endured. American farmers puzzled over the remnants of pottery and the shadowy carvings in the cliff faces. Some scratched their own markings over the carvings as if to establish ownership. Scholars learned to recognize that the mounds and the carvings of the birdlike human were common to a region from the Ohio River southward. If the artifacts seemed to defy interpretation, the Osage and Winnebago memory keepers understood. They still made pictures of the birdman. While their stories had changed in detail over the generations, their tellings echoed their ancient ancestors. Thus, the Indian elders understood the connections in ways their Christian counterparts, when viewing their own ancient religious iconography, might feel distance and some bewilderment yet could discern primary meaning. Like their ancestors who lived on the banks of the Big Muddy, the memory keepers mapped the cosmos with an upper world divided into several levels, a watery lower world composed of its own dark realms, and the earth delicately balanced between the two. The elders pointed to places in the landscape along the Missouri River, the Ni-sho-dse in their tongue, that disclosed this cosmic order in microcosm. They told stories of the birdman, Morning Star, He-who-is-hit-by-deer-lungs, and He-who-wears-human-heads-as-earrings. If they had come to the cave at Piney Creek or the rock faces at Millstone Bluff, they might have with time recognized the signs signifying the upper world, where falcons and thunderers kept domain, or the references to a watery lower world, where dreaded serpent creatures lurked ever ready to disrupt the realm of humans above. They too understood that there were portals in the landscape leading from this world to others, that balances must be maintained in the eternal cycles of life, death, and rebirth and between the powers of these three worlds.

Looking to the skies, the Osage, much as their ancestors had, saw layered spheres where celestial powers dwelt.[19] The creator Wa-kon-da called into being all that was visible and all that was invisible. According to the tradition keepers, he lived in the sun. Each morning believers awoke to sing the song of greeting. Wa-kon-da's son Hon-ga A-hui-ton is the Morning Star who first appears to announce his father's coming and then vanishes. Each day his coming and going represents the powers of fertility and rebirth, the cycles of birth and death and birth again. On earth he appears as the falcon or the birdlike human. Accordingly, the ancestors who once lived on the banks of the Ni-u to-ga depicted this birdman on rock walls. This was a great sign of power. So, too, Winnebago elders told stories of Morning Star whom they remembered as Red Horn.

Osage and Winnebago told the story of Morning Star's death and rebirth. Once, the Winnebago recounted, a band of giants attacked the village of Morning Star, sometimes known as He-who-wears-human-heads-as-earrings.[20] Finally, Morning Star, with his warrior companion Turtle, challenged a giantess in a series of deadly competitions, with the loser's head at stake. First, they met in a round of ball games. After several contests, the giantess was hotly pursing Morning Star until she looked at his ears. The heads hanging from his ears stuck out their tongues and winked at her. Then the giantess burst into laughter and lost the match. Several contests followed, one of dice, another with bow and arrow, and Morning Star and Turtle continued victorious. Then Morning Star agreed to a wrestling match. This time the giantess prevailed. Morning Star and his companion were killed. The giants took Morning Star's head to their village in triumph and hung their trophy from a pole before the lodging of their chief.

Then the light went out, and all was cloaked in darkness. But Morning Star had two sons. When they grew to their full strength, the heroes set out in search of the giants' village. "After walking for some time," they found their father's killers and slew them all. On finding Morning Star's head, the older brother gave it to the younger: "Take it to your mother, and tell her to lie in bed with it." She refused, however. So the brothers took the head and placed it in their lodge. The next morning they returned to find their father made whole again. And then, according to the storytellers, the light was reborn.

When Morning Star stood at the edge of the skies and looked down, he beheld a dark and watery lower world. Like its celestial counterpart, the underworld was a many-layered domain but teeming with frightful creatures.[21] Within the waters lurked monstrous winged serpents. So said the Osage. The Winnebago described panthers with dreadful horns. No matter the difference, both looked at a turbulent, threatening realm possessed by menacing powers ever ready to wreak havoc and death upon humans.

When the ancestors lived on the great river, Ni-u To-ga, they pointed to the dark, churning waters with foreboding. They told stories of the unfortunate ones who had been pulled beneath the waters never to be seen again. They assembled at their sacred places and carved representations of the deadly serpents on the rock walls. They did so habitually in the rocky bluffs and along streams feeding into the great river at Piney Creek and farther south into the Ohio River near Millstone Bluff. To the north along the great river, the people carved into the rock walls a huge image of the winged monster with fearsome horns who lurked below. When passing by the carving, they offered presents to propitiate the creature.

From this underworld came the powers that brought illness and wellness, death and fertility. The universe was held in balance, turning on a celestial axis. The powers visible in the stars were kept in equilibrium with the forces below. The rotations were visible in the night skies with the coming and the going of Morning Star. At night the sky dwellers disappeared beneath the horizon's rim and into the world of darkness. And then the inhabitants of the underworld emerged in the night sky. There was the dreaded serpent. In the warm summer months the people pointed to its frightful presence in the southern skies but dared not tell the stories about its powers until it had vanished during the cold winter nights. It was the task of humans to keep the cycles rotating in order and thereby to maintain the three worlds in their proper alignment. And some uniquely empowered humans—shamans— performed the rituals necessary for mediating between the worlds.

The keepers of the past told the stories of how their ancestors, the Little Ones, had descended from the skies.[22] One time the Little Ones had existed as souls without bodies—like twinkling lights in the starry heavens. And the sky dwellers conferred: "The Little Ones have become persons. . . . Should not the Little Ones go below to become a people?" And they went to the god of day, the god of night, Evening Star and then Morning Star, "who sitteth in the heavens." Each listened and made it so that the little people had bodies. And Morning Star said: "When the Little Ones go below and become a people, the Little Ones shall find in me the means of reaching old age." Then Falcon guided the people down through the heavens' four levels. Still farther did they descend toward the watery world. But there was no land for the people to set their feet. The great and sacred Elk, when told that "it is not possible for the Little Ones to dwell as a people upon the surface of the water," threw himself upon the waters. "And the depth of the waters began to lower." Four times he did this. "And he made the land of the earth to appear, to become dry and habitable." Then he made the winds of the earth, "my breath of life" and source of good health. From his hairs he made the grasses, from his backbone the ridges of the earth, from his horns "the streams of the earth."

These were the Sky People who came to earth. Their children lived along the waters of the Ni-u to-ga at places that would later be named Vogel Mound and Fountain Bluff. Regularly they entered the dark cave at Piney Creek, where they pecked out and painted their representations of the cosmos and their place within it. As these ancients watched Morning Star appear, disappear, and appear again, they witnessed the cycles of birth, death, and rebirth and the upper, lower, and middle worlds turning in wondrous equilibrium. At the center stood the sacred tree that stretched its branches up into the heavens and pushed its roots down into the murky world beneath. Fixed at the stationary North Star, this sacred axis kept the upper, middle, and lower layers in harmonious rotation. Like the Osage storytellers on the Oklahoma plains, they understood that at night Morning Star descended into the lower world, and the serpentine powers of the lower world appeared in the darkness above to descend again on the ascension of Morning Star.

Religious leaders pointed to crevices in the earth that served as entry to the lower world and to waters seeping from the rocks that signified magical presences below. The shaman, endowed with shape-shifting powers to move from human to animal form, could pass through these entryways into the lower world. There he did combat with the serpent so that he might gain the powers necessary for good health. Above in the sky another portal opened. With death, the soul took leave of the body and began its passage toward the heavens.[23] The rock carvers on the river Ni-u To-ga represented the pathway by the image of the outstretched hand with an eye gazing from the palm. In preparation for the journey, the living buried the body often facing south with implements and supplies. Soon after, the soul departed on the journey toward the edge of the earth. On coming to earth's end, the soul set up camp and waited for the opportune moment when the heavens would come close enough to make the perilous leap across and continue on the path of souls. The living pointed to that place where the stars came together to represent a hand. Just at dawn, only during the winter months and only briefly, the constellation appeared and then dropped below the earth's edge into the watery world below. This was the moment for the soul to jump. On making the leap successfully, the soul encountered several trials—one with a ferocious dog and another with the frightful great serpent from the underworld. In time the traveler came to the village of the ancestors. On a starry night, the living could trace the path that their forebears had followed and one day they too would walk.

While reading the cosmic mysteries, these people expended great energy to represent that understanding by shaping the earth into mounds and carving their sacred symbols into rock walls. Not far south of Vogel Mound, they had been gathering for generations at a remote rocky ravine (Millstone Bluff) overlooking a stream that flowed into the Ohio River.[24] There they selected three adjoining rock faces for depicting the cosmos—one for the upper world, another for the lower, and between the two their own middle world. There they painted and carved the traditional symbols evoking the powers that shaped their lives. On the face designating the upper world, they represented the famous birdlike human or Morning Star who possessed life-giving powers and the warrior's courage and strength. At the opposite end of the triptych, they carved images of the horned serpents who wielded sinister domain over the lower realms. Between the two ends, the artists rendered the human world where the powers from beneath and from above came together with the Sky People; on that rock face falcons and serpents mingled with human images. The people returned to this place regularly, each time adding the traditional geometric signs signifying the four points of the universe held in equilibrium.

The birdman was present everywhere. Artists at settlements near the Vogel Mound had created his image on the rock walls at Piney Creek, Peters Cave, and Fountain Bluff. Traders from afar brought a copper plate engraved with his likeness. Like the people at Millstone Bluff, the artists who gathered in the caves at Piney Creek pecked out their representations of the many layered cosmic order replete with horned serpents, humans, birdman, and encircled crosses. While gathering at these places, the people reminded themselves of the transcendent and ever-present powers that brought birth and death, chaos and order into their lives. There they saw depicted the shape-shifting shamans who ventured into the other worlds and there battled to keep the earth whole. Artists pecked out the images of boats making celestial passage to the birdman's world.

Gathering at Piney Creek to gaze upon the numerous pictures that their forefathers had made, the Little People acquired a sense of themselves rooted deeply in place and time. As they passed by dark crevices in the ravines, they remembered their fathers describe the monsters lurking underground. On the death of kin, they took the body to the same place where the ancestors were buried. Sometimes, while scraping the earth away, they encountered a skeleton that they recognized as an ancestor, and the storytellers recounted the descent that the more distant ancestors had made from the sky to this place. When erecting their houses, they chose the sites where their forebears had once lived.[25]

The children of the Little Ones who came from the sky were reminded of their origins when they tilled the earth. At times they found stone implements left behind. Perhaps the maker had fashioned the chert in a foreign manner, and the new owner might reshape the tool according to his preference. If at times a river washed away a bank revealing the skeletal remains of an unknown creature, they interpreted this discovery as the remains of a monster from the underworld. Accordingly, a human skeleton was an ancestor.

Though the priestly leaders and the shamans mustered their powers to maintain this world, the Sky People felt life along the river becoming perilous. Violence between settlements grew bloodier. Increasingly, the beleaguered peoples invoked the birdman's powers to sustain the warrior and empower him against the enemy. Threatened communities shrank in size, and the spheres of protective palisades continued to contract as they were rebuilt after each skirmish. Slowly the city at Cahokia dwindled away, and trees grew over the mounds where once the chiefs had lived.

The Sky People moved westward across Ni-u To-gaup and up the Ni To-ga.[26] In time, with each generation's passing, the memories faded of bluffs and rock faces where they had once assembled and the marshes where they had hunted. Soon the memory keepers could only recall their origins somewhere near the confluence of the two great rivers. They could still tell the stories of the birdman and of the ancestors and could map the cosmos in its several layers, much as their forebears who had lived along the Mississippi River had done. Reference to He-who-is-hit-by-deer-lungs or He-who-wears-human-heads-as-earrings may have evoked different meanings. Yet the essences endured, remaining intact enough so that the descendants of the Sky People on the Ni To-ga could make connections with the carvings and paintings their ancestors had left behind in Jackson County.

* * *

WHEN THE PEOPLE with property deeds to Jackson County worked the land, they routinely stumbled upon reminders of the Sky People. The stone pipes, pottery, stone tools, burial mounds, skeletons, and carvings on rock faces stirred imaginations. Robert Allyn was not alone in his speculations. For generations the troubling questions nagged at the edges of community consciousness: Who were these people? Had Jackson County's property owners been complicit in the stealing of land? To assuage consciences, the property owners persisted in reciting the answers that had satisfied Allyn when he wrote his explanation of "the aborigines." A generation later, George Washington Smith was teaching a similar lesson in his history classes at Southern Illinois Normal University and discussing it in his multivolume history of the region. The archaeological evidence, he observed, demonstrated that a people "of considerable advancement in civilization" had once occupied this region and built the mounds. But this nameless people had been chased off by savage invaders, whose descendants were the Algonquin-speaking peoples of the Illinois confederacy. The people that European explorers first encountered were, in contrast to the mound builders, lazy and benighted. Smith needed few words to characterize these people. They managed their affairs by a primitive "tribal form of government." They lived in rude "temporary shelters called wigwams" and sustained themselves principally by hunting and fishing. Some tried their hand at growing crops, but their abilities were "indifferent." Accordingly, "they had an indefinite notion of a future life."[27]

These Indians of Jackson County, Smith lectured his students, had earned a reputation for their bloodthirsty "savagery." For the sake of progress, their removal became a necessity. Writing in the wake of the Spanish American War, Smith did not see reason for considering the moral implications of government policy directed against the American Indian. While some Americans may have indulged themselves in sympathy for the plight of these vanishing peoples, the professor assured his readers and students with the belief that the process was natural and inevitable.

Without reflection, Professor Smith drew upon deeply embedded conventions of his culture and joined with his peers and neighbors in silencing the voices of the past. The artifacts remained ever mute. Smith knew storekeepers, farmers, and doctors who made it a hobby to collect artifacts.

As their acquisitions increased, the collectors sorted their treasures for display according to size and shape and sometimes into balanced symmetrical designs of their own making. At once they were fascinated and unable to imagine contexts and meanings.

The university in Carbondale had established a museum, and the curators were making room for the local curiosities.[28] Their displays followed long-standing conventions. Since the beginning of the century museums had created cabinets of curiosities in which they arranged the exotica collected by the agents of European expansion. Art from the South Seas and stuffed animals from the tropics were offered to visitors in the hopes of expanding horizons. Meanwhile, as interest in the local past grew, museums acquired housewares from pioneer days, clothing once worn by the ancestors, and the unearthed relics from a vanished Indian past such as arrowheads, pottery, baskets, and even moccasins. Arrowheads were arranged in glass cases with a stuffed jaguar and peacock feathers nearby.

According to convention, the curators in Carbondale collected and displayed curiosities while paying scant attention to interpretation. The objects, be they stuffed animals from South America, unusual rocks, specimens of coral, or stuffed birds, were kept locked behind glass doors with brief labels of identification but without explanation of context. Visitors discovered a "coral cabinet" in the same room with a randomly arranged "animal cabinet." With these curiosities stood the boards of mounted arrowheads and rows of pottery, some from Central America and some from Jackson County. All was curiosity and nothing more.

At the same time Wa-tse-mon-be of the Sky People became convinced that a museum was necessary if the young were to know their past. His museum would not only preserve the "relics" from the past but also keep the stories that rendered meaning. As he and other elders from the several Osage clans mused over their future, they dreaded that time when tradition keepers would be gone and no one would tell the genesis stories to the young. So, too, Mon-zhon-a-ki-da, Guardian of the Land, looked ahead to a dark future when all would be forgotten.[29] Then an ethnographer commissioned by the Smithsonian arrived with a proposal to record the stories and the songs for posterity. Mon-zhon-a-ki-da, Wa-tse-mon-be, and other elders listened but with caution. Would it be better that the stories be forgotten than becoming possessions of others? Some were loath to give away the ancestors' words. Others agreed reluctantly. Mon-zhon-a-ki-da began to recite the traditions, and so did Wa-tse-mon-be. Some began and then stopped suddenly. Tse-zhin-ga-wa-da-in-ga agreed to chant his clan's songs. Then he died suddenly and mysteriously in a house fire. Neighbors said that he brought disaster on himself for "giving" his songs to the ethnographer.

* * *

GUIDED BY HABITS of belief deeply embedded in his culture, Robert Al-lyn, like his historian cohorts throughout the region and nation, was able to cram evidence of a native past into a box that prevented imaginations from speculating on its significance or implications. Voices were silenced, connections to the present severed. What remained was a pile of curiosities devoid of meaning. History from Allyn's perspective began with the arrival of his people. The foundation for a white settler narrative had been laid in a few brief paragraphs. Reinforcing this perspective were equally powerful beliefs that enabled local pastkeepers to glide over, to forget, living memories of the Native Americans who occupied this place on the arrival of the first white settlers. That interpretive device came with other boxes, squares drawn by surveyors on the map at the county's creation.

CHAPTER TWO

SQUARING THE CIRCLES,
FILLING THE SQUARES

DURING THE WINTER of 1810, the Indians at Sand Ridge watched a band of strangers trudge methodically across the frozen bottomlands that stretched below the great ridge overlooking the Mississippi River.[1] While one held the end of a length of chain, his partner walked forward with the other end in hand. They paused and then repeated the ritual again and again until the sun set. While the surveyors drew their chain measure forward to mark an invisible line across the land, others with axes blazed a path ahead. Their leader recorded his observations: the timber—oak and hickory—was plentiful; the soil was rich and promised a bounteous future for farmers who would come. He had been talking to the few squatters on the land who had given this place its name: Sand Ridge. They pointed to a large hill they had named Big Hill. With his coordinates designating the location, the leader noted an "Indian Town on the East." Then they moved on.

This moment of encounter on the frozen bottomlands would be lost—forgotten—if it were not for this brief note buried among the mundane jottings in a surveyor's field notes. The chainmen Isaac Glen and George Roswell—both illiterate—scratched their marks in the notebook. Then they vanished. The axmen who had cleared their trail remained nameless shadows. The surveyor wrote no more than his assignment required—the soil and timber resources that might guide future settlers. He too disappeared. And the villagers watched silently. Whatever their impressions, they left no record. Soon they too would disappear. What remains is a map with the surveyors' straight lines running north and south, east and west. Yet beneath the map's grid lies this moment of encounter that marked the end of one history and the start of another. That map with its squares stands at the front of the 1878 county history, immediately after Robert Allyn's cursory discussion of the American Indian antecedents and before the longer narrative of the settlers who came. It serves as a bridge between Indian time and European time. But it also covers over the process of transition. The indigenous Americans at Sand Ridge are erased, forgotten.

The act of mapmaking represented a meeting of two historical experiences with different understandings of this land and the significance of that moment. The villagers knew themselves as the Kaskaskia people. They carried a history with them.[2] They remembered when they came to the west bank of this muddy river and planted a village, and when the French had recently claimed this land and named the river La Vase. In their native language the river may have been "r8caki8i." But they told the American newcomers who came with the surveyors—pioneers like Benningsen Boon's father—that the river was called by its French name. Soon Boon and his neighbors translated that name to the Big Muddy. The names were changing. While the Americans took the Kaskaskia word for the "Missisipi8i" River to make it their own, they were filling the squares in the surveyors' empty gridwork with their own names—Sand Ridge and Big Hill. They were taking possession. Soon they were fixing their own names to the land—Walker's Hill, Jones Ridge. They pinned their own imaginings to the land—Devil's Backbone and Devil's Oven—or their own associations—Rattlesnake Creek and Swallow Rock. As the population grew they filled in the names of settlements—Brownsville, the first county seat, and Murphysboro, the second.

These small acts of naming advanced the process of dispossession and possession. Cumulatively they represented deep differences in understanding this small world and in telling its story.[3] The Kaskaskia by tradition mapped the land in personal terms—distances by the days a person walked from one point to another, places recalled for the stories associated with them. They remembered places where they had buried their ancestors. By habit they mapped the world they knew with circles. The individual stood at one such imagined circle looking toward the rising sun. The other directions were designated by the right hand or left and by the back directed toward the point on the horizon where the sun set. Circles represented spiritual wholeness, power; they designated sacred places on the earth.

The European stood on the same piece of earth but mapped it with squares. The survey with its regular lines drawn invisibly across the land marked that place so that it might be identified by persons who had never walked upon that ground, never heard its stories. The stories were irrelevant. The place became an abstract numerical coordinate that any persons, be they speculators in land in Philadelphia or London, could identify. And with these two mappings came contrasting understanding of this place in time. To explain the arrival of the surveyors, the Kaskaskia told their stories that turned on acts of dispossession by distant imperial forces. The surveyors and the people they represented far away talked about that piece of earth as something called property, identified by strange lines and numbers that could be bought and sold by strangers. They looked at the grid as the way to secure land and happiness for future generations who might move west. The squares, the numbers, promised fulfillment of something called a republican dream. They had no past—only a present and a glowing future. For the villagers at Sand Ridge the invisible squares were boxes squeezing them relentlessly, irresistibly, from this place.

* * *

IN WATCHING THE strangers with the chain, the villagers were witnessing the closing episode in a history that stretched back four centuries. They were newcomers to this place. The names of peoples who had once lived here and the stories they had told had been forgotten. What these villagers knew rested on disjointed fragments of recent memories. They likely recalled the stories of a time a century earlier when their ancestors the Kaskaskia had lived in a great camp to the north on the Illinois River. Then they were part of the Illiniwek Confederacy that had flourished over a region stretching from the Illinois River and along the Mississippi River to the Ohio River. If these people stopped to ponder that Illiniwek meant "original people," they sensed somehow their disjointed condition—that their past on the Illinois River was disconnected from their lot at Sand Ridge.[4] By naming themselves "original," the Illiniwek, like the Sioux to the north, claimed a special identity rooted in time at the earth's creation and in the place where they had come to the earth. So their fathers had listened to the stories from their fathers and now tried to tell their children. But by retelling the origin stories, they reminded themselves that they had become a people without roots.

When they dug in the earth, they discovered remnants of an earlier people that had once lived on the banks of the Big Muddy. Perhaps they, like other American Indian peoples, were tempted to claim the skeletons as their ancestors. Yet memory of life on the Illinois River was too vivid to permit such a leap. If they had looked closely at the strangers' survey map, they would sense that they did not fit.

It was the brokenness of their stories that made the Sand Ridge villagers one with a succession of now nameless people who had drifted into and out of this region like shadows flitting across the landscape, leaving little mark of their presence. For four centuries this place had seen a succession of such wanderers. Societies had formed and then reformed, appeared and then vanished to be replaced by others. For the most recent arrivals, the Kaskaskia, the broken shards of pottery and portions of human skeletons remained mute, silent, seemingly impenetrable. Yet at some level their recent experience put them in touch with these nameless presences and reminded them that they stood poised on a precipice. This shadowy story of past transients in time was their own.

This history, whispered only in oral traditions of people long absent, began when the mound-builder chiefs felt power slipping from their grasp.[5] No longer could they command the workers to build or maintain the mounds. Their communities dwindled in numbers. One by one the chiefdoms collapsed. When the people at Cahokia abandoned their urban center in the fourteenth century, smaller complexes continued around Twenhafel and Millstone Bluff. Trade networks from the Great Lakes to the Gulf of Mexico, though frayed, did not vanish entirely. While increasing numbers crossed the great river and moved west and north, others remained often in ever-smaller settlements tucked away in the hinterlands.

Perhaps the world of the mound builders had declined because growing populations taxed the environment's ability to support them. Perhaps the exodus was spurred by environmental change. Decline or exodus, however, did not mean a complete emptying of the region. With the waterways—the Mississippi, Illinois, and Ohio Rivers—the soils, and the forests, this land provided well. Small communities settled into a seasonal migratory cycle. In the spring they planted themselves in the bottomlands where the women cultivated fields of corn, beans, and squash and the men fished the rivers and hunted deer, elk, and buffalo. In the winter, they broke into small bands and moved into the interior in search of game. With the thaws, they returned to the bottomlands to hunt migratory birds flying north and begin the cycle of planting.

Environmental change brought new opportunities and new people. The climate had been growing warmer at the end of the mound-building era, and the prairie grasslands to the west were spreading eastward into Illinois.[6] The buffalo followed, and people who once relied on agriculture became increasingly dependent on the large herds. Strangers appeared. The Oneota migrated westward and southward toward the Mississippi River. And other Siouan speakers, the Winnebago and the Iowa, were moving into and through the river region in pursuit of the herds.

A swirl of peoples was forming and reforming around the larger Mississippi region. The Algonkian-speaking Illiniwek were leaving the Ohio River area. Moving northward, they brushed against the emerging Iroquois Confederacy, then turned westward along the southern shores of the Great Lakes and toward the Illinois River. In their search for food they clashed with the Winnebago and Fox and became enduring enemies. And as they entered the Illinois River region, one group, the Kaskaskia, settled on the river near Starved Rock. As their numbers increased, the Great Village emerged to become the center of their world. Other groups, including the Michigamea, followed the great river southward past the Ohio River. From the Great Village, this region around Sand Ridge seemed a shadowy zone sparsely settled by transitory populations where raiding parties confronted one another.

The Illiniwek—the Kaskaskia with the Cahokia, Peoria, Tamaroa, Michigamea—told the stories that they were the "original people" and thereby took possession. When they encountered the great mounds, there was no one who remembered the names of the people who had built them or the stories that gave meaning to these places. On occasion they unearthed the burial places of these forgotten people and claimed them as their ancestors. And so to root themselves in this landscape, they buried their own atop the forgotten people. Sometimes they lived on the same ground where the earlier people had lived. Thus, they connected themselves to the ancients and made both the land and its past theirs.

On encountering ancient carvings on rock walls, they felt the presence of transcendent mystery. What the images of the birdlike men or the horned serpents once signified they did not know. The legends of Morning Star, the Little Ones, and the water monsters had been forgotten or had been carried across the river. Instead, this new "original people" filled the silences with new stories.[7] Oftentimes while gathering in the same places where the ancient ones had once sat, the storytellers recounted the origins and workings of their world. Kitche Manitou created all. The Great Spirit made rock, water, fire, and wind and breathed into each its unique essence. As if echoing the

29

stories once told by the mound builders, the storytellers recounted that moment when the first human descended from the sky world but could find no earth on which to rest her foot. When the creatures dwelling in the watery world below looked up, they took council with one another; Turtle swam to the surface so that she might stand on his back. Thus the earth was made. While the Great Spirit had withdrawn to the realm of the rising sun, the process of creation continued. The storytellers explained death and the afterlife. They recounted the time rabbit willed that the earth be kept in perpetual light. But possum protested that darkness be given its time. They argued, and possum struck rabbit in the mouth, thus leaving him and all his children with a split lip. And because possum prevailed, light and dark shared the world together.

Rabbit would transform himself into human shape, a figure known as Manabozho, sometimes as Nanabush. Sometimes trickster, sometimes hero, he lived with the animals, befriended some, and matched wits with others. One day he encountered Big Skunk. "Come," said Big Skunk to Manabozho, "I will teach you how to kill those who enter your lodge." Skunk then instructed him how to fart. So delighted was Manabozho with this talent that on his way home he used it to blow down a large tree and shatter a boulder to dust. Once home he learned to use his power well. When a herd of moose entered his lodge, he farted and killed them all at once. Thus his family had enough meat for the long winter.

Manabozho did battle with the evil ones. Once his brother who assumed the shape of a wolf had been caught unawares by monsters lurking in the deep waters and had been pulled into the murky depths to his death. Seeking revenge, Manabozho went to the water's edge and took the shape of a tree stump. He waited patiently until the monsters came ashore. When they were asleep, he resumed his shape and with his bow and arrow slew them all. According to the storytellers, Manabozho's brother went to the land of the dead where he protected departed souls from harm.

While fixing their stories to this riverine world, the Illiniwek listened to reports from the south about strangers who had appeared suddenly and who had left the land soaked in blood. In the mid-1500s, traders recounted their tales of fearsome men riding strange animals. These conquistadors, inspired by their predecessors who had laid waste to Aztec society, had cut a bloody swath across the south in search of treasure. They had slaughtered entire communities without mercy. In their wake they left disease that ravaged the survivors. Then they vanished. Communities collapsed, and powerful chiefdoms disintegrated. Meanwhile, other Spanish adventurers appeared from the west determined to find riches whatever the cost in lives. They too disappeared, but they were not forgotten. The survivors told the stories to their children and grandchildren. Generations later, when these strangers reappeared, they were remembered for their bloody deeds.[8]

The Illinois people listened to the stories. But because the strangers did not penetrate north of the Ohio River, the stories may have seemed remote and were forgotten. A hundred winters later they heard similar accounts, this time of men coming from the north and east. The reports grew frequent and more vivid. Soon the people of the river encountered these foreigners who came from Quebec to secure the French king's hold on the continent's midsection. One afternoon in the late summer of 1673, the people of the Great Village received a small party of Frenchmen led by a missionary and an explorer-adventurer paddling down the river. The next day they listened to Father Marquette tell the story of Jesus and his sufferings on the cross. He later returned to build a mission. Fur traders came and established trading posts along the great river. Farmers arrived and planted a community on the riverbank at a place they named Kaskaskia.

By this time, the world of the Kaskaskia had undergone profound alterations. With the coming of the Canadian traders, the local people attached themselves to a fur trade that drew them into an economy with Montreal at its center. New goods and technologies became commonplace. Family and community life changed as French *voyageurs* joined with native women and formed families. And so fundamental beliefs mixed as the indigenous people gathered around the missionaries to hear the promises of salvation. Perhaps they did not abandon their ancestral beliefs as quickly as Father Marquette had hoped. While still telling the stories of Nanabush, they opened their traditions to accommodate the image of Christ on the cross.

Meanwhile, the people of the Great Village were absorbing the shock of continual and brutal wars to the east. The conflicts for empire among Europeans and American Indians assumed myriad patterns. While Indians watched the French and British combat for control of the continent, the tribes joined with one side or the other and against other tribes in pursuit of what they believed to be their interest. Entire societies from the Atlantic to the Mississippi were decimated by warfare or ravaged by disease. Survivors sought refuge with other tribes. Those who appeared for the moment more powerful asserted control over the weaker ones or adopted them. Thus tribal identities were shifting.

When the missionaries arrived, the Kaskaskia appeared to be a thriving people numbering more than five thousand. The French thus named the community the Great Village. While the villagers began to open themselves to the words of the missionaries, they attended to reports from the east of the bloody devastations. The powerful Iroquois Confederacy, seeking control of the fur trade, launched a series of bloody attacks on their neighbors that reached progressively westward. The survivors fled toward the Mississippi River, some to the Great Village. By incorporating these strangers, the village became, like other indigenous communities on the continent, an amalgamation of refugees. Meanwhile, Iroquois raiding parties came ever closer and in 1680 fell upon the Great Village and laid it to waste. By the turn of the century the Kaskaskia had abandoned their Illinois River habitat, migrated south along the Mississippi, and reestablished themselves nearby the French farming community that had appropriated their name for its own.

The transplanted Kaskaskia had become a mixture of refugees. Belief systems and memories of the past changed shape and, bit by bit, were forgotten. Inherited religion was stretched to make room for the Blessed Virgin, the Immaculate Conception, and the Christ. Children born to French fathers and Indian mothers were baptized by the priests and given French names. While calling themselves Kaskaskia, the name assumed new meanings with each passing generation. The process of cultural mixing became more complex when they encountered the Africans in French Kaskaskia.[9] These people came as slaves. Some had escaped and were adopted by Native American communities. Others, living as property of the French, grew in numbers so that they constituted a third of French Kaskaskia. Some mixed with native Kaskaskians. They came into this world with memories and beliefs from Kongo, Senegambia, and Benin. And even while the appearance of some in the parish baptismal records might confirm the priest's hopes for the obliteration of inherited beliefs, evidence of African folkways persisted.

Uprooting themselves, the Kaskaskia had not escaped distant empire. Slave traders in South Carolina were offering good prices for captives, and indigenous tribes, most conspicuously the Choctaw and the Chickasaw to the south, were making themselves into slave hunters. Raiding parties crossed the Ohio River into Illinois territory. In turn, the Illiniwek listened to their French neighbors who encouraged them to raid nearby tribes for captives.

Meanwhile English merchants in Philadelphia, yearning to extend their trade into the midcontinent, enlisted American Indian allies to attack French settlements such as Kaskaskia on the Mississippi River.

At mid-eighteenth century the Kaskaskia felt the French and British wars coming closer.[10] Though diminished, they still enjoyed the reputation to command both sides' attention. Like other indigenous peoples, they calculated their separate interests and watched and listened to British and then French representatives entreating for their loyalty. The Kaskaskia let it be known that they were sitting with the British so that the French worried for their loyalties. But finally, whatever their separate interests, the Kaskaskia had become deeply enmeshed with the French. They had "French hearts"; "the French were their own blood."[11] And as for the British, the Kaskaskia had heard enough from refugees such as the Delaware, who recounted the great swindle that had stripped them of their lands in Pennsylvania. The British, they concluded, had greedy hearts. The jockeying for position ended, however, with the French defeat in 1759. Then this "original people" stood alone, exposed to the British.

American Indians struggled to adjust to the transition. While the Kaskaskia watched neighbors, both French and Indian, seek refuge from British dominion in Spanish territory across the Mississippi River, others remained behind to watch an uncertain and unstable political scene and to discern a path to safety.[12] The British were slow to arrive and few in number, and Indians were not impressed; rumors circulated that the French would return. Indian leaders were summoning the tribes to join in united resistance against the new imperial arrangement. The Illiniwek attended to reports that Pontiac, an Ottawa, had laid siege to British Detroit and considered his appeal that they join him. Meanwhile Charlot Kaské of the Shawnee was petitioning the French to support the resistance. Both leaders visited Kaskaskia town in 1764, and the people listened. Though Pontiac had failed to take Detroit, the British had not established domination over the region. And though the Kaskaskia harbored few illusions about the British, they felt so weak that they chose to avoid entanglements. Pontiac persisted but could not turn their hearts.

Yet, for the next generation, no one seemed able to prevail in the country of the Illiniwek. The British, though weak in numbers, continued to meddle in the region's affairs. When the American colonies revolted, Virginia dispatched troops under the command of George Rogers Clark to secure the region. Immigrants began to follow. Yet the new republic seemed incapable of securing its territorial claims. From Canada the English continued to encourage and aid Indian resistance. And new Indian leaders with their own agenda emerged to call for ridding the land of the Americans.

The Kaskaskia understood their condition. Refugees from the east recounted their experiences with the English.[13] Echoing the Delaware, the Shawnee came with stories of their futile attempts to keep their lands from English incursions. Meanwhile a new generation of spiritual leaders renewed the call for united resistance. While neither the English nor the French deserved the respect they had sought, these spokesmen for national renewal singled out the Americans for special condemnation. This was a people that Nanabush had once driven from the earth to dwell in exile in the murky underworld among the evil spirits. Now they returned to do evil. The Shawnee leaders Tecumseh and his brother Tenskwatawa, the Prophet, added their voices in 1810. The Americans were created by the underworld serpent; their ways must be rejected. Calling for spiritual renewal, the brothers summoned the downtrodden peoples of the midcontinent to spurn alcohol and to return to the ancestors' traditions.

Tecumseh traveled through the Mississippi River Valley seeking to awaken the tribes and unite them against these evil intruders. He sought aid from the British in Canada and from the divine. When, in 1811, a horrifying earthquake shook the land for days and turned the Mississippi River backward, he interpreted the disaster as a sign that "the Great Spirit is angry with our enemies."[14] His brother had correctly prophesied an eclipse of the sun. While many joined the patriot movement, the Kaskaskia, like other tribes, preferred caution. They need only count how few warriors remained. And they witnessed the swarms of white immigrants crossing the mountains to the east.

Even before the Americans had crushed Tecumseh's followers at Prophetstown, the Kaskaskia were seeking accommodation with the Americans. Jean Baptiste Ducoigne spoke to this necessity.[15] His father a French Canadian and his mother a descendant of prominent Kaskaskian elders, Ducoigne understood this unstable world where European and American Indian identities were mixing and believed that with skillful diplomacy he might maneuver between antagonists. While the American colonists were fighting for their independence, he joined their cause. And in the peace, he used his reputation to secure his people security with the new republican government.

Thomas Jefferson wrote, assuring him: "We, like you, are Americans, born in the same land, and having the same interests."[16] In the 1790s, when the western tribes rose up against the Americans, the Kaskaskia refused to fight and even gave aid to the American armies. When the resistance was broken, the Kaskaskia were invited to the negotiations, where they witnessed the defeated tribes cede millions of acres. The tactic paid off: in recognition of Kaskaskian loyalty, the American government granted the tribe an annuity of five hundred dollars.

The Kaskaskia had become the clients of the land-stealing republic, and their vulnerability became ever more apparent during later treaty negotiations. As they watched the government wrench territory from other tribes, they turned themselves into supplicants pleading for security and whatever scraps of land Washington deigned to allow them. Powerless, they bargained away millions of acres of loosely defined territories for assurances of clear, well-defined parcels that were laid out by the American mapmaking surveyors. When Ducoigne and friends came to treaty negotiations, they had made themselves into ratifying witnesses to the incessant land grabbing.[17] In return, they earned the animus of neighboring tribes. As their numbers dwindled, they became increasingly vulnerable to attack from neighboring tribes who felt betrayed. In turn, they became ever more dependent on American protection. And so they received a larger annuity and assurances of provisions.

When Tecumseh and the Prophet called upon the tribes and the British entered the hostilities against the American republic's expansion, the Kaskaskia had been reduced to accepting small tracts such as that at Sand Ridge.[18] When they offered to join the United States against a common enemy, they were dismissed. The cash payments that had been solemnly promised were no longer paid. Though some Americans protested that their government had disgraced itself, the Kaskaskia received no redress. But the Kaskaskia had correctly calculated the futility of taking up arms against the Americans. Tecumseh, like Pontiac and other patriot chiefs, was crushed. Remnants of the Indian peoples continued westward toward the Mississippi; the Delaware and the Shawnee were crossing the river and drifting into the territory of the Osage.

While the Kaskaskia watched the surveyors pass through Sand Ridge, and simultaneously while they listened to the Prophet's call for spiritual awakening, they were witnessing themselves in history. Somehow they felt themselves trapped where place and time converged.[19] The land they stood upon was not theirs. This they knew in an unsaid sense that was truer than the words on the treaties they had accepted. Once, their fathers had taught them the ways to picture the land by imagining themselves standing on a specific place and telling stories attached to that spot. When the leaves began to fall and they looked to the rising sun, they heard the geese in flight. Their left hands pointed to the geese flying toward them, and when they turned to their right, they watched the birds vanish in the distant horizon. They knew the places at the river bottoms where they might smell the rich black earth. And when they prepared for a journey, they sat facing one another drawing lines in the dirt to explain the route, talking about landmarks to be encountered and the accompanying stories, and measuring the distances by the number of walking days. There were the bluffs overlooking the river where frightful monsters lurked, waiting for the unsuspecting traveler, the tree trunks with the carvings, the stream at the edge of grasslands where the traveler might encounter the buffalo wallowing.

Now the sons and daughters confronted strangers who came with compass and chains to describe the land. The Kaskaskia were forced to learn a new language that used numbers to designate invisible coordinates. Men far away who had not watched the heron perched on the edge of a wetland and the early morning mists or had stalked the deer along the forested bluffs could point to the lines on pieces of paper and claim the land theirs. The Kaskaskia could no longer rely on tradition's stories to describe their place on the earth. The sacred circles that signified the well-ordered cosmos, with the spheres of the earth suspended in balance between the upper and lower worlds, had brought power and well-being to life. But now the circle was boxed in the strangers' squares.

The fathers' world was flattened. The men who came with a new religion made mock of trickster rabbit and of Nanabush. Repeatedly they demonstrated that their power was mightier than the shaman's. The wondrous beings that lay beneath nature's surface, that revealed themselves in the places where water seeped from rock faces or in the healing medicines of plants, were fading from sight. Instead, the square makers were cataloging the natural world into resources that might be seized and employed for profit.

As they watched the surveyors, the Kaskaskia understood that they had lost. Memories of the Great Village where the ancestors had lived reminded them that they had been dispossessed. While they turned away from

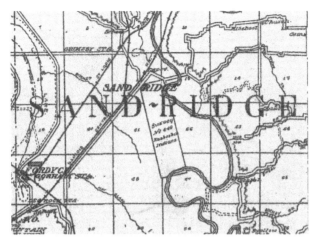

Detail map of Jackson County with Kaskaskia reservation against survey grid. *Standard Atlas of Jackson County* (Chicago: G. A. Ogle, 1907), 7.

Tecumseh, his words spoke truth. As they watched the Delaware wander through and listened to their stories of the land stealing, they recognized themselves. This place had become a waystation. They had become nuisances, vagrants, to be pushed aside.

If they had looked at the map that designated the lines demarking their lands, they would have understood. After the surveyors left and the Americans arrived to lay claim to their parcels, they filled the squares with property lines that conformed to the larger gridwork. Lines designating the land reserved for the Kaskaskia remained on the map, but these cut diagonally across the prevailing pattern of verticals and horizontals. The most cursory glance confirmed that this remnant of the Great Village did not belong.

* * *

OTHERS, MEN WHO had not stood on the bank of the great river, were filling the empty squares with names of their own and with their own stories. Surveyors Glenn and Roswell had been hired to clamber over the ridges, tear themselves through the briars, and slog through the wetlands so that they might implement a historical narrative imagined by men like Thomas Jefferson. From his study at Monticello Jefferson assiduously scanned the maps and pored over the reports from those who ventured into this region.[20] At first, he was looking at what was designated according to colonial charters as the western extension of his own Virginia. During the struggle for independence, he had worked with Governor Patrick Henry to dispatch troops into the Ohio River Valley to secure the territorial claims of his fledgling commonwealth from British control. Even after Virginia ceded its western claims to the national government, these territories between the Illinois and the Ohio Rivers remained fixed in his imagination. Military leaders and explorers returning from these lands brought him the relics of an ancient past—notably, the bones of mastodons—curiosities obtained from the American Indian peoples such as a battle scene depicted on a buffalo hide, botanical specimens, and living animals. He designated a special room—Indian Hall—for his collections that became a museum of the West.

Looking west across the Blue Ridge Mountains, Jefferson saw vast blank spaces inviting him to impose his own story complete with names of his devising. He envisioned an unfolding narrative of American continental expansion, of successive generations migrating westward, and of commerce binding east and west together. Working with state and national government, he initiated proposals for land development and sales and for the creation of new states in this vast Northwest Territory.[21] While fixed on this future of unfolding boundless opportunity, he labored over the smallest details, in particular the mechanisms for laying out the grids necessary for the sale of lands. As he studied the maps and imagined the lands that would be surveyed, he proposed the locations of future states with their approximate boundaries and their names. While recommending that towns be named in honor of the French alliance during the war for independence—thus Marietta (Ohio) for Marie Antoinette—he proposed to fix American names upon the states. The first two due west of Pennsylvania were to be Washington and Saratoga. Other names were plucked from his classical learning and sometimes fused with local derivations. Thus the territory "thro' which the Assenisipi or Rock River runs shall be called ASSENISIPIA." Others were "METROPOTAMIA" and "PELISIPIA." The future state north of the confluence of the Ohio and Mississippi Rivers was to be "POLYPTOTAMIA," and the land due north and to the Illinois River was to become the state of "ILLINOIA."

While imposing his squares upon a land that he would never see and by naming places that he could only imagine, Jefferson was sketching the outlines of a historical narrative that would be applied to the empty spaces such as Illinoia and even Sand Ridge. His story was powerful not because it was the product of private fantasy but because he spoke and wrote to the sentiments of his generation of revolutionaries. When he and his colleagues created a republic, they assured themselves that they were marking the dawning of a historic epic in which the natural rights of humankind would be progressively secured and advanced. What happened in 1776 promised to become an example for the world at large. Yet, the lessons of history taught that republics were fragile and short-lived entities. With success and prosperity came luxury and corruption. As populations grew and prospered, some grew rich and others grew ever poorer. The emerging landless and dependent classes became subject to corruption and manipulation by the rich. Thus Roman republicanism had turned to Caesarism.

The question that haunted Jefferson and his contemporaries was stark and simple: Would the cycle leading to degeneration be repeated on American soil? Specifically, would the independent, yeoman farmers of America be replaced by renters who, in turn, would grovel before their new economic overlords? Economics was crucial, and that was what guided Jeffersonian concerns for the West. Since republicanism rested on the virtuous independent agriculturalist—in sum, on self-possessing, self-determining, property-owning farmers—the equation was simple: land scarcity turned the independent farmer into a dependent renter. Escape from the pressures of population and corruption lay in the seemingly limitless lands to the west. History would not repeat itself as long as there was this safety valve.

The republican vision translated into a geometry imposed upon the western lands. Jefferson and his colleagues puzzled over the empty spaces on their maps and wondered how to administer the territories and transfer land to prospective migrants. From their Philadelphia conference rooms, the simplest answer lay in drawing horizontal and vertical lines that intersected to form squares. Implementation, in turn, required a system for surveying the land. The square appealed to Jefferson's sense of symmetry and balance. Square measures of property were simple and easily understood by the most common farmer. Thus the square was in essence democratic. Traditional conventions of demarking boundaries by natural boundaries or hearsay would be abandoned. Transfers of land would no longer depend on such vagaries as the distance covered in a day's walk. Cheating would be made difficult. Above all, land would become a measurable commodity that could be identified, sold, and traded among people miles apart and far from the commodity itself.

Jefferson devised an orderly system of western development that would satisfy his colleagues who feared that the new territories would turn to republican degeneracy. Those who left the well-ordered society of the East, conservatives warned, would disappear into a howling wilderness, forget the virtues of a well-governed civilization, and descend into barbarity. Government would dissolve into anarchy. Rough frontiersmen would squat upon the land without title. Others warned from another perspective that vast tracts would be gobbled up by speculators who would enrich themselves and thereby deny opportunity for those in need. Would the West become a scene of anarchy and savagery? Would it become the playground of the profiteer? Lest history be repeated, Jefferson worked to institute an orderly basis of settlement, urged the creation of a system of sales that would forestall the influence of speculators, and laid plans for the creation of republican state governments.

As Jefferson expected, his plans were compromised. The states he had imagined were not created. His dreaded land speculators could not be kept at bay. But the fundamentals of that vision—the orderly process of square making and the blueprint for the establishment of state and local governments—remained.

While his squares contained vast empty spaces waiting for the arrival of hardy republican farmers, Jefferson could not ignore the indigenous inhabitants like the Kaskaskia at Sand Ridge. Ever the keen observer of Indians, he addressed the subject directly and struggled to fit these people within his republican geometry. American Indians, though on first impressions a benighted lot, evinced potential to partake in civilization's progress. Thus he wrote to Jean Baptiste Ducoigne, promising that the Americans and the Kaskaskia would live together in harmony. The hides on which the Kaskaskia had mapped their land claims hung on his walls at Monticello; he would "always keep them . . . in remembrance of you and your nation."[22] Assured that the denizens of the wilderness could learn and so be uplifted, he promised that the new republic would send them teachers. "We desire above all things, brother, to instruct you in whatever we know ourselves . . . and to learn you all our arts and to make you wise and wealthy." The philosopher president promised a future in his republic to those who would forsake their wilderness ways in favor of the American.

The remnants of the Illiniwek might keep a place in Jefferson's squares if they transformed themselves into republican farmers. As president, he revealed the practical elements of his policy. In a secret communiqué to the Indiana territorial governor William Henry Harrison, he shared his understanding of the Indian future. The Indians must "withdraw them-selves to the culture of a small piece of land."[23] "We wish to draw them to agriculture, spinning and weaving." The promise of government subsidies would lure them to abandon their primitive ways. That goal once realized, the Indian would recognize the uselessness of the large tracts of the land they claimed. Finally, Jefferson forecast that the Indian farmer would be-come dependent on American trade goods and eventually fall into debt. He would "be glad to see [the Indian peoples] run in debt, because we observe that when these debts get beyond what the individuals can pay, they become willing to lop [the debt] off by a cessation of lands." Thus, by peaceful means the American Indian presence would no longer work as an obstacle to the narrative of progress, and these peoples would be erased from his map.

Jefferson was imposing a narrative on this land that collided with an-other advanced by the American Indian patriot leaders who called for a confederacy from the Great Lakes through the Mississippi River watershed to repel the land stealers.[24] The land, Tecumseh had reminded his listeners, was not a commodity on which surveyors would draw their lines; it must not be turned into private property so that individual farmers might have the liberty to pursue their personal fulfillment. No one, he scolded the chiefs who had bartered land for peace, could hand the earth over by fixing his mark to a piece of paper. If surveyors were to attempt the implementation of the land cessions, he promised fierce armed resistance. According to his vision, the heart of the continent would not serve as a safety valve guaranteeing the future of American republicanism but would become the home for an independent pan-Indian confederacy. Accordingly, he translated Jefferson's liberty and self-sufficiency into license for greed.

A history of the area could take alternative forms with different geo-graphic shapes and with contrasting narrative content. Since the mid-eighteenth century, Europeans on the Atlantic coast had been concocting competing schemes for the future of the region. Some were speculators and others settlers. In Philadelphia, for example, the Company of Suffering Traders, which claimed grievous losses in the Indian trade, sought com-pensation by pursuing a land grant for a colony somewhere between the Illinois and the Ohio Rivers and recruited Benjamin Franklin to support its scheme.[25] At the periphery of the new republic settlers from Vermont to the Carolinas and westward across the Appalachians envisioned republics separate from the United States. If American Indian ability to establish a self-determining confederacy waned, the new national government seemed to lack the institutional strength and the loyalties of its presumed citizens to move its paper projects to reality. The actions of Jefferson's vice president Aaron Burr and his general James Wilkinson, as well as his trusted friend George Rogers Clark in the Mississippi River Valley, undermined what some hoped would be a natural course of national republican expansion westward toward the Pacific Ocean.

* * *

LINES DRAWN ON the map were fluid; the names were changing. Jefferson's Illinoia never was. Sand Ridge, which had been in his Polypotamia, became part of the new Indiana Territory. In turn, Illinois Territory was carved out of Indiana in 1809, and its capital was installed at Kaskaskia. Meanwhile, county lines were shifting, with Sand Ridge first in St. Clair and then Randolph County. The territory that would become Jackson County was for a time divided between Randolph and Johnson Counties. In 1816, Jackson County's boundaries were drawn on the map, and nine years later its northern border was nudged southward in favor of Perry County.

Jackson County's history was as fluid as its boundaries.[26] While a republican narrative advanced by self-sufficient, self-determining freeholders was implicit in land policy, its adherents wrestled to gloss over contradictions in practice. Americans had been explaining land stealing first as divine providence and then as manifest destiny, but they consistently did so by erasing the indigenous presence from history. Fitting the republican narrative into Jackson County's empty spaces required squaring republican ideals with African bondage.

Edward Coles looked to Jefferson's Illinoia as the realization of republican ideals.[27] Born in Virginia at the end of the Revolution, he learned to admire the author of the Declaration of Independence as the architect of a shining republican future. A member of the slavocracy by birth, Coles wrestled with his society's contradiction between its egalitarian and universalist professions and its dependence on unfree labor. And so he appealed to Jefferson to lend his moral authority to the ending of slavery in Virginia. His logic was simple and Jeffersonian. He understood Jefferson to be the guiding genius behind the Northwest Ordinance that had provided for the exclusion of slavery from the territories. Moreover, the justness of the cause was self-evident. "The principles you have professed and practiced," he wrote Jefferson, made him the obvious spokesman for "getting into operation some plan for the general emancipation of slavery." Gently but firmly, Jefferson declined. Coles was undeterred even when his family rebuffed his appeals.

Like other conscience-stricken Virginians, Coles looked westward where immigrants could begin anew, unburdened by traditions and inherited instruments of oppression. In the spring of 1819, he left his home with a dozen slaves. Traveling first by wagon and then by flatboat down the Monongahela River, the party reached the Ohio River. Halfway across the river, Coles gathered his slaves. The sun was "shining bright, and the heavens without a cloud," he recalled. Nature's beauty and the "finest feelings of our nature" were in "harmony." He watched their faces, "curious to see the effect of an instantaneous severing of the manacles of bondage, and letting loose on the buoyant wings of liberty the long pent up spirit of man." He spoke to the point: "They were no longer slaves, but free."

James Hall also brought a narrative ready to be stamped upon wilderness Illinois.[28] Like Coles, he centered the story on the Northwest Ordinance and the prospects for republican fulfillment. From his native Pennsylvania he witnessed that story's enactment as he watched the waves of immigrants surge westward toward the Ohio Valley. Once moving to Illinois, he actively promoted public awareness of the unfolding process of development. At the initial meetings of the Antiquarian and Historical Society of Illinois, he warned that contemporary Americans were mesmerized by the Founders. By looking backward at the "classic purity and heroism in the achievement of our gallant ancestors," today's generation felt diminished: "What hero or statesman could hope to win the applause of a people whose heart dwelt with reverence upon the exalted standards of civil and military greatness exhibited in the founders of the American republic?" Moreover, settlers in Illinois, while celebrating the birth of the nation, might feel disconnected by geography from the story. Illinoisans must awaken. They were historical actors in the next chapter of the national saga. If they would look up from their daily wrestling with the wilderness, they would open their eyes to a grand historical narrative: "The history of nations does not present a more beautiful picture than that exhibited by the settlement of the Western Country." Here they witnessed republican "theory carried into complete practical operation."[29]

Hall's colleagues in the historical society agreed: the history of the new state had just begun and must be seen in context of "a living stream of freedom." Their story turned on the manifest newness. "All is new," Hall rejoiced.[30] As historians surveyed the rude cabins and settlements, they witnessed a process of exodus out of the civilization of the East. Among the unlettered pioneers were leaders, many of the revolutionary generation who carried the principles of '76 in their hearts and were determined to implement them free from the encumbrances of the past.[31]

Hall wrote to awaken Illinois to its place in history. His portrayals of the landscape worked to complete the abbreviated descriptions left by the surveyors and corrected distortions published in the East. He assured readers that were they to visit his land, they would be dazzled by "the most attractive scenic exhibition of our Western hemisphere" with flowered prairies edged by thickets of trees resplendent with red and white blossoms. The land with its "inexhaustible fertility" lay waiting for improvement. Enterprising and virtuous easterners were already transforming what might once have been viewed as inhospitable wilderness into a vista of welcoming settlements. The prospects for future immigrants were abundant. Reports of disease, he assured his reader, were much exaggerated. The rich bottomlands along the Ohio and the Mississippi Rivers awaited the plowman to yield their bounty. The spring floods were mere inconvenience that did not deter the growth of settlement. Indeed, he ventured that with growing population and the spread of towns would come warmer climes, less snowfall, and thereby diminished flooding.[32] In time this growing, prospering region would become the center of the nation and the older eastern states its appendage.

While fixed on a vibrant present unfolding into the realization of republican ideals, Hall and his colleagues glanced backward to discover confirmation of their narrative. A French presence, remaining in scattered settlements and names on the map, reminded the historian of a first faltering step toward liberty. These earlier settlers had come to the banks of the Mississippi expecting an "Arcadia of simplicity" far from the "despotism which had ruled them at home." While escaping courts, sheriffs, lawyers, and tax collectors, they abused their liberty and "rioted in free, unbounded action." Hall remembered them for their "curious manifestations of character." Their "happy and careless" ways provided material for local color and taught a sobering lesson. "Freedom sometimes degenerated into a stormy licentiousness which has left dark and enduring stains upon their memory." The French could not be credited with civilization's progress. As Hall wrote, they seemed to be dwindling in number and slipping down the river into the Louisiana bayou country. Even the names they had left were being erased: La Vase would soon be the Big Muddy.[33]

Historians also attended to the American Indian population, in part from the need to rid themselves of responsibility for dispossession and in part from antiquarian curiosity.[34] On considering the small settlements like Sand Ridge, they fixed on squalor and misery. Were these desperate conditions, they asked themselves, the result of innate character traits and thereby irreversible, or were they the dark side of their cherished historical narrative? When they discovered the mounds, they were predisposed to surmise that they were looking at the remains of a people distinct from the present Indians. While admitting that the evidence seemed inconclusive, Hall was inclined to accept that the mound builders were capable of creating a thriving society and were therefore "superior" to today's "savage" denizens of the forest. Would "a wise Creator" have made such a verdant land to be the home of such a people found at Sand Ridge? By their present wretchedness, these people seemed unworthy of the bounty the creator had laid before them.[35] History began with the coming of a people guided by republican virtue, quickened by the spirit of industry and enterprise, and inspired to turn nature's bounty into western Eden.

By importing the elements of American republican culture to the Illinois scene, Hall and Coles were translating the Jeffersonian historical imagination into local historical awareness. They were sketching the story that would be applied to the empty squares. When the surveyors passed by Sand Ridge, a handful of immigrants had already planted in the area. William Boon, Benningsen's father, a settler from North Carolina, watched them cross the horizon. Soon after, Conrad Will, an enterprising doctor from Pennsylvania, set up a saltworks nearby. Though neither imagined writing a history, they participated in shaping its contours.

This transplanted historiography, at once republican and imperial, as-sembled a cast of actors and shunted others into the shadows. Will and Boon became the embodiment of the Jeffersonian improver. And accordingly, they improved with unfree labor.[36] Of the 1,392 inhabitants counted for the territorial census in 1818, 53 nameless persons were identified as bonded workers. Jackson County and Illinois were participating in a national repub-lican emergence. The Jeffersonian vision, while universal by implication, was moving toward consolidating deeply embedded exclusivist habits. At the na-tional level, the government was defining who made history and who did not.

Citizenship, the congress had enacted, was reserved for free Europeans—not Africans. The states worked to make real the idea of a white republic by ratifying similar legislation denying the rights of citizenship to persons not white. Not only did the franchise specifically exclude nonwhites, but marriage laws denied recognition to interracial couples.

Emerging political leaders like Boon and Will balked at the Northwest Ordinance's prohibition of slavery.[37] Illinois's natural riches lay before them unused and would remain so until likeminded enterprising settlers were allowed access to bonded workers. They slipped through legal loopholes permitting importation of slaves, ostensibly as indentured servants. Black codes, reflecting practice in the slave states, were enacted to restrict African American assembly and speech. When the Illinois territory prepared for its transition to statehood in 1818, lawmakers and their constituents debated the issue. While Edward Coles declared for the prohibition of slavery in the state constitution, he confronted stiff resistance. The debates turned on economic progress: could the new state realize its potential with or without slavery? Coles put the choice clearly: he would "rather see our rich meadows and fertile woodlands inhabited alone by the wild beasts and birds of the air, than that they would ever echo the sound of the slave driver's scourge."[38] But the champions of unfree labor could not be ignored. The new constitution, while in compliance with the Northwest Ordinance, left open provisions for importing bonded labor for limited terms. Entrepreneurs like Conrad Will continued to lease slaves from Kentucky, and debates over slavery continued into the 1820s.

Will was creating a shadowy world where both "humanity and justice" flourished and the free lived with the unfree. Not content with the compromise settlement in the state constitution, he pressed his vision of a white republicanism. Elected to the state legislature, he lent his voice to a coalition dedicated to relaxing restrictions on the importation of bonded labor. His constituents, he argued, suffered under policy imposed upon them by eastern politicians who lacked any inkling of conditions on the banks of the Big Muddy River. Progress from savagery required the ability to buy and control labor. Settlers would not come unless the time limits on keeping slaves were relaxed. "By this qualified introduction and modification of slavery . . . the country would derive all the advantages in point of wealth and improvements it so much needs." By "admitting slaves to be brought into the state," Will assured his colleagues they would be advancing the republican ideal.[39]

These frontiersmen made Jackson County a bastion of pro-slavery sentiment. The election for governor in 1822 turned on the labor question. Edward Coles spoke for cleansing the new state of all vestiges of involuntary servitude. Overwhelmingly Jackson County voters preferred a strong pro-slavery candidate and gave Coles only one vote in ten. But Coles won and in his first legislative session pressed for the prohibition of kidnapping African Americans and for the absolute abolition of slavery. Representative Will and Senator William Boon read the governor's message with consternation and responded by joining a movement to call for a convention to revise the constitution in their favor. Their constituents voted their approval by a margin of two to one.[40]

No matter that the majority of voters in the state rejected the convention, African bondage remained part of Jackson County's society. Will and Boon continued to hold unfree laborers. During the debates over slavery and a constitutional convention, Dr. John Logan, arrived to join their cause. People noted that he came from Missouri with a slave. An enterprising and experienced trader in slaves and horses, Logan quickly established himself in Brownsville. Neighbors recognized him as an avid horse trader and suspected that he continued to speculate in bonded labor. Runaways were regularly slipping through southern Illinois. And Logan earned additional income by catching the fugitives and returning them for reward.[41]

The doctor taught his son to love horse trading and to loath the African with uncommon passion. As a young, aspiring politician, John A. Logan spoke vehemently against the antislavery movement and its Yankee adherents. On election to the state legislature in 1856, he proposed to cleanse the state of free black people with legislation prohibiting new arrivals from staying more than ten days on penalty of a fifty-dollar fine. Any white citizen successfully accusing an African American of violating the law reaped half the fine as reward. And the guilty immigrant would be jailed and sold to the highest bidder. The bill passed the legislature with unanimous support from the southern portion of the state.

While this white republicanism framed the past by obliterating alternative tellings, the possibility of a counternarrative persisted. Reminders of the French period endured.[42] French names were on the land. Jackson County's entrepreneurs like William Boon looked to Kaskaskia as a trading center. There they heard French still spoken. If they had cared to observe more closely, they would have spied the elements of another history that turned on Kaskaskian, French, and African peoples mixing. By his presence, Jean Baptiste Ducoigne reminded these Americans of this ethnic blending.

Africans in French Illinois were not only conspicuous but might have served as a reminder that they were integral to the region's history.[43] One in three inhabitants of French Kaskaskia had been African. Slaves escaped French masters and found refuge with Indian communities. Others mixed with the indigenous people at Kaskaskia as well. Many remembered their African origins and clung to their beliefs and customs. Their presence, though sometimes shadowy, continued into the republican era. Contrary to the wishful fantasies of white republicans like Logan, free Africans were planting pioneer communities in the wilderness to the south of Jackson County and to the north along the Mississippi River.

White republicans worked to dismiss these reminders. They glossed over the region's French pioneers who, like the indigenous peoples, became a measure by which to confirm the progress of American republicans. One traveler noted that the French "conformed in great measure to the more numerous savages by whom they were environed." The French were lazy; they did not understand the advantages of private property owning. Doubtless their consorting with others across the color line confirmed these prejudices. Thus, Thomas Ford began his history of Illinois at 1804 when he arrived. History began with his people. What he offered was a blossoming of the Jeffersonian republican promise. John Reynolds looked farther back, but from Ford's perspective. By the "decrees of Providence" the "Indians must emigrate, leaving Illinois—the finest country on earth, for the peaceable occupation of the white man." The French, though "innocent and honest," had taken but modest steps from savagery to civilization. These farmers cared "little for the future."[44]

* * *

THE SURVEYORS AT Sand Ridge, like their counterparts throughout the region, had stamped Jeffersonian self-evident truths and the accompanying history upon the land. Their squares enabled the enactment of a white settler narrative. The Americans Indians' circles—their rich cosmology and the understanding of their place upon the land—could not fit within this gridwork. Instead, the squares promised property to the self-determining farmer and thereby became the stage for ever-progressing generations. Always these historical actors were white. When they told their story, they relegated American Indian and black people to the margins, vanished and forgotten. While the emerging story focused on settlement—white settlement—it could endure by forgetting that for many this was not a place of settlement but a waystation and that domesticating this wilderness was achieved by deeply engrained habits of violence.

CHAPTER THREE

SETTLERS AND TRANSIENTS

HISTORY BEGAN WITH Benningsen Boon. Neighbors knew him as "the first white man" born in Jackson County, and he would regale friends and strangers with stories from his childhood at the county's creation. He grew up in a log cabin on the bottomlands near Sand Ridge. Though but four at the time, he vividly remembered the great earthquakes of 1811. As he told his friends and neighbors, his father William Boon had loaded a flatboat with coal dug from the banks of the Big Muddy River for sale in New Orleans and had left with his slave Peter. On the night of December 15, the boy awoke to a violent trembling. Weeks later his father and Peter returned with stories of the "terrible" scenes they had witnessed. The days had been uncommonly warm; the air hung heavy with mists so thick that the boatmen could not make out the riverbanks. Boon and his slave had tied up the boat just above New Madrid. Suddenly in early morning, they were jolted awake by the first rumblings. In the darkness they felt the river roil and toss their boat violently. The air seemed filled with sulfurous vapor. At dawn they discovered that riverbanks had collapsed into the water; trees were everywhere uprooted. Through the day the shocks continued, with the most violent forcing the river backward.[1]

Benningsen recounted his memories of frontier life, and with practice he became an accomplished storyteller. In time—by midcentury—he represented the surviving connection to a world that was fading from memory. He had grown up in the company of men who had fought against American Indians and listened to their tales. In 1812 his father fought the Indian enemy, and twenty years later, when Black Hawk mounted the last Indian resistance to invasion, Benningsen volunteered his service.[2] Boon recalled the voices of the storytellers, their faces, and their names. William McRoberts was a miller. He walked with a pronounced limp. He loved to tell jokes and to reminisce about life in western Pennsylvania and the day General Anthony Wayne drilled troops at Pittsburgh in preparation for his campaign against local Indians. Though McRoberts drank to excess, his neighbors deemed him an honest man, a "good citizen," and a "good farmer." Boon enjoyed retelling his father's story of two settlers, one named Reed and the other Jones. Reed's Creek was named after one and Jones Pond the other. Jones, "for some cause" quarreled with Reed and shot him dead. He fled to Walker's Hill, where he was arrested before being taken to Kaskaskia for trial, found guilty, and hanged. He was "the first white person" hanged in the county. But, Benningsen reflected, "what became of their families, I know not."[3]

Sometimes details eluded him; on occasion he could not recall a first name. Neighbors moved on, he knew not where. "There was a family by the name of Brilhart." Jacob Brilhart worked for Benningsen's father and then migrated "to the south-west somewhere." Sometimes Benningsen stumbled over dates. His world was slipping away ever more rapidly. In his sixties, he encountered a rude log cabin that stirred memories. He mused over the images of household life, of families eating from a few pewter plates. Knives and forks were scarce; "the butcher-knife and jack-knife were quite as commonly used as table-knives." The furniture was of the "rudest construction." Shoes were rare and moccasins commonplace.[4] In post–Civil War Jackson County, children perused the newspapers filled with advertisements for manufactured clothing and household wares. White frame houses replaced cabins. Now the shriek of the railroad whistle cut through the rural quiet, reminding him of time's accelerating pace.

Sometime in his mid-sixties, doubtless moved by his own sense of mortality, Benningsen Boon prepared to write a history. He started with what he remembered—his father's stories, the tales told by neighbors at the store-front at Brownsville, the first county seat. But while assembling his notes, he discovered that however indispensable oral traditions were, they were not sufficient. Paper records, however, were scant. Fire had destroyed much of the county archive before 1843. But Benningsen persevered in his search for documentation and cobbled together the bits and pieces as best he could. The Morrows—the brothers John and Thomas and their father—had moved from the Ohio River Valley. Benningsen began to reconstruct the family's marriages and children. The family held land "on the north-west quarter of section 18, T. 10 T. S. 3W." He had seen the land title for the Kaskaskia reservation "Recorded in Book 'A.' Page 3, July, 4th, 1818." And for corroborating perspective he kept John Reynolds's *Pioneer History* at his desk.

Benningsen's preliminary draft of a county history was ramshackle, the "Sketches" a hodgepodge of anecdotes. Yet, by assembling the bits of family histories and genealogies of land titles, he was filling the squares on the survey map. Beneath the clutter lay a tradition of history writing that turned on conquest and its erasure. Like the earliest European colonizers who had invaded the continent, he began with first settlers. Without reflection—as if by reflex—he could not imagine the need to attend to the original inhabitants and the possibility of their past. History began with the arrival of his people.[5]

In his own way, Benningsen echoed that white settler historiography. He told a story with authority derived from his reputation as the county's first white child. After giving passing gesture to the original people, some of whom were "hostile" and others "friendly," he turned to his own—"the first white people who crossed Degognia Creek" from the north. What later historians would name *invasion* he called *settlement.* For a brief transition period, settlers defended themselves from Indians. Soon they replaced their blockhouses and "Indian proof" dwellings with frame houses, laid out fence lines, and created community.[6]

Benningsen treated the story as if its deeper meaning were self-evident, not worthy of elaboration. Significance emerged from the details—the "sketches" of the men who came. He gave his readers a mosaic of genealogies of land titles, of men who claimed those titles, of their family trees, and of the men who later purchased these properties. These venturers came from North Carolina, Georgia, and Tennessee, from Pennsylvania and Ohio, and some from the British Isles. The Creath family came by flatboat in 1810, lived for a time in a house owned by William Boon, and then purchased land "at the bluffs." The Glens planted nearby "at the foot of the bluff a short distance above Kinkaid Creek." Robin Glen had two sons, Ewing and Isaac, by his first wife and four by his second. He died at age eighty. His son Isaac remained with a family of "several children," only two of whom still lived.[7]

Character provided the energy for settling this rude world. The pioneers lived simple lives, endured "many privations," and were "content." How they fared depended on inner resources. The Brooks men "were hard-working and industrious farmers" who "attended to their calling." George Cline "was a good man and a good farmer. He was well off when he died in 1837, leaving five children." Many "lived temperately, that is, they used very little whisky." But for some, whisky was their undoing, and they died "drunkards." Others like the Brooks and Cline men lived prudently, saved instead of squandered their money, bought their farms, and thrived.[8]

* * *

THIS ACCOUNT, LIKE the national historiography, glossed over disquieting meanings. While Benningsen's sketches focused on the property owners and developers, the land itself carried its messages. The Indian presence persisted; the mounds and the arrowheads whispered that the improvers were conquerors and land stealers. Other shadows appeared at the edges of the settlement—the people who did not settle but lingered for a time, then moved on and vanished somewhere downriver, into the western prairie, or even across the Rocky Mountains. These were the squatters who first cleared the land, the hired hands whose labor was indispensable to the propertied developers, and the bonded workers who slipped through the records as nameless entities. And finally, beneath Benningsen's story of settlers domesticating a wilderness lay a dark and bloody experience linking generations in a collective consciousness. He related something more than anecdotes illustrating a passing moment in the county's history. His settlers on the banks of the Big Muddy had been raised by parents who themselves had been engaged in violent conflict on the Appalachian frontiers. Their sons, in turn, would move west expecting to repeat that experience. In sum, this was a restless people in motion, carrying memories and behaviors born of generations of frontier warfare. For these transient conquerors, Jackson County was a waystation.

Benningsen himself lived in the contradiction between attachment to place and an itch to migrate. On the one hand, he staked his identity on this county and cultivated a reputation as caretaker of its past, thereby imagining writing a history for his public. While gathering anecdotes and rooting through courthouse records, he composed a first installment of his history for a local newspaper. At times he laid the project aside. After quarreling with the editor, he could not see a way to print. And then the aspiring historian decided to follow his son to Oregon. Perhaps he intended the move to be permanent, as he mislaid the manuscript history. Eventually, however, he returned home, picked up his project again, and wrote another installment for publication. If printer Edmund Newsome had not saved his copy of the history, Boon's work would have been lost.[9]

Many like Benningsen felt this restless itch. Throughout the nation they told each other that personal and national progress came from a willingness to yank themselves free from their roots and move westward. Attachment to place and local tradition seemed an enervating sentiment. President Andrew Jackson had said as much: "To better their condition our forefathers . . . left all that was dear in earthly objects." Leaving one's birthplace, bidding farewell to loved ones, may bring pain to the hearts of some. But, the president assured himself and his fellow citizens, "our forefathers" did as much when they bade farewell to their homes. "Does humanity weep at these painful separations?" "Far from it. It is rather a source of joy." And so will each succeeding generation gladly depart so that it may begin anew. He spoke compassionately on behalf of the indigenous peoples he proposed to send packing to unknown western territory. "Doubtless," American Indians will find it "painful to leave the graves of their fathers." This is the price paid for reaping the benefits of progress.[10]

While Benningsen sketched his story of settlement, his evidence suggested that this place was a waystation for transients. The Brooks family broke up, sold their land, and moved south to Baton Rouge. Jacob Brilhart, who once worked for William Boon and later married Nathan Davis's daughter, moved with that family to "the south-west somewhere." A contemporary of Beningsen Boon observed that southern Illinois included settlers and "floating people." The floaters, though numerous enough to shape the county's history, were discounted. Benjamin Walker, his wife, and three sons were living near the Mississippi River when the surveyors came. Soon Walker sold his lands to Samuel Cochran and, according to Benningsen, disappeared "in his old age into the hills."[11] Of the twenty-four men holding title to land in Benningsen's neighborhood on the eve of statehood, half had vanished in two years. Some, like Pierre Menard, a prosperous French merchant in the Kaskaskia region, owned several tracts near the Boons but never intended to relocate. Many stayed long enough to be counted for a census. Of the 239 families listed in the 1818 enumeration, 39 percent were gone two years later. Boon witnessed that pattern continue. Of the 230 families counted in 1820, more than half (126) had uprooted themselves by the next census.[12]

When the Boons visited Brownsville, they were sure to meet new faces. In 1840 the county's population had increased twofold over the past decade with 3,479 white and 44 black residents. During the next decade, the count had risen to nearly 6,000 whites, while the black population had declined to 33.[13] Many were floaters: over a quarter (28 percent) of the families on the 1830 census were gone by 1840. Of the families listed in the 1840 census, 29 percent had disappeared from the next enumeration. And, of course, the rate of transiency would be higher if enumerations had been taken between decennial listings. Benningsen watched the floaters in his own backyard. Charles Sczerkowsky appeared in the 1830s with his wife and two young sons and purchased three parcels of land amounting to over a hundred acres. A Gottwald Sczerkowsky acquired forty-three acres nearby. Both families had vanished within a decade. Postmaster John Clodfelter and his family appeared on the 1840 census and then disappeared.[14]

When they appeared, the floaters often seemed indistinguishable from persisters. They drifted into the county after several moves. They came with an eager eye, scanning the landscape for opportunity but not necessarily with the intent to plant something called community. If they stayed, their decision came by chance or perhaps from age. William Boon was born during the Revolution in North Carolina. While a child, his father moved the family to Kentucky where he established a gristmill. At age eighteen, he picked up and eventually arrived in Missouri where he worked in the lead mines for a few years. Then he drifted off again, crossing the Mississippi into Illinois Territory; he lived in Kaskaskia long enough to find a wife and begin to raise a family. Around five years later he was scouting the land to the south. In 1807 he moved his family beneath the bluff area near the Kaskaskia village. He acquired land and slaves. In addition to farming, he periodically floated a flatboat south to New Orleans, where he sold his goods and the boat and walked home. By happenstance perhaps, William Boon had ceased his wanderings and stayed. Son and grandson, however, inherited an itch to move on.[15]

Conrad Will was scouting the area in 1811. The Pennsylvania doctor came with entrepreneurial instincts—his immediate purpose was to buy cattle at Kaskaskia and drive them home for sale. During his visit, he detected potential along the Big Muddy River for starting a saltworks. After selling his livestock, he sank his profits into large iron kettles for boiling spring water down to salt and returned to begin operations. Labor, however, proved scarce, and he routinely crossed the river into slave territory to rent workers. Will continued to practice medicine, opened a tannery and then a distillery, and entered politics. His neighbors elected him to the state legislature. Sometime between his business ventures and elections, he had chosen to stay.[16]

Soon after his arrival, Will met Henry Dillinger. Born in North Carolina, Dillinger had been moving westward in search of opportunity. While in Kentucky, he had met George Creath who was preparing to move his family to Illinois. The three men—Creath, Dillinger, and Will—were soon active together. Will and Dillinger bought land in 1818 and built a sawmill and a gristmill. Dillinger operated another mill in partnership with Creath. Soon after, Dillinger and Creath applied for a state license to construct a toll bridge across Beaucoup Creek on the road connecting Kaskaskia with Shawneetown on the Ohio River. Speculating on future growth and a market for building material, Dillinger began to quarry limestone on a ridge overlooking the Big Muddy River. But finding the cost of transporting the stone prohibitive, he built a kiln for burning the stone to lime.[17]

Their eyes always roving the landscape, men like Will, Dillinger, and William Boon ventured in schemes to shape the land for profit. At first they had planted in the Sand Ridge area under the bluff and westward toward Big Hill. The place attracted small clusters of settlers who awakened to the commercial advantages of living near the convergence of the Big Muddy and Mississippi Rivers. Will, ever the entrepreneur, recognized the need for a trade center more conveniently located than Kaskaskia. On conferring with William Boon, Jesse Griggs, and John Byars, he called like-minded neighbors to lay plans to create a new county with its government seated on the banks of the Big Muddy. On granting land to the county, Will and his associates named their town Brownsville. Will opened a store. Business flourished, and a lawyer hung out his shingle. Carpenters, a blacksmith, and a wagonmaker came. A hotel was built.[18]

Alexander Jenkins had been looking for such a place. After leaving South Carolina and an abusive father, he had been drifting westward. About 1820 and not yet twenty, he appeared in Illinois. Somehow he had acquired carpentry skills, and Brownsville seemed to promise a living. Soon he opened a store. In his spare time he studied for the bar with an eye on political office. In time he won a seat in the state legislature and later was elected lieutenant governor. Soon after setting up shop in Brownsville, Jenkins met John Logan, the son of Irish immigrants who had settled in Maryland and then moved to Ohio. Young Logan had been roving the Mississippi River valley. While trading in horses, he was encouraged to apprentice himself with a doctor in Natchez. Four years later Dr. Logan was moving northward, perhaps to escape debt collectors. Soon after arriving in Cape Girardeau, Missouri, he met a widow who had inherited substantial lands. Within a year they were married. Seven years later she died, and Logan set out for Illinois. On arriving in Brownsville, he met Jenkins's sister Elizabeth and made her his wife. The doctor's medical practice flourished. The alliance with Jenkins did so as well. Both were stalwart Jacksonian Democrats, and Logan followed his brother-in-law to the state legislature.[19]

Another fortune seeker appeared at Jenkins's store. With his New England accent, Daniel Brush drew attention. He thought of himself as a man in motion: his family had moved first from England to Long Island and then to Vermont. He remembered the family farm vividly. His father, however, was talking with neighbors about better prospects in the "western wilds of the Mississippi Valley, then the Eldorado of many enterprising Yankee minds." Daniel remembered packing the wagons and proceeding slowly through New York, along the southern shore of Lake Erie, southward across Indiana, and then to Missouri. After a brief stay, the family backtracked across the Mississippi River and up the Illinois River, where they formed a settlement with other New Englanders. A year later, Brush's father died, and the family scattered. His mother remarried; soon after, his sister married Alexander Jenkins and moved to Brownsville. Daniel, pushed by his stepfather to leave home, followed his sister. Soon he was managing Jenkins's store and in time became a partner. When Jenkins turned to politics, Brush bought complete ownership of the store.[20]

Brush congratulated himself on finding his place in Brownsville. By 1839 he had resigned his position as postmaster and was holding three offices at once: judge of probate and clerk of both the circuit and the county court. But he felt his relationship with Jenkins cooling and his rivalry with Dr. Logan growing. By identifying himself as a New Englander and a Whig, he distinguished himself from the majority of his neighbors, including Jenkins and Logan, who were Democrats. Brush condemned slavery and preached against liquor, thereby setting himself apart from the Logan-Jenkins coterie. Logan's love of horse trading and racing earned his scorn. With the death of his sister, his relationship with Jenkins soured. Brush discovered himself encircled by a "Jenkins-Logan clique" conspiring "to effect my ruin and to take away my living."[21]

Creating a town brought profit, especially for those who owned the core properties. In 1843 fire consumed the county courthouse and most of the public records. Jenkins and Logan seized the opportunity to relocate the government to a more healthy location where they owned property. The town would be named Murphysboro. Brush fumed. He publicly condemned the "underhand and sneaking tricks of the enemy," but to no avail. "Free whiskey" and "lies" carried the day. During the public auction of new town lots, Brush realized that Logan's "cronies" manipulated the bidding to close him out. But by the "quiet arrangement with a friend" who bid in his stead, the Yankee outflanked his enemies and acquired an entire block of prime real estate. Brush opened a store, floated flatboats laden with corn, pork, and dried fruits to New Orleans, and operated a sawmill. And he prospered. But always the "Logan tribe" schemed against him.[22]

The encircled but enterprising Vermonter scanned the countryside for the means to free himself from the Logans. In 1852, Brush lit upon a scheme to make his own town. The Illinois Central Railroad was preparing to lay track from Chicago and through the eastern section of Jackson County. One day Brush explored the area in search of a site for his town. Envisioning a commercial center, he fixed on a point midway between Murphysboro and the town of Marion in Williamson County. This was a gamble, because the railroad had planned its depots elsewhere along the line, one at DeSoto and the other Makanda. Moreover, prime real estate in those towns had been gobbled up. And so Brush joined with other speculators to buy the land for a town and then persuade railroad officials to alter their plans so that the train would stop on their property.

Brush and his fellow adventurers laid out the town in a gridwork of streets and lots. A square was reserved at the center for the depot and freight office. They divided half the remaining lots among themselves and sold the rest at public auction. Lots were also reserved for a school and churches. Brush became the town's largest landowner with twenty-two lots. Eager to turn this venture to profit, he proposed to build the railroad's freight office and the first church. He planned well. He erected the first store directly opposite the depot. In addition, he served the railroad as ticket agent and telegraph operator. The town grew rapidly. Three brickyards began operation; four hotels opened their doors. Murphysboro businessmen were following Brush to his town.[23]

Entrepreneurial energies and rivalries were shaping and reshaping the county landscape and its stories. The names on the land were changing, and so were the people. When Carbondale was being laid out, the Worthens, who had been Brownsville's first settlers, watched their town fall into the earth. William Worthen had worked for Conrad Will. While the family acquired land, neighbors were leaving. William's grandson Richard walked the deserted streets. Property was cheap, and he bought the abandoned buildings, burned them down, and converted his holdings to a farm. Memories of this boomtown were dissolving.[24]

Benningsen Boon's actors were disappearing from the scene in search of advancement. Jenkins moved to Springfield following his election to lieutenant governor in 1834, and he later became president of a short-lived railroad. Cairo looked promising, and he invested in railroads and canals in that city.[25] Jenkins's nephew John A. Logan grew up with his father prompting him to look beyond. He and his siblings were sent away for their education; John later studied the law in Kentucky. Hardly had he returned home when he began to rove from one community to another, eventually landing in Chicago.[26]

The Duncan brothers, Matthew and Joseph, were fixated by the transient's imagination. They came from Kentucky on the eve of Illinois statehood. Matthew had studied at Yale, returned home to begin a vocation as printer, and on coming to Kaskaskia quickly won the contract as printer for the state government. After several ventures in the capital, he moved to Jackson County, where he joined his brother at Big Hill near Sand Ridge. The brothers operated a gristmill and a distillery. Together they plunged into local politics. Joseph rose rapidly from the state legislature to the national congress. In 1833, he won the race for governor. They had prospered. Benningsen Boon remembered that Joseph owned "the best house in the county." And both moved away. William had left before his brother was elected governor. Joseph never returned after serving his term.[27]

Families vanished, their names soon forgotten. Remnants of their presence littered the landscape. Passersby noted the abandoned shells reminding them of the once-thriving village of Brownsville. Clusters of huge iron pots sat rusting together near the riverbanks—the silent vestiges of Conrad Will's saltworks. Adventurers had probed the earth along the Big Muddy in search of coal. Some succeeded, others abandoned their shafts. The scars they left were disappearing in the underbrush. Mining towns popped up. Miners came, houses were erected, shafts were dug, the town was abandoned, and the houses were torn down. The life of Fiddler's Ridge was so brief that few could recall its existence. Iron furnaces had been built at Big Hill, later renamed Grand Tower. Their crumbling shells remained. And coke ovens were falling into the earth.[28]

In celebrating the hardy adventurers who turned nature's bounty to profit, the county's pastkeepers chose to emphasize half the story of boom and bust. The failures were embedded in the landscape. But the pastkeepers did not write the patterns of transiency, of fortune hunters coming and then vanishing, into their narrative. And while they noted the enterprisers who invested their energies, they ignored the workers who provided the muscle. Labor remained in the shadows, faceless and nameless. Slavery was recognized because it proved indispensable to the pioneer developers. But except for rare cases, slaves as individuals did not appear. Benningsen Boon remembered the name of his father's slave, and that was all. He passed over the moment when another slave—Juliet was her name—sued him for her children's freedom. But that slave was exceptional. Census takers counted black faces but did not record black names.[29]

While recounting the adventurers who tapped the mineral wealth in the land, the pastkeepers were disinclined to attend to the workers who were brought to the mines. After briefly noting the Scots and Welsh miners who had come to dig coal on the banks of the Big Muddy, historian Newsome turned his reader's attention to superintendent Edward Holden, a "perfect gentleman" who harbored a "deep seated hatred" of the Irish and would not employ them on "any terms." The miners and their families remained nameless; neighbors had known them well enough to call the community "Scotchtown" in remembrance of their presence.[30]

Another theme, this one of bloodletting, threaded beneath and through the pastkeepers' memories. While they called up the stories of frontier fighting, they habitually glossed over the deep significance of their tales. In recounting the anecdotes, they forgot how the collective experience of killing stretched over generations and became an unsaid part of their cultural inheritance. They made the stories into isolated episodes, part of local color. The stories illustrated the hardships that their rugged forebears overcame.

By habit they framed the local history within the larger historical scheme of progress advanced by Jefferson and Jackson. The harrowing anecdotes served as measures of this progress out of savage wilderness. That past became transition, something to be tucked behind.

They looked away rather than ponder how deeply this experience had embedded itself into the lives of their families over generations. The scalping, the tortures, the slaughtering by all parties, the captivities—all fused into a collective unsaid awareness. Like the Boons, most immigrants to southern Illinois came from the frontiers of southern Appalachia—the Carolinas, Georgia, Tennessee, and Kentucky—where their families had engaged in ongoing bloody conflict with the Creeks and Cherokee. Others like Conrad Will, the Kimmels, and the Dillingers who came from Pennsylvania crossed the blood-drenched ground where the French and Indians had laid waste an entire British army. The details of General Braddock's rout in 1754 may have been forgotten, but the broken ribcages and the remnants of skulls still littering the ground reminded the westbound traveler.[31] These migrants had occupied shadowy ground with the indigenous peoples, where distinctions between friend and foe seemed to blur. The bonds of intimacy were complicated and deep. These peoples traded with one another. Europeans and Indians raised children together. Boon's cousin Daniel had been captured and adopted. And they killed one another.[32]

Benningsen Boon's neighbors came to Sand Ridge with vivid memories of the bloody conflict zone in the East and retold their harrowing stories at the Brownsville storefronts. Many from the Carolinas recalled their lives of service in the Revolution fighting both Tories and Indians. Joseph Williams told stories about growing up on the Virginia frontier, in Pittsylvania County, which had been named after the English prime minister credited for crushing the French and Indian foe. Conflict for empire had not ended, however. In 1776, Williams joined the militia against the Cherokee who resisted English intrusions into lands west of the Appalachian Mountains. After a three-month campaign, Virginia forces brought the Cherokee to a conference on the Holston River in western North Carolina. Williams attended and watched while the enemy ceded claims east of the mountains as well as western sections. Later, near the end of the Revolution, he fought the Tories in the Carolinas.[33]

Joshua Tyner brought family stories from the bloody Georgia frontier. One day, while his grandfather was absent, a band of Cherokee attacked the homestead, killing his wife and two children and taking another daughter Ann Eliza captive. Ann Eliza endured the journey into the wilderness, eventually became the wife of one of her captors, and bore him a son. Later she escaped with the son, returned home where her father received them, and renamed the boy Joshua after her father. When revolution came to Georgia, young Joshua and his neighbors were drawn into what he later described as "almost constant warfare surrounded by the Indians, British and Tories" that raged even after independence had been secured. Tyner volunteered to serve as a scout in search of the hostile Creek. He recounted his stories of attacking enemy encampments, skirmishing with raiding parties, and giving warning to what would otherwise have been unprotected American settlements and stations. After roving the frontiers for more than two years, he returned home, later moved to Tennessee, and finally appeared in Illinois.[34]

Tyner and Williams had planted in Jackson County when Jesse Gordon arrived. At the outset of the Revolution, Gordon was living in North Carolina. He had fought the Tories at Cape Fear and then marched against the Cherokee. He was with Williams at the Holston River conference with the Cherokee. Soon after, Gordon drifted into Georgia where he fought the Creek and later settled near the Tyner family in Wilks County. Soon, he recalled, the county became "the seat of an almost constant war . . . with the Indians on two sides and the British and Tories on the other two." As a militiaman, he seemed always on the alert and often on the march. "Although occasionally at home a few days at a time," he had "no time to attend to any business" before the alarm summoned him. Even after the war officially ended, hostilities continued against remaining indigenous peoples and embittered Tories.[35]

Allen Henson had lost his scalp on those bloody grounds. Benningsen Boon remembered him vividly. The Hensons had come from the North Carolina–Tennessee frontier and settled near the Boons. William Boon had helped them build their log cabin. Young Benningsen listened to Henson recount the time when hostile Indians had overcome him and took his scalp. Neighbors had found him and carefully nursed him back to health. As a final touch to his story, Henson removed his headpiece revealing the place where the skull had been cut away. Boon could not forget peering into the place where "the brain could be seen plainly." Sometimes Henson succumbed to "crazy spells." "At such times he would go among his friends and sing funny songs, and was very child-like in his ways and acts."[36]

Living in this violent world joined people over generations and space.[37] Physically these migrants had cut themselves loose from the sites of past conflict, but the memories they carried shaped their understanding of life in this new Illinois frontier. Stories told and retold wove connections between bloody past and present. Virginians who had taken up arms against the English marched to Illinois to secure this territory for an independent Virginia. Later, some like James Davis returned to claim what they had taken. When they rode to Brownsville for supplies, they took time to tell their stories of fighting in Illinois and Virginia. These migrants also encountered grim reminders of their violent pasts. The American Indians they had learned to fear in the East were moving through this region as well. Scattered bands of the ubiquitous Shawnee and the dispossessed Delaware drifted through. Once again encountering the Cherokee and Choctaw, these pioneer settlers renewed stories connecting distant bloody scenes in the past with Jackson County.[38]

The Boons had no sooner come to Sand Ridge than they awoke to reports that Tecumseh and the Prophet were summoning the indigenous peoples from northern Illinois down the Mississippi River to reclaim their land. A confederacy of Shawnee, Creek, Choctaw, Cherokee, Chickasaw, and possibly Osage across the river to the west seemed imminent. Tecumseh had passed through the vicinity a few miles to the east. Skirmishes had broken out in the north. News spread of American defeats. The emboldened Indian enemy penetrated into southern Illinois. The Creek killed families on the Ohio River. Hostile warriors attacked a family living on the road linking Shawneetown and Kaskaskia. Small bands, Benningsen Boon recalled, were lurking in the wilds near his home.[39]

The territorial governor ordered that a string of blockhouses be constructed at twenty-mile intervals from the Illinois River south through Jackson County. One blockhouse was erected on the banks of the Big Muddy River near the Boon home. To keep watch, the militia patrolled between each blockhouse. The young Boon remembered his father, who was elected captain of the local rangers, telling stories of the desperate conditions. A family in flight to a blockhouse was caught by a raiding party and killed. The father was with Boon's rangers. When Boon's men arrived at the scene, they found the women and children hacked to pieces. One small boy was found decapitated. Boon's men set out in pursuit of what they assumed was a small party. After several days, they spied the enemy in the distance and recognized that they had stumbled upon an encampment of several hundred. Benningsen remembered listening to his father tell the story how he and his comrades quickly withdrew and "beat a hasty and successful retreat." Terror spread, and the legislature posted a bounty for each male American Indian killed.[40]

The Boons lived in a garrison society that had been moving westward for generations. For Benningsen and his friends, listening to their fathers relive their harrowing exploits made fresh again the bloody tales from the eastern frontier. Young Boon watched neighbors raising the conventional "Indian-proof" homes. Each neighbor provided "a protection to the other against the wild Indians." The men habitually carried a "rifle kept in order" with "flint, bullets, bullet-moulds . . . butcher-knife and tomahawk." Years after Tecumseh's defeat and death during the War of 1812, the militia still trained. Young Boon was taught that "every able-bodied man was enlisted, enrolled, and had to attend the different musters."[41]

And veterans of the wars told their stories on training days. At Brownsville one old warrior thrilled the young with memories of Revolutionary days when he marched with George Rogers Clark to Illinois. He still carried his flintlock "Old Trusty." Pointing to a deep gouge in the stock, he gathered his young listeners about him. After the Revolution he returned to the western territories. Once he was captured by the Wyandottes. Helplessly, he watched as another prisoner was beaten mercilessly and then slowly burned to death at the stake. The gouge marked the place where an enemy arrow had struck in one of his numerous scrapes with the enemy. His heirs kept "Old Trusty" over the mantle and still told the stories. Neighbors passed on tales of living in a blockhouse for weeks while listening for sounds of an enemy lurking in the dark forest. Others shared stories of capture.[42]

Like heirlooms, the stories passed across the generations, perpetuating a deep awareness of the grim world Benningsen inherited. While Benningsen was putting his memories to paper, Lyman Draper, a historian of the frontier conflicts, was traveling the region in search of stories like the Boon family's that reached back to Virginia and the Carolinas and illustrated the personal trials of generations of westward-bound migrants. Draper sat up late with men, drinking liquor and indulging themselves in reliving the atrocities and heroics. He listened to an elder woman at the common table who remembered parents and siblings captured and killed in the east. Some remembered Jean Baptiste Duquoin of the Kaskaskia, others Daniel Boone.

Many shared secondhand impressions of frontier times, of fights with the Delaware and the Creek, of heroic pioneers, and of the death of innocents. The stories were grisly in detail. A husband and wife were captured by Indians; the husband was "tied to a tree." The woman watched in horror as their captors "cut his body open from his chin down and disembowled" him, "the blood spurting out on the sapling." The family explained the reasons for the atrocity: the husband and his brother were known for "Indian killing, & this was in retaliation." Draper recorded the bloodletting with attention to detail. In a skirmish, an ancestor had shot one male dead and then a woman. He seized her knife from her fist; it was a "long butcher knife . . . used perhaps in preparing the breakfast with a painted green handle" and "with it took the Indians's scalp." The storyteller hastened to assure Draper that the man, not the woman, was scalped.[43]

Benningsen Boon was nearly thirty and had married the daughter of Conrad Will. One morning in 1832 he awakened to reports of renewed troubles to the north. The Winnebago resisted intrusions into their homelands but were forced to surrender their claims in northern Illinois. Shortly after, the Sauk leader Black Hawk spoke to the times: nothing would satiate the Americans' hunger for land; they must be repelled. As the news of sporadic skirmishes filtered southward, memories quickened. Governor John Reynolds, himself a veteran of the War of 1812, summoned the state militia to join in common defense of the northern borders.[44]

Benningsen joined the war with fifty-one others from the county. Alexander Jenkins, who was sitting in the legislature, dropped his duties at once and rushed home to command the volunteers. His brother-in-law Dr. Logan enlisted as surgeon. In all, 15 percent of the county's men between age sixteen and forty rallied to the governor's call. While eager to engage the enemy, the troops were ordered to guard supplies at Fort Hamilton until Black Hawk was forced to leave the state.[45]

In the decade following Black Hawk's expulsion, Boon watched the cleansing of his neighborhood. He had grown up aware of these indigenous people on the margins of his world. In addition to the small band of Kaskaskia, he noticed other nameless American Indians slipping across the land. By the 1830s his Kaskaskia neighbors were preparing to cross the Mississippi as well. Ignored, their treaties forgotten, promised annuities unpaid, the villagers could see their numbers shrink while the American settlers flourished. Then they vanished. Their disappearance seemed inconsequential, a natural, inevitable product of taming the wilderness. Neither Benningsen nor other pastkeepers felt moved to note their exit. Still these indigenous peoples floated through Benningsen's world. But they remained shadowy entities scarcely worthy of mention and were thus forgotten.[46]

The people of Jackson County left scant record of the hundreds of dispossessed Indians, principally Cherokee, who in 1838 passed by on what would be remembered as the Trail of Tears. Andrew Jackson's decision to remove the Indians to territories west of the Mississippi realized deeply engrained attitudes and long-established policy. Implementation required the establishment of three routes, with one cutting through Illinois just south of Jackson County. Over ten thousand Indians were gathered into separate parties during the autumn of 1838. The hundreds who proceeded through southern Illinois camped often for prolonged periods to wait for icy conditions on the Mississippi River to improve. Desperately in need of supplies, they traded with the local settlers. Several died before the ferry at Willard Landing was able to carry them to Missouri.[47]

The thousands passing through in steady procession, one party after the next over several months, could not but be noticed. Doubtless memories were revived. While the Gordon, Tyner, and Williams families had once encountered these people in the east, others shared memories of struggles with other indigenous peoples, of relatives killed or captured, of scalpings and torture. Marks of the campsites and the graves remained on the landscape as reminders. Yet pastkeepers did not consider this episode as part of their history. At least publicly or in writing there was no mention.

Families, however, told the stories in private. The ferry owner had looked into the desperate faces as he transported them across the icy Mississippi. His daughter vividly remembered his stories of that grim winter. The cold was intense when the Indians approached the river. They waited—three thousand camped on a farm and another thirty-five hundred nearby. Army officers hired her father to mill grain. The mill was kept in operation all day and often all night. She remembered two Indian chiefs; their names were "Bushyhead" and "Nowatts." Sometimes her details became fuzzy: she got dates wrong, and perhaps the names were incorrect. Yet she conveyed a veracity in her memory of her father's experience.[48]

The Tyners also kept stories and mementos from their days in Georgia, before the Revolution, that intersected with the Trail of Tears.[49] When Ann Eliza had escaped her Indian captors with her son, Joshua, she had left behind an infant son. Like many captives, Joshua could not let go of his connections with Indian culture. Neighbors knew him as the "Indian herb doctor." His descendants remembered that he chose to end his days with the Indians. They also remembered that Joshua knew his brother, who still lived with the Cherokee and was part of the forced migration. Somehow the brother slipped from the encampment to visit Joshua. Joshua's family provided him with necessities for the journey, and when they separated, the brothers exchanged gifts. The leather goods that Joshua received became family treasures passed on with the stories through the generations.[50]

The Cherokee passing through, the Kaskaskia moving on—neither episode seemed relevant to the white settler narrative. On occasion, the Indian appeared as anecdote for local color. Edmund Newsome shared what he deemed a humorous but finally inconsequential episode. One day "Bob" Worthen was walking along the banks of the Big Muddy. The river was at flood stage. He came upon several "Indian children at play." "Just for fun," Worthen "began to pitch them into the swelling river." What he found great "sport" frightened the "the young savages." "Not appreciating the joke," they screamed for help and "brought their mothers to the rescue." The women promptly threw Worthen into the river "and left him to get out as well as he could."[51]

Newsome and Benningsen Boon participated in glossing over the collective experiences and memories rooted in frontier violence. Indians remained on the edges of the narrative, largely as shadows of a fast receding past. The collective terror of frontier life was reduced to isolated anecdote. Accordingly, Newsome briefly described the story of John Murdock, who witnessed the bloody massacre of innocents and became an "embittered and dedicated Indian hater." The pastkeeper echoed James Hall's vivid rendering of an "Indian Hater" who was driven for the same reason. Both writers used the isolated character to illustrate the transition from wilderness to civilization. In turn, the pioneers underwent a metamorphosis into hardy, brave, enduring progenitors of a whitewashed Jackson County.[52]

Accordingly, the writers glossed over a larger framework of imperialism. Consciously or not, Benningsen's pioneers were advancing the expansionist imperatives that drove this white American empire ever westward. They gave Andrew Jackson, Indian fighter and later Indian remover, overwhelming majorities in the 1828 election for president (91 percent) and again in 1832 (74 percent) and embraced his expansionist rhetoric. Already families were looking to lands across the Mississippi in Missouri and Arkansas and even farther beyond. Many were lured by stories of opportunity in the northern Mexican territory of Texas.[53]

The Creaths were getting itchy.[54] George Jr. remembered his father bringing the family to the Jackson County frontier. Though the family prospered, the younger generation looked south and across the Mississippi. In the early 1830s George bade farewell to his sister Sarah and her husband as the couple set out for Texas. When Sarah returned for a brief visit, he listened to her relive that day when Indians had killed her husband. Still, she intended to return to her new home—she had also since remarried. George resolved to accompany her. After floating downriver to New Orleans and then riding westward, they joined Sarah's new husband. Soon after, Indians attacked, killing George, Sarah's husband, and their child and capturing Sarah. Eventually she escaped and, undeterred, resolved to stick it out in Texas.

Sarah's story wove seamlessly into those told by immigrants from eastern Appalachia. The Halls had migrated from Virginia to Kentucky and then to Jackson County by the time of statehood.[55] They were farmers, blacksmiths, and operators of a gristmill and a distillery near Beaucoup Creek. James Hall Jr. (not related to the author) was elected with Conrad Will to the first state constitutional convention. While his sons Phineas and Samuel continued to manage the family enterprises, his other son—James III—moved to Texas. Relatives followed.

In the spring of 1847, John A. Logan prepared to go to Texas with a company of his neighbors. In 1844, James Polk, Andrew Jackson's heir, had won the presidency by promising annexation of Texas from Mexico as well as Oregon from Britain.[56] "Young Hickory" had quickened deep expansionist passions. While carrying Illinois by a slender margin (54 percent), he swept Jackson County by a substantially higher rate (65 percent). For Logan and his neighbors, Texas lay just down the Mississippi River waiting to be seized. The southern portion of the state, in contrast to the north, jumped to the call for volunteers and enabled Illinois to fill its troop quotas.[57] In early May, Lieutenant Logan and his men marched north to Alton where the state's forces were assembling.

Young Logan wrote home seeking his father's approval with his thirst for battle and military glory. He was soon disappointed. The Jackson County men did not see Texas but were dispatched up the Missouri River to Fort Leavenworth and then westward across the parched prairies toward Santa Fe. Instead of doing battle with Mexicans, the troops kept alert for hostile

Indians. Stationed in Santa Fe, young Logan's military ambitions were slowly quashed by the routine of garrison duty. By the following spring, he was readying his men to return home. Dr. Logan, while reading his son's account, recalled chasing Black Hawk a decade earlier and cautioned his son to beware the Indian menace.[58]

When county historians began to organize their thoughts, they swept this war to the margins. Perhaps they did so because the conquest of Mexico was so brief, perhaps because it happened outside the county, in distant lands, and thereby did not fit with their conception of local history. Men like Logan marched out of Jackson County and into a history larger than the local. Then they returned. Yet that war flowed together with the wars against Black Hawk and the ceaseless fighting on the Appalachian frontiers, creating an intergenerational consciousness integral to the local mentality. Sons listened to the veterans tell stories about their favorite gun. They watched the militia assemble for regular training. The beliefs that impelled young men, like their elders, to pick up their weapons to do combat with a distant, even imagined, enemy need not be elaborated, so pervasive were they. In turn, the aspiring local historians had breathed this atmosphere so deeply that they looked past this culture of violence as commonplace, not worthy of comment or reflection.[59]

Standing on the land that Mr. Jefferson had planned to be theirs, local historians had absorbed his faith in the unfolding progress of liberty and of civilization. Bloody conquest was thereby reshaped into expanding opportunity for the pursuit of happiness. Nor could they imagine that they were engaged in another war, this time against the African. But Jefferson had said as much when drafting the Declaration of Independence. Later, musing in his Monticello study, he imagined that if he were a slave, he too would rebel against his oppressor.[60] In southern Illinois majorities made Elijah Lovejoy, the outspoken enemy of slavery, a pariah and rejoiced when an Alton mob murdered him. When Logan's troops gathered at Alton in preparation for invading Mexico, they elected their officers. In one company a candidate nominated himself by boasting that he had killed Lovejoy with his bare hands. His comrades made him their leader. Logan reported the story to his father without comment. Slave catchers openly rode the southern Illinois countryside ferreting out their victims without thought of reproach. In 1860 one catcher appeared at the Carbondale railroad platform with an African American in chains. When they prepared to board a southbound train, one citizen spoke up protesting this violent act. Immediately a crowd gathered warning him to leave if he valued his life.[61]

The slave catcher and the African American were characters from a story that did not fit the design of Jackson County's pastkeepers. Their history turned on the efforts to cleanse the land of black people and on the habit of denying their presence. Yet they were there, running across the land. People said that slaves who had stolen themselves from their masters were hiding in a secret place at the northern edge of the county. There were others as well. The original people still lurked on the edges even after the Kaskaskia had forsaken their lands. When the railroad was laying tracks through the region, American Indians appeared with game for sale to the work crews. And there were the workers who laid the railroad tracks and dug the coal who were often transients. Many were Irish and Catholic. While the owners of the land depended on these laborers, these same owners of the past had by habit given them passing notice.[62]

The image of settlement might have on closer look dissolved into way-station. Even the owners of the land who were crafting their story held this idea in the recesses of their thoughts. The Logans seemed to have their bags packed. When John A. was preparing to return from the Mexican War, he and his friends discussed seeking their fortunes in California. While many of the Halls had been going to Texas, William, a grandson of James Hall, set out for the western gold fields. Or that was the story, for he seemed to have vanished. Others, like Benningsen Boon's sons, were looking to Oregon. At the dinner table Benningsen listened to the young men talk about leaving. After his second wife's son Francis Marion Lee—named in memory of the legendary frontier fighter of South Carolina—went to California, his own son Daniel set out on the Oregon Trail. While John A. Logan read the letters from California warning him not to come, he was looking elsewhere.[63]

In balance, original settler families like the Kimmels and the Bilderbecks would stay, but persistence represented a portion of the story. The remainder was found in the "floating people." The census takers documented the rate of transiency. In 1860 nearly half the people enumerated (49 percent) had not appeared on the 1850 census. And of those listed in 1860, two-thirds had left by the end of the decade. Benningsen Boon himself represented both types. Attached to place, he felt the itch to uproot. While preparing for Oregon, he attended to his stepson's caution to beware of Indian attack. The advice revived boyhood memories of stories he had heard.[64]

Benningsen's rudimentary history was the first step toward creating a community ritual of remembrance. In the decade after the Civil War, concerned citizens like Edmund Newsome were forming an Old Settler Society and an Old Folks Association for staging public acts of remembrance. Salesmen scoured the countryside searching for authors to write a county history as they peddled subscriptions to the promised publication. What emerged from these projects was elaboration of Benningsen's original.[65]

In 1880, Daniel Brush rode to Murphysboro to address the Old Folks Association. For some time he had been cultivating his reputation as caretaker of the past. He had been preparing his memoirs of life in southern Illinois, a history of Carbondale, and a history of his regiment in the Civil War.[66] As he looked upon old friends and associates, he summoned them to reflect: "Think of Fifty Years ago Ye Old Folks, and Sigh for the good times long departed!" Those Brownsville days were "the best of times," when hardy settlers led "clean and simple" lives. They dressed in plain homespun. The liquor they drank was homemade peach brandy, and they drank it in moderation and for refreshment. Since this was the occasion to remember the dead, he listed them by name, dozens in all, including his old rival Dr. Logan. These were the owners of the earth who had built for the future. And that generation had built well. "Take our County. Old Jackson—where is there a better heritage?"

But he warned the younger generation not to look back with envy lest nostalgia distract from the present and the future. "Ponder not" those bygone times, "Ye Young Folkes, lest they cause regret for the Change that has come and render you dissatisfied with the present." Today is the "most important and wonderful period of the World's history." The numbers told the story of progress. The county population had grown to over nineteen thousand. "Labor saving machines" such as the sewing machine had become available to the children of the pioneer settlers. "Wealth accumulated—population increased." Coal production in the county as well as farm surpluses promised prosperous tomorrows. Already Jackson County was selling to the world. "We now feed Europe" and soon would be feeding China. "What an Empire in Extent?"

No matter his cautionary note, Brush kept Benningsen's view of pioneer days. The frontier past remained a place for nostalgic fancy. In glossing over that grim and bloody time, he invited his listeners to forget. Instead, his past was populated by the owners and improvers of the land—all white. He and his audience chose not to remember this place as a waystation where so many, often less fortunate, had passed through. The heritage he worked to preserve was rooted in images of the virtuous and industrious. Their spirit promised a bright future. "God has given us this great land of Freedom & Equality, where each man & woman starts out the equal of every other to run the race of life—where there is no Royal road to wealth or honor—but with integrity, industry, morality & virtue governing the heart, success in life is assured—and Earthly honors may come."[67]

* * *

THE NARRATIVE EMERGING from the land survey raised images of propertied self-determining settlers who had domesticated a wilderness. While satisfying to the owners of the past, it rested on illusions or the habits of forgetting. Forgotten were the rootless drifters. Indeed, the pastkeepers themselves displayed that pervasive itch to uproot themselves. So, too, the story of hardy pioneers settling a wilderness enabled historians to slide over the multigenerational violent traits that were expressed in frontier warfare against American Indians and civil wars against African Americans. While frontier warfare was receding from the county's experience, white residents of the county would become bitterly divided over the place of black people during the Civil War.

CHAPTER 4

CIVIL WARS AND SILENCES

ONE SUNDAY MORNING in early spring a year after the Civil War had ended, three veterans talking on the steps of the Crab Orchard Christian Church grew silent as the widow of a comrade entered the burial ground with her children to lay flowers on her husband's grave. The veterans had watched the graves being dug in Carbondale's Woodlawn Cemetery. Twenty had been buried there. They recalled comrades who lay buried in distant, sometimes unmarked graves, some hastily covered with a few spades of earth. If they had dared to reflect, they might have remembered the animals digging that earth for meat. That same week, they rode to town and spoke to the need for a public act of memorial.[1]

On the last Sunday in April more than two hundred veterans gathered at the cemetery. General John A. Logan spoke. He had commanded these men at Belmont and Vicksburg, at Kennesaw Mountain and Atlanta. They remembered when he was wounded grievously at Fort Donelson. He spoke with certitude, assuring his audience that the dead had given their lives for a noble cause. He had rehearsed the address and would deliver it often. "Every man's life belongs to his country, and no man has a right to refuse when his country calls for it." He summoned the living not to forget, to preserve "tenderly the memory of our heroic dead, who made their breasts a barricade between our country and our foes."[2] The general made it his calling to honor the soldiers who had returned, some whole, many maimed, as well as those who had died on distant battlefields.

Regularly the people of Jackson County gathered in public places to remember. Soon Daniel Brush of the Illinois Eighteenth Infantry would deliver his own memorial address. Yet there were others, perhaps like the widow and her children at the church cemetery, who remembered silently in private. Julia Bowers kept a letter from her son Peter written from the front, assuring her that he and his comrades were well. He had been wounded but slightly. Shortly after receiving the letter, she learned that he died. A widow with two daughters, Julia kept the letter and made it a family remembrance for future generations.[3]

The reminders became an enduring part of daily life. The veteran who struggled to make a living without an arm, others crippled, wheezing, suffering with ravaged digestive systems, or complaining from stiffened joints were commonplace. There were the widows and the orphans. And there were the absences. Many returned, seemed unable to cope, and wandered off. Many shied from remembering. In the wake of the war's carnage, veterans often stayed away from public memorial celebrations; they declined to join the veterans' association, the Grand Army of the Republic. Some had thought they could keep the memory for posterity. When Daniel Brush and Edmund Newsome joined the fight, they carried journals to record their experiences. Newsome published his, and likely Brush expected to bring his to print. But words that might capture experience seemed inadequate, somehow illusive. A chasm remained. On one side were the silent and visible reminders of unspeakable horrors, and on the other were the public speeches and memoires extolling heroism, service, and sacrifice.

Public remembering worked to distract from the silent witnesses and the trauma. The writers of local history perpetuated the process of denial. The war's effects cut deep. This the historians knew when they looked about at the men who had witnessed the blood and gore and had heard the screams on the battlefield, or when they pondered over the fathers and mothers, wives and children of those who had not returned. The war could not be denied. And so the writers included in their histories honor rolls of those who had served and died. Perhaps the columns in print served as public memorial. Perhaps because the soldiers had marched out of the county to participate in a larger national history, their deeds were not considered part of local history. But the experiences the survivors carried home, tucked in their memories, did become part of community life. There seemed to be no words to address what remained present.[4]

* * *

JOHN A. LOGAN and Daniel Brush framed the county's wartime experience within a narrative, conventional and unchallenged, that extolled patriotism and elevated the soldier's loss to hallowed sacrifice. Looking back, they addressed audiences as if the war's meaning and the reasons for remembering were manifest and lay in loyalty to the Union. In their repetition, the rites of remembrance flattened the experience into a conflict between the friends of Union and its enemies, between the Union and the Confederacy. Speakers, like Brush and Logan, invited audiences to forget differences that had recently raged among neighbors. If either speaker had looked back carefully, he might have dredged up memories of recent deeds and understandings of the conflict that changed from the election of Lincoln to the surrender at Appomattox.

If the war had been fought for the Union, many in southern Illinois had bitterly and publicly opposed the president's call to arms in the spring of 1861. Naysayers identified with the South: either they or their parents had migrated from the Carolinas and Tennessee. Kin remained south of the Ohio River. This civil conflict was reduced to family feud. Thus only an insignificant fragment of the county had given its votes (three hundred of two thousand) to Lincoln and the Republican Party in November 1860. As the prospect of secession turned to reality, some marched south to join the Confederacy's armies. Those who rallied to the president's call to arms were deeply troubled by the war's purpose. Lincoln's call for union and liberty raised questions over whose liberty.

Moreover, these white citizens worried as they witnessed the emergence of an overweening national government that intruded upon the individual's rights. They were accustomed to a world where the federal authority was a distant presence. Although they participated in national elections with enthusiasm, they rarely encountered representatives of that government except for a local postmaster and the candidate for a seat in the national congress. Survival dictated that government expand its powers. Federal marshals roamed the countryside in search of friends to rebellion; neighbors were thrown into prison without due process. A military draft was instituted, and the government compiled a new census of eligible males for conscription. Even a tax on personal incomes was invented. While summoned to the Union cause, Jackson County's voters worried that their union of states governed by white males was disappearing. As the people watched the death counts rise, their concerns assumed urgency.[5]

The General Logan who had fought Mr. Lincoln's war was not the Logan of 1860. In the wake of the 1860 election and before Lincoln took office, the congressman cautiously tested the shifting currents. Echoing the sentiments of his constituents, he had vociferously expressed his contempt for the "black Republicans." His standing with the public rested on his sponsorship of legislation to cleanse Illinois of African Americans. A staunch Democrat, he had stumped for Senator Stephen Douglas's reelection against Lincoln's challenge in 1858. Again he supported Douglas's bid for the presidency in 1860 while dreading Republican victory. When the votes were counted, Lincoln carried the state easily but was trounced in the southern counties by a margin of three to one.[6]

Congressman Logan heard his constituents' southern accents. He attended to the reports from the southern states, especially South Carolina's call for disunion, as harbingers of a "fearful future." While colleagues in Washington believed conflict was "irrepressible," he prayed that a compromise might be achieved and that the fire-eaters would fail, as they had before, to rouse a united South. In contrast to those who spoke of a clearly demarcated sectional division, Logan refrained from placing Illinois in a North. Nor could he cast southern extremists outside the national community. "They are not our enemies with whom we should be willing to measure swords." Logan's own mother, born in Tennessee, had raised her children with southern sympathies. As the secession crisis deepened, she vocally supported the South, as did Logan's brother. The congressman prayed that "with forbearance and moderation" the government might achieve reconciliation.[7] Meanwhile he hesitated and waited in hopes that the crisis would pass. Observers wondered where his loyalties lay.

If Daniel Brush had looked back to the election, he might have recalled that he had harbored the same misgivings as had Logan. Like his longtime rival, he dreaded the prospect of Republican victory. An active Whig, he despised the Democrats, especially the Logans. Yet when his party disintegrated, he, unlike Lincoln and other Whigs, had been loath to join the newly founded Republican Party. While attending to the Douglas and Lincoln debate and the growing crisis over the extension of slavery, Brush found himself more often in agreement with Lincoln than not, but he could not lend his support to the Republican. That party's association with the most vociferous abolitionists seemed recklessly provocative of sectional discord. Like Lincoln, Brush disapproved of slavery. For Brush, the institution nurtured indolence and immorality among masters. But he heard no argument that persuaded him that the slavocracy and its right to own human property should be challenged. Nor did he feel moral discomfort with the plight of the slave.

Brush had, like Lincoln, traveled down the Mississippi and witnessed slavery firsthand. Unlike Lincoln, witnessing the plight of humans in chains did not prick twinges of empathy. Like Logan, he preferred to imagine Illinois as the white man's domain. Later, during the war, when contemplating the possibility of emancipation, he hoped that measures would be devised to keep black people in the South and out of his state. Brush found himself adrift. By habit reluctant to endorse Logan's Democrats and by principle repulsed by the Republicans, he found refuge in the newly formed Constitutional Union Party and its candidate John Bell of Tennessee. Hastily cobbled together by habitual compromisers who feared slavery's divisive effects, the party assured men like Brush that it would preserve the Union and the constitution by doing nothing on the major political issue of the day. Bell's candidacy seemed the last recourse for the despairing. It appealed to less than one in ten Jackson County voters.[8]

While men like Brush and Logan hoped that the crisis would pass, they felt themselves swept by events. In April 1861, when Carbondale learned that Charleston's batteries were firing on Fort Sumter, Brush watched "Secession Sympathizers, of whom quite a number resided in this town and vicinity," conspire to withdraw the southern counties from the state and to join the Confederacy. The president's call for troops provoked these men to desperate measures. On learning that troops would pass through town on the southbound train, they plotted to seize the telegraph office and burn the railroad trestle over the Big Muddy River north of town. Meanwhile Logan learned that his brother-in-law Israel Blanchard was meeting with secessionists who conspired to "use all means in our power" to "attach ourselves to the Southern Confederacy."[9]

Whatever his misgivings about Lincoln, Brush jostled against southern sympathizers on the street. He stopped them from seizing the telegraph office. When he announced his intention to lead a rally of Unionists, "Rebel sympathizers—and they were not a few—swore the Meeting should not be held" and "Threatened" to "trample [the flag] in the dust." As he spoke to his assembled allies, he heard the threats and the "rebel yell across the square, to down the flag." Later that month he enlisted. For nearly two more months Logan kept colleagues wondering. Finally, in June, he addressed troops in Springfield and, to the surprise of Colonel Ulysses S. Grant, "breathed a loyalty and devotion to the Union" into the recruits. Soon after, he toured his home district, rallying the undecided behind the Union cause. When he accepted a military commission, his mother refused to admit him to her home.[10]

By war's end, remembering entailed a foreshortening of the story so that uncertainties and inner conflict were glossed over and divisions pitting neighbor against neighbor, often violently, were swept aside. So simplified, the story became a recounting of Union against a southern foe. While the veterans were honored, their experiences were considered separate from the local history because their stories unfolded elsewhere, outside the county. And by this accounting, whatever experiences they brought back as memories—the friends lost, the people they had killed, the grueling hardships, the terror of battle—appeared irrelevant to life in their communities.[11]

Forgotten too were the conflicts that raged within the county. Neighbors questioned each other's loyalties and prepared for civil discord to erupt in their backyards. They wrote to Governor Richard Yates reporting conspiracy and summoning him to prepare for violent resistance to the government: "Pay attention to the Rebells in this End of the state" who boast they will "shoot every Republican" and "drive out every free Negro and 'Black Republican.'" They saw a "regular organized band of ceccionists [sic] in the adjoining towns of Jackson County." This "formidable conspiracy" awaited a rebel army to cross the Ohio or the Mississippi River and invade the state.[12]

Families worried about sons and husbands who boarded the southbound trains to Cairo and marched into the land of rebellion. They anxiously pored over the letters for assurances and expected the writer to send news of friends, whether they were wounded, killed, stricken with disease, or healthy. Neighbors shared news with one another. While waiting, they heard rumblings of cannon fire on the Mississippi River. They heard the trains passing south laden with soldiers for the war and returning with others on furlough. They recognized the wounded returning home to recover. Many died. Some who were discharged struggled against disability. Mothers and wives, fearful for their loved ones and hard pressed to manage a household alone, wrote urging men to come home at once—to desert. Deserters lurked in the woods dodging arrest. The war seeped into domestic life.

Those who stayed at home were enmeshed in the war. Unionists worried about the Knights of the Golden Circle—an underground militia supporting the Confederacy. It met regularly at the Makanda hotel and had grown in number, some said, to nearly two hundred strong. The Knights encouraged resistance to military service, gave shelter to deserters, and openly challenged Unionists searching for deserters. In Du Quoin, just north of Carbondale in Perry County, a crowd clashed with soldiers arresting deserters. Fighting broke out sporadically in the woods near Makanda. Emily Wiley wrote to her husband Benjamin, a cavalry colonel, that "we may expect some war in our own state if not on our own co[unty]." By some calculations, nearly twenty were killed in her neighborhood. From Carbondale, a Unionist wrote the governor that "Threats of violence are being Constantly made against the lives and Property of loyal men." "Many Citizens Swore they will resist drafting."[13]

At sixteen when the war began Hiram Lee was too young to enlist. The farm boy envied his friends as they left for adventure. No one anticipated the losses. The Thirty-First and Eighteenth Infantries, drawn principally from Jackson County, had encountered heavy fighting at Fort Donelson. Thomas Richards wrote home: "John Brookman pore fellow he is dead he was shot rite the head and killed dead. . . . It is the worst looking site ever I saw in my life to walk over the battle field and look at the dead and wounded." Total Union deaths approached a thousand. Weeks later at Shiloh the Eighteenth and Ninth Regiments lost twice that of Donelson. In the war's first year, Jackson County lost forty men from battle and disease.

Families began to feel the war. William Etherton had enlisted in the Sixth Cavalry, and after less than six months he returned discharged for debilitating "chronic diarrhea & exhaustion." He did not recover and died four months later, leaving a widow and six children. Meanwhile Micajah Etherton had joined the 109th Infantry, served for three months, deserted, and fled to Canada. At the end of 1862, Daniel Brush reviewed the grim tallies endured by his regiment. Of the original 930, 212 had died—65 in battle, 30 from wounds, and 117 from disease, and 164 were discharged for physical disabilities. More than 20 had deserted. The count of widows and fatherless children grew. Hiram Lee watched the wounded return, some "minus a leg or otherwise wounded." Two from his Kinkaid district had died of disease. Undeterred, the youth waited impatiently for his birthday. "I was crazy to enlist," he remembered, "and when Lincoln made the call in the spring of 1862 I did."[14]

The calls for volunteers, the lengthening lists of deaths quickened concerns about the war's purpose. Were soldiers risking their lives for the Union or for the African slave? Despite the president's repeated assurances to the contrary, suspicions could not be allayed. Logan, while committed to the preservation of both the Union and a white Illinois, shared his fears with his old friend Lindorf Ozburn. Together they had served in the Mexican War and now were in Mr. Lincoln's war, this time in the Thirty-First Infantry. While Logan preferred discretion, his friend could not contain his rage at that "black hearted," "fanatical" party of abolition. Similar grumblings could be heard in the ranks of the 109th Infantry. Soldiers were taunted by their families for risking death in behalf of African Americans. Desertions increased.[15]

Across the Mississippi River, Union general John Frémont had declared martial law in Missouri and ordered that the slaves of rebels be freed. Though the president reversed the proclamation, suspicions simmered. Frémont had been the Republican candidate for president in 1856 and consorted with notorious Illinois abolitionists. Opponents of the war spoke out openly. Logan's brother-in-law Israel Blanchard was arrested and summarily dispatched to a Springfield prison camp. On Logan's intervention, Blanchard was released and the next year handily won election to the state legislature. Republicans endured statewide defeats at the polls in 1862 with Democrats gaining control of both houses of the state legislature and winning eight of thirteen races for congress. In southern Illinois, Democrats nominated for congress an outspoken opponent of the war who trounced the Republican candidate by a margin of more than two to one and won 85 percent of Jackson County voters.[16]

If it were not for "the infernal negro," Private Matthew Pate wrote his brother, he could accept the "harde" life of the soldier. A young Murphysboro farmer, Pate had joined the Thirty-First Infantry, had witnessed the heavy losses at Fort Donelson, and had been marching through eastern Tennessee and northern Mississippi under General Grant in preparation for the siege of Vicksburg. With his comrades he cursed the news that President Lincoln's proclamation would free slaves in rebel territory and give arms to blacks.[17]

When Pate's brother read the letter, he was witnessing the local implications of emancipation. As Union forces drove into southern territory, slaves were escaping northward and seeking refuge with the army camp at Cairo. Their numbers rose to nearly two thousand. Federal authorities, looking for a method to relieve themselves of this growing burden, realized that communities northward along the railroad were desperate for workers. Farmers and government officials entered into labor contracts. Chapman Ward, a

Murphysboro carpenter, received one black worker in the fall of 1862; Isham Worthen, a Murphysboro farmer, took on four. In De Soto, William Parsons and Stephen Hall each brought in seven. In Makanda, Colonel Ben Wiley of the Fifth Cavalry who had returned home to recuperate from illness hired two black laborers.[18]

A few railroad stops south of Makanda, in Jonesboro, Democrats rallied to express their outrage: "In memory of our fathers and a rich legacy to our children, the soil of Illinois shall be held sacred to the uses and purposes of the white race." Citizens were incensed to learn that a neighbor had bought a cotton gin and contracted for forty escaped slaves; they forced him to return his workers. Authorities began prosecutions under Logan's black codes. In all, Jackson County brought proceedings against thirty-four of its residents.[19]

Soldiers coming home on furlough listened to friends and family rail against this abolitionist war. When they returned to the army in preparation for the campaign against Vicksburg, they heard the same grumblings echoed in camp. Soldiers in the 109th infantry openly vowed that they would not fight for the slave. In the Thirty-First, Lindorf Ozburn brazenly expressed his contempt for the "black republicans." General Logan worried for his sympathies for deserters. The two clashed, and Logan summarily sent Ozburn home. Soldiers like Matthew Pate heard the general's brother, publicly intoxicated, cheering the Confederacy and President Jefferson Davis. Desertions in the 109th had risen to such a level and the remaining troops proved so unreliable that the regiment was sent home.[20]

At home in Jackson County the war engulfed the people. Neighbors charged neighbors with disloyalty. Race fears inflamed passions. Finally, it was the absences, the waiting, the losses that deepened the crisis. When Peter Boyer wrote to his mother, he understood that she, as well as her neighbors, waited anxiously for news. Thus he listed the names of friends who were well, knowing that the news would be shared with families. The war fell heavily on women like Altisadora Reese. She awaited her husband John's letters and read his harrowing accounts of long marches and fierce battles. Alone at home, without her husband's labor, she cared for children and ran the farm. Widowhood haunted imaginations. In turn, the soldiers who returned brought with them images of scenes that could not be put to words.

In August 1862 Edmund Newsome boarded the train at the Carbondale depot to join the Eighty-First Infantry encamped at Anna. Arthur McCullough and Edwin Loosely had taken the same train from the Du Quoin station in Perry County; John Reese from Cobden in Union County joined them. All four served in the Eighty-First. A third of that regimental roster came from Jackson County, the rest like Reese and McCullough from the immediate region. Whatever their addresses, the soldiers were a homogeneous lot. After encamping at Cairo and Fort Defiance, they marched south into the bloody Vicksburg campaign and later pursued the enemy from Arkansas and Missouri to Georgia and Alabama. But for the occasional furlough, they were absent for three years. Meanwhile their families kept households together and waited for news. Mary and Edmund Newsome were older and could entrust their twenty-one-year-old son with the printing business. Loosely, McCullough, and Reese left wives with children no older than six. McCullough died of persistent maladies at the war's end. The other three returned home. One third of the regiment had died by the summer of 1865.

When Altisadora Reese bade John farewell, she had three children, all under three. Husband and wife had discussed the management of the farm—the time to butcher the hogs and the season to plant.[21] They agreed that neither John's father nor hers was able to help. She would need to hire workers; he promised to send his pay to cover the family's expenses. If unable to plant crops, she might simply rent the land. The prospect of widowhood weighed on her mind. Forty men from the regiment had died of sickness in the four months after his departure. Alone, dependent on his pay, she wrote regularly inquiring for his health. She kept secret that she was carrying a fourth child.

And while John wrote home, every few days, expressing his affection, he reminded Tisa of deep resentments toward his family for mocking him for soldiering on behalf of African Americans. Both his parents and his wife's were rooted in the South. John had been born in Tennessee; a brother had enlisted in the rebel army. Even while he angrily protested that he did not harbor abolitionist sympathies, his father-in-law continued to write, especially after the Emancipation Proclamation, to ridicule his service. "I'm tired to have it thrown in my teeth," he wrote, "that I am fighting for Negro Equality. . . . It seems that I have lost all my friends at home." He did not wish to discuss the matter further and directed his family to cease their ridicule.[22]

Health weighed on both their minds. While John assured Tisa that he and his men fared well, he could not hide the thought of death. Two days after reporting that he and "the Boys from our Neighborhood are all in good health and spirits," he shared his thoughts while listening to a man die in the adjoining tent: "It is a hard thing to die away from home and friends. Oh I hope I will not get sick in the Army where you can't be with me." Four men in his company and thirty-four more in the regiment had succumbed to disease. A month later—January 1863—Tisa read that John was recuperating from "Yellow Jandice [*sic*] and the worst cold I think I ever had in my life." She was in her eighth month of pregnancy.[23]

Reese and his comrades were uncertain what General Grant planned. After his earlier attempts to advance against Vicksburg from the east and by land had failed, the general tried one route after another to bypass the Confederate batteries.[24] From February to mid-March 1863, the Eighty-First encamped at Lake Providence, watching escaped slaves dig a canal toward the Red River. Tisa pored over each letter. John shivered in the cold rains. While assuring her that he had "nearly got well of my cough," he composed a list of the men they knew who had died of sickness.[25] Jack Jenkins was ill. Tisa learned that Joe Stone "is very sick I fear he will not get well." Burdened by household chores, she wrote less often but always asked for his health. Had he enough to eat? Soon after, neighbors told her that Jenkins had returned home to recuperate. Later she learned that he had died. John pled for her to knit a pair of warm socks.[26]

Death was always in their thoughts. Reese knew that comrades in his company were receiving letters from wives urging them to desert. Some did. Though friends at home called him a Lincoln "hireling," he felt honor bound to serve for the war's duration. "I am in this thing I entered to stay until the War is over if I should live that long." Loyalty dictated his course. He hoped that Tisa would teach their three children "to love the stars and stripes." Writing with grim determination, he concluded one letter with "Your husband until death." His letters were becoming darker. He prayed that Tisa would not counsel desertion. Then in early March, the army prepared to move southward.[27]

In a few days, while his regiment was moving down the western side of the Mississippi River toward a crossing south of Vicksburg, Reese awakened to Altisadora's announcement that she had given birth to a son, John Daniel. He attempted humor: "I think you played a yankee trick on me for you never told me." But the news roused a cry of anguish for the burden he had put upon his family. "I have left my wife and little children and my home, left everything that is dear to me." Always he grasped for solace or self-justification by assuming the role of selfless patriot that verged on martyrdom. He had, he continued to Tisa, "offered my self if need be upon the alter of my Country. I have endured hardship and Privations and periled my life and I am ready to do the Same thing again when called on."[28]

John Reese wrote that he heard cannon fire along the river. While trying to assure Tisa, he could not disguise his concern that he might "fall upon the Battlefield." He imagined Tisa's condition; springtime and planting were upon her. "I expect you see a hard time of it." While promising that his pay would support her, he was frustrated that he was paid irregularly. Other than sending her money, he was resigned that he could do no more. His advice on farm management seemed inadequate from the distance. After suggesting that she hire a plowman, he let go: "Do with the Mony as you think Best." Still he wrote to justify his absence. "Tisa you know I have Been Right on the Union question all the time and . . . I am Ready to seal my Principles with my hearts blood."[29]

For the next month, the Eighty-First moved rapidly, crossing the Mississippi south of Vicksburg, driving though enemy resistance at Port Gibson and Raymond, and then raced toward Jackson.[30] The troops lived off the land, snatching whatever food they found, slept little, and when they did it was on their arms in the cold, damp open air. The conditions were "awful," Reese wrote. He fell sick but doggedly slogged forward with the company.[31] In two weeks Grant's army marched into Jackson, stayed long enough to wreck supply systems and burn down factories, turned about, and sped toward Vicksburg. At Champion Hill it drove rebel forces into retreat behind the formidable redoubts protecting the city. The regiment's losses seemed minor with only five killed since the crossing. The army outnumbered the enemy by more than two to one. And the quick succession of victories instilled the troops, however exhausted, with confidence that the city would fall easily.

On May 22, Grant directed an assault on the fortifications at the top of the bluffs defending the city. For the steep uphill climb against cannon and infantry, Union forces were equipped with scaling ladders and bayonets. They met catastrophe. Four days after his shattered company scrambled down that hill, Reese tried to collect his thoughts and feelings. What he experienced was not a battle, he wrote, but a "slaughter." Eighteen in the regiment had been killed and another eighty had been wounded. In all, more than five hundred had been killed and more than twenty-five hundred wounded. Many of the wounded lay abandoned in a ravine at the bottom of the hill. Reese and his comrades still heard them crying in agony. If they visited a field hospital, they were struck mute by the "mangled" bodies.[32]

Horror mixed with anger as Reese reflected on the carnage. On that morning when Federal troops readied themselves for the assault, they were ordered to fix bayonets and not to fire their weapons until they had achieved the heights. When Reese's company began the climb, others in advance were tumbling down in bloody tatters. "We went with fixt Bayonett" within a hundred yards of the fort. "The Rebels commenced firing Shell and grape shot as soon as we came in sight and when we came in Range of their Muskets and Rifles they poured a Murderous fire on us." The details flooded his mind. The hillside seemed shorn clean of grass. "Not a twig" remained. Maybe his company advanced within "70 steps" of the enemy. Then the men dropped their ladders and scrambled downhill in retreat. "Oh it was a frightful Massacre if we had been allowed to fire we could of saved ourselves." By his calculation, "The 81st lost 1,07 men in ten minutes." The Seventh Missouri Infantry that had advanced and retreated with his regiment "lost 1,00 in the same time." "How any of us escaped is Wonderful."[33]

Reese was stunned. Why were he and his comrades ordered not to fire? The air was heavy with the smell of decaying human flesh; the dead still lay on the hillside and in that ravine. He could see the bodies. Each day a wounded friend died in the field hospital. Images of the horror returned as he wrote to Tisa. He saw "a Brave Boy in our Co named W P Mcoy fall shot through the heart." Burt Morris had fought valiantly. Specific faces came to mind: "By my side Lt Lamar and 3 others were wounded." "None of the Boys from our Neighborhood were hurt except Seargt Ede he got a painful shot in the foot." But "The col was killed the Adgt lost one leg 2 Lieutenants were killed and 5 wounded also five captains were wounded." So fixed on the horror, he wrote without imagining Tisa's response when he recalled that in the thick of this melee he "was hit in the left arm with a glancing Ball." A few lines later he mentioned a cannon striking the earth near him.[34]

During the routine of the siege Reese unburdened himself to Tisa. By habit he assured her that he and "the Boys from our Neighborhood" were well. Then he returned to the dying: a sergeant from Carbondale was shot while on picket duty. When reading her letters, he felt her anxiety and tried to allay her fears. Then he opened a window for her to peer into a dark world beyond her comprehension. The air was full of bullets and shells screaming past. On spotting a puff of smoke from an enemy piece, the men ducked before the shot arrived. They laughed and joked. He invited her to imagine the unimaginable. The "narrow escapes from death I see every day you could hardly believe." While "writing this letter 2 Rebel shell bursted in our Camp." No doubt Tisa could "form no idea of our Situation While I am writing the Bullets from the Rebel fort are continuously passing over my head if they don't hit is all we care for."[35]

Tisa read his accounts and wrote her concerns. "So Tiss don't get uneasy about me just think that I will live to get home. . . . If I live to see Vicksburg taken I intend to come home." In one letter he described meeting an enemy soldier who had been trying to kill him. One night "I hollowed to the Rebels . . . and told them to meet me half way." They agreed and they approached each other. John "set down" with "a Big live Rebel," "shook hands . . . and had a half hours social chat." The soldier was "an intelligent good looking man" from the Twenty-Third Mississippi Infantry. He asked if John was the officer in command of the "sharpshooters at the rifle pit." When John nodded, the man volunteered that "he had taken several pulls at me that day."[36]

On July 4, Federal troops marched into Vicksburg. They had bought victory with nearly five thousand killed and wounded. When the soldiers returned home on furlough, they might have expected the war to end soon. Rebel forces had been defeated at Gettysburg, also on July 4. Instead, the Confederacy demonstrated dogged determination to fight for its survival, and the war continued, with men from Jackson County engaged continuously. While the Eighty-First chased the enemy in the west for another year before marching eastward against Nashville, the Thirty-First and Twenty-Seventh Regiments had moved eastward toward Atlanta. After the Twenty-Seventh was mustered out in September 1864, the Thirty-First, Logan's own, continued with the campaign into the Carolinas. At the war's end, more than fourteen hundred men from Jackson County had served in ten infantry and two cavalry regiments. The losses counted, though never complete, came to more than three hundred. Twenty-one percent of the county's soldiers had died.

When the Eighty-First was mustered out in Chicago, it had sustained heavy losses of over three hundred, with more than eighty from Jackson County. Captain Reese set out for his farm, and Captain Newsome returned to his Carbondale print shop. Private Loosely soon moved his family to Murphysboro and opened a bakery. Sergeant McCullough, who had moved his family to Carbondale on enlistment, had died while stationed at Montgomery, Alabama, a month after the war's end. While the experiences that soldiers brought to their homes and that wives, widows, children, and parents had endured affected local life in the subsequent decades, the survivors pushed memories of war and the ensuing private struggles off the pages of local history. Newsome, for example, composed a history of developments within the county. Briefly, in a single paragraph, he glossed over that time: emotions were "stirred," soldiers came and went, and families waited. This was a "long dreary time." "Everything stopped"; nothing happened. The economy, he observed, was stagnant for the duration of the conflict. What he witnessed at the siege of Vicksburg and later campaigns seemed extraneous to understanding the life of the county.[37]

Yet, the war had become a presence, often without words to identify its place in the lives of families and neighbors. The numbers alone mutely point to a collective experience. On the eve of the war, the census counted nearly ten thousand residents of the county. Two years later the government compiled a census of males between 18 and 45.[38] The list comprised one-fifth the county population. Everyone knew young men who enlisted, some for a hundred days at the war's onset and many for four years. In Carbondale slightly more than half the 377 military-age males went to war. In Murphysboro, the rate of enlistment was even higher: 119 of 153 males (77 percent). The enlistments were lower in rural areas, with slightly less than half (46 percent) of Ora Township's 177 eligible males and 33 percent of Somerset Township's in uniform.

Newsome mentioned without lingering long enough to recall their names the "many women" who waited "in vain . . . for those who never came."[39] The numbers render a sense of proportion to his words. Of Carbondale's 192 soldiers, 41 (21 percent) died. Only three of Ora Township's 69 soldiers died (4 percent). The men of Somerset Township sustained a higher rate, with 8 of 45 soldiers (17 percent). Men from Murphysboro suffered the highest rates with 32 deaths of 119 soldiers (26 percent). Jackson County men served in regiments that suffered heavily: the Eightieth Infantry and Logan's Thirty-First lost over 450, and the Eighteenth nearly 400. By contrast, the Twenty-Seventh counted less than 200 dead. The 109th sustained 94 losses, principally from sickness, before it was sent home.

The numbers need not have been tallied to sense the depth of trauma. Some names and faces slipped from memory: the young transient day laborers who appeared in the county on the eve of the war, enlisted, and disappeared on a distant battlefield or in a field hospital. But the living reminders bore witness by their presence. Neighbors recognized the widows and the children. In Carbondale they knew Laura McCullough, who kept house and raised her son Frank. In De Soto, they recognized Mary Purdy, the widow of Henry who had succumbed to illness in Tennessee; she was responsible for five children. Widow Lucinda Etherton was left raising six children. Neighbors knew the grieving parents. Esther Stearns's son Frederick had come home to recuperate from his wounds and died. Some families had felt the war severely. Nine Haglers of Carbondale served together in the Eighty-First Infantry. One came home disabled, and two died in Memphis hospitals within days of one another.[40]

The disabled reminded neighbors. Nearby the widow Bower, Elias Worthen farmed his land without an arm. Four amputees lived in Ava, one in Carbondale, two in Grand Tower, and four in Murphysboro. Veterans limped from crippling wounds, they were missing a hand or fingers, some had lost an eye or were nearly blind, others suffered visibly from injured spines. They coughed incessantly. They complained of diarrhea and rheumatism. Ambrose Crowell and Alfred Elmore had marched together in the Eighty-First. Crowell returned home with his right arm impaired. Elmore, who had ended the war in Andersonville Prison, returned with a chronic cough and shortness of breath that prevented him from sustained labor. Martin Whipkey, also from the Eighty-First and a prisoner at Andersonville, returned to his De Soto farm complaining of a "Rupture of the lower bowels" and "disease of the kidneys."[41]

Crowell and Elmore talked with one another about their ailments and likely shared reminiscences. When applying for pensions, they relied on each other for corroborating testimony and turned to neighbors who compared their conditions before and after the war. In doing so they sustained a memory community that kept the war a continuing presence. Yet the veterans felt a distance separating themselves from those who had stayed at home. They had "seen the elephant." They listened to speechmakers praise the soldier's valor on the battlefield. Once they had been moved by such words, but they had been to that place, heard the deadly fire and the screams, and smelled the powder and the rotting flesh.

In early 1863 Edwin Loosely looked forward "for the first time to see the real elephant." "We shall undoubtedly have a deal of fighting to do," he wrote home. In early June he stood before Vicksburg, still stunned by the fruitless uphill charge against the enemy. As the men of the Eighty-First clambered up the steep incline, enemy artillery "threw bushels of grape and canister from both flanks while infantry in front was pouring deadly volleys at us." He had seen his comrades "shot down like dogs." In a few brief moments "2 out of every 3 in our Company was shot. . . . I was to the left of the company and in a few minutes everyone in both ranks to my right for 10 yards was hit, the last one of them, leaving me solitary and alone and company 'C' on my left suffered nearly as bad." Any moment he expected a "ball to come and do its work" on him. With "about half the regiment . . . killed and wounded we were ordered to charge." "Our loss was fearful . . . our Colonel . . . [was] shot through the head the top being shot off. . . . I felt that I lost a friend."[42]

Soldiers had seen comrades' faces disintegrate into a bloody mass.[43] They carried images of the once unimagined. The minié ball inflicted ghastly damage on the human body. Men screamed in agony as they clutched at gaping holes in their abdomens, others fell with their brains splattered across the earth. Men shot in the neck stumbled aimlessly, chocking in their blood. Soldiers saw a minié ball rip a hole through a friend's artery, watched a fountain of blood shoot upward, and felt themselves bathed in the warm redness. They saw men with their eyes shot out, blood running out their sockets, groping in darkness. Cannon tore through the ranks, shredding men to pieces. Soldiers remembered being struck by flying arms and legs. They had watched men crawling in pain across a field, their intestines dragging behind them. Daniel Brush was horrified at the scene after one battle: the bodies were "mutilated and blackened by the . . . power & bursting shells—arms off—legs off—heads off—It was awful to behold—the heart sickened at the sight."[44]

At battle's end they gazed numbly at the bodies strewn across the field, some mangled beyond recognition, others near death and writhing in pain. Bits of flesh littered the earth and dangled from nearby trees. They remembered slogging through pools of blood and stumbling over the unrecognizable corpses. Soon the stench of rotting flesh, human and animal, filled the air. At the field hospitals they gawked at the ambulances, blood dripping from their bottoms.

The living returned home carrying images of the bodies unburied, bloated, black, decaying in open fields or shrouded in woodland thickets.[45] Soldiers told stories of vengeful rebels desecrating bodies. Mourning families made arrangements to retrieve the dead for safe burial. Veterans thought about comrades lying in distant forgotten ground, about the skeletons lying somewhere, unidentified, alone, without as much as a marker. Edwin Loosely reflected with his wife on the soldiers lying "far away in an enemies country with not even A stone to mark the resting Place." There "they will lay far from home . . . to the crack of doom."[46]

John Reese revisited the Vicksburg battlefield where a year before he had witnessed the "slaughter" of "true warm friends." As he read the names roughly inscribed on the markers, "a shade of Sadness passed over me." As he read the names, "their features came Back in imagination." He mused over the families, people he knew, waiting for homecoming but "in vain." "Husband and Father can never come home." Loosely wondered too: "How many thousands of widows will remember the past year as the saddest in their life's history. And how many sweet dear little innocent orphans will still wonder why 'Papa' don't come home, too innocent to know and appreciate that their dust lies far away."[47]

The veteran had "seen the elephant" and could not forget. In camp soldiers felt a comradeship that came from the long grueling marches followed by the exhilaration and horror of battle. Anticipating that they would soon be separated, they vowed to keep memories alive. Reese asked Tisa to buy an album for him to keep photographs of his comrades. Memory keeping became a business, with photographers following the army and taking portraits. Reese sat for his photograph. He acquired portraits of his friends and sent them to Tisa to be mounted in the album.[48]

Memories separated soldier from friends and family. It was noon when the Eighty-First infantry crashed through an enemy artillery unit at Compton Hill. Rebel soldiers, dead and dying, lay scattered across the ground. Suddenly Reese froze before a wounded rebel, twisting in agony, who had been shot once in the leg and a second time in the belly. Screaming, he pled with Reese to shoot him. Reese refused. The youth cried to be given a revolver. Still Reese refused. During the siege, Reese recognized himself as a killer. One day he and his men were exchanging fire with the enemy when "I saw a rebel crawl upon the Breast Works." He remembered the scene vividly. The man had laid aside his weapon and "forgot himself so far as to expose his full length to me." Reese took aim and pulled the trigger. He could see that he had shot the man "in the side." He watched the man lie on the embankment "until someone in the fort pulled him Back."

Reliving that moment, he wrote: "So I guess I am guilty of killing one of my Southern Brethren."[49]

The war had seeped into lives of soldiers and civilians and lingered at the heart of county life. Its presence was at once palpable and ethereal. The soldier without a leg became a silent witness, evoking imaginations, his reserve testifying to experience that eluded words. The soldier who had yearned for homecoming felt the distance. The thundering, unrelenting roar of cannon, the artillery crews bleeding out the ears from the pounding, the sight of an artillery shell turning a friend into a mass of raw flesh, the very moment of killing, the stench of humans rotting—these sights, sounds, and smells could be understood only by others who had "seen the elephant." Thus, veterans, reluctant to share their experience except perhaps with one another, were wont to shy from public celebrations in their honor.

The veteran also seemed to recede into the background. Soldiers, who had endured long marches and exposure to cold and wet and had returned with lingering and debilitating ailments died earlier than their contemporaries who had stayed home. They also disappeared from sight. In Carbondale, one in four soldiers who survived the war remained by 1870. The rate of exit was nearly twice that high in Murphysboro. In Bradley Township sixteen of the sixty-one surviving soldiers stayed to the decade's end. In Elk Township six of thirty-four remained. Significantly, the rate of departure was higher for soldiers than for contemporaries of military age who did not serve.[50]

In time, other veterans publicly claimed their identity by joining the Grand Army of the Republic (GAR).[51] After two decades of membership lagging well below the eligible applicants, the numbers rose appreciably. When a local post posed for a photographer, the assembled represented the men of substance—merchants, professionals such as lawyers and physicians, farmers, and skilled craftsmen. The group carried weak connections with the local wartime experience, however. Members were likely to come from regiments recruited elsewhere in Illinois or in states from Kansas to Ohio, Pennsylvania, even Maine. The Carbondale post had thirty-five members with eighteen from county regiments. Significantly, pensioners were more numerous than GAR members. Of the fifty-nine who gave a Carbondale address, only nine joined the Grand Army. So, too, of the eighty-seven Murphysboro soldiers who returned, only twelve joined the twenty-three-member post. The other half had come from other states. Ava boasted the largest post with thirty-six of sixty survivors joining. Pensioner participation remained within the norm with nine of twenty-two on the roll. The little Mississippi River town of Grand Tower seemed the exception with farmers and laborers setting the tone of membership. Like neighboring posts, however, only four of the eighteen members served in locally recruited units.[52]

The missing veteran remained a presence. Unable to adjust to the peace, he became the tramp. In the decades following the war, communities throughout the nation felt overwhelmed by these footloose men who were reminders of vanished veterans. In Carbondale, people knew "Jerry the Bootblack." Homeless, he wandered from town to town, appearing periodically across the railroad depot. Hardly Barely able to eke out a living, he spent most of his earnings on drink. He regaled customers and passersby with stories about his adventures in distant lands and his wartime service. Jeremiah Williams had served in the Pennsylvania infantry. Townspeople preferred not to believe that he was once a soldier. Indeed, he represented the common lurking image of the veteran who had fallen to immorality and no longer possessed the character to support himself. He could not be a veteran, townspeople told themselves; if so, he would have joined the GAR. But they remembered his stories. When he took himself to the county poor farm and died, the Carbondale newspaper put the story at the top of the front page. Unlike those of other vagrants, this story was somehow worth telling. Appropriately, he was buried in potter's field with the fitting epitaph: "Known to thousands, yet mourned by none." Veterans, many like "Jerry the Bootblack," lurked on the margins of community life and appeared briefly in public records as social nuisances. Others exhibited unstable mental conditions and were admitted to state institutions for the insane at increasing numbers.[53]

The presences and the absences pointed to the question: why had the war been fought? From the outset soldiers and civilians alike had been addressing the question. Men like Reese had insisted that they fought for Union. Yet the war carried them by its own momentum to address the slavery question and in turn the place of the freed slave in their society. In camp the soldiers were reminded. While people in Jackson County awakened to the arrival of black contraband, soldiers often for the first time in their lives met black people. As Union forces moved south, escaped slaves appeared in camp as servants and cooks. In the Eighty-First Infantry, for example, Edward and Jerry Woods; Levi, Joseph, and Abraham Evans; John Lucas; Alexander Fortson; and Samuel Stratton cooked meals. Officers employed escaped slaves as personal servants. Several vanished. Though a lingering, often nameless, presence, they became reminders of the question.[54]

While Daniel Brush kept two escaped slaves as personal servants, his experience had not softened deeply engrained contempt for the African's ability to lead a self-sufficient life. Others, however, felt drawn to reflection as they witnessed slavery firsthand. John Reese felt himself faltering in his opposition to abolition. He argued strenuously against emancipation as if to convince himself. No doubt, the plantation system was best for the African: "The government will inflict an irreparable injury upon the Darkey here if it frees them." In the same letter to Tisa, he was troubled to discover that "there is plenty of Mulatoes Down in Dixie." The widespread sexual exploitation of slaves testified to the moral depravity and hypocrisy of the master class. A month later he was becoming open to the implications of the president's Emancipation Proclamation and the possibility of a "union without slavery." In recovering from the horror of the siege of Vicksburg, he recognized the war's logic. "I am satisfied," he wrote home, that slavery "was the imminent cause of the War." Too many lives had been lost to deny this truth that "as long as Slavery remains as it is in the country there will be perpetual war with its horror." Like his English comrade Edwin Loosely, he saw that secession was the handiwork of the slavocracy. Some might call him an abolitionist, "But it is my honest opinion and I can't help it."[55]

Reese and his comrades witnessed the black man don a Union uniform to risk his life. Prejudices softened. They knew that by order of the Confederate government black troops would be given no quarter. Once during the Vicksburg campaign, Reese and his comrades witnessed black soldiers engage with the enemy, momentarily break ranks, and then were reminded of the futility of surrender. Prisoners "were Butcher[ed] in cold Blood, the Negros saw that it was death to give up . . . and Rallied again." It was "a terrible fight." Black combatants "neither asked or gave quarter" and "Routed the Rebels." On July 4, black troops marched with white into Vicksburg. A year later at Memphis, Jackson County men would have been routed by rebels under the command of Nathan Bedford Forrest if not for the arrival of the Fifty-Ninth Colored Infantry.[56]

Union forces came to know General Forrest for his cruelty in ordering the killing of black troops even while trying to surrender. On overrunning Fort Pillow, his troops had slaughtered hundreds of black soldiers. Fort Pillow became a watchword among Union troops black and white. Reese seethed with anger at the mention of Forrest's "cut throats" and hoped "to get close enough to use my pistol on them." When he heard that the "Darkies" were escaping their masters "and gone off Shooting Rebels," he approved their actions as "the best Business of the Darky."[57]

At war's end Captain Reese glimpsed meaning in the years of killing. His regiment was encamped at Montgomery, Alabama. One day, he wrote home, two "negro women and one negro man" stumbled into camp. Their ears had been sliced off and their skin hung loosely from their faces. The sides of their faces were gone. "The poor creatures sufferd terrible." The war was over; Lee had surrendered weeks before. "The Rebels done the deed without provocation. . . . They think it mere past-time to shoot a Negro." The war was fought for good reason: "I am glad to have had this war for such a state of society as exists in the south is a disgrace to Republican government." The deed "chills my blood." If these monsters were caught, "their days are numbered."[58]

When returning home, soldiers discovered Jackson County's social landscape being reshaped. Veterans of the Eighty-First recognized Alva Curtis. He had freed himself by finding refuge with the army outside Vicksburg. Colonel Andrew Rogers, a Carbondale attorney, took him on as a personal servant through the war and then invited him to come north. The town was changing noticeably. During the war the number of black families increased from one to thirteen. Five years later when Curtis left, the population had grown to thirty-seven families in town with equal numbers on the outskirts. The county's total black population had grown to nearly one thousand. While two-thirds lived in towns along the Illinois Central Railroad, one-time slaves were coming to such western communities as Murphysboro and Grand Tower.[59] Like Alva Curtis, many, such as the Bosticks from eastern Tennessee, had liberated themselves when the Federal army drove southward, enlisted in the army or navy, and made their way to Murphysboro. Nearly twenty servicemen came, settled, and began to raise families in Jackson County.[60]

For the county's whites, African Americans were a discomfiting sight. They had simply assumed that freed slaves were incapable of assuming self-sufficient and productive roles in society. But because these one-time slaves had donned the blue uniform, and because white veterans had witnessed their conduct in battle, ingrained assumptions were challenged. The former slave who remained a day laborer may have confirmed racist assumptions. But several were buying lands, promoting community life, and thereby conspicuously defying convention. While the Bosticks planted a flourishing settlement south of Murphysboro, the Burkhalter, Williams, and Jackson families—all born in slavery—were following similar paths on the opposite side of the county.[61]

Three explanations of the war and slavery bumped against one another.[62] Two were white. The first rested on a traditional narrative that was fastened to an ideal of an ever-progressing but always white republican society and ignored the egalitarian principles that sparked the conflict. The other, while embracing the Union cause, consciously attended to the blemish of slavery on the national conscience and supported the conflict as the means to resolve the tension between egalitarian profession and its contradiction.

The third view was African American and, while joining with the white abolitionist, was informed by vivid personal experience that made for a separate memory community. Rooted in generations of bondage and kept alive by family elders passing stories on to the young, this personal and immediate perspective was anchored in genealogies of families and of their owners. The storytellers recalled the names of ancestors with the succession of masters. They remembered the cruel owner and the one less so. They remembered the sales that shattered families. And they kept that inner light that illumined the path to liberation. Their civil war began generations before the firing on Fort Sumter. Resistance was expressed by the runaway, the slave striking a master, and the groups that rebelled. Many black migrants to Jackson County came from Williamson County, Tennessee, where they had grown up with stories of local rebellion.[63] They had overheard slave owners whisper of uprisings elsewhere and the prospects of local rebellion. Slaves pointed to the places where friends and relatives met in secret. They whispered the names of the daring souls who slipped away from the plantation and evaded the slavecatchers.

For generations they had been watched, regulated, sold, and punished in what the master class had made into a garrison society. Experience had taught them what Mr. Jefferson had momentarily spied while penning the nation's declaration of principles: that slavery itself was an act of war. While Mr. Jefferson and his associates worked to forget this moment of self-recognition, slaves understood. After generations of resisting, they listened for reports of advancing Federal forces, prepared for emancipating themselves, and made Lincoln's war their own. A black identity and faith transcended the immediate condition of bondage. Those born in freedom from as far as Canada came to join the cause. Free blacks in Illinois whose families were exempted from the black codes had also volunteered. Richard Bass, whose family had lived free in the county immediately south of Jackson before the passage of the black codes, joined the fight. They enlisted knowing their fate if they fell into Confederate hands.

Thus, with victory secured, Jackson County's freed people celebrated Emancipation Day on the first of August. They might have selected the anniversary of Lincoln's Emancipation Proclamation or later the ratification of the Fourteenth Amendment that secured them the rights of citizenship. Sometimes they did. But the August celebration carried deeper meaning that transcended the national experience. On that date, a generation earlier, slavery had been abolished in the British empire. The American struggle for freedom merged with a larger international, indeed black Atlantic, cause.[64]

At war's end Carbondale publicly recognized the abolitionist telling by observing Emancipation Day. In the summer of 1868 the town's small black population was joined by another thousand from the area and "a goodly number of whites."[65] In the war's immediate aftermath, towns throughout the region prepared similar public events. In 1869, Elihu Palmer, minister of Carbondale's Baptist Church, joined in Cairo's festivities. Choosing that date to celebrate the peace put the conflict into a transcendent narrative pointing toward the realization of ever-progressing egalitarian principles. Confirmation of that history came when the state legislature repealed Logan's black code. That Logan himself had embraced emancipation, openly consorted with black political leaders, and joined in the speechmaking seemed additional proof. Some predicted that someday soon the freed slave would receive the vote. And to advance this agenda, black leaders embraced the Republican Party.

At first glance white champions of antislavery and their black counterparts struggling for freedom and citizenship seemed to stand on common ground. But white citizens, no matter their attitudes about the institution of slavery or their contact with freed slaves, seemed oblivious to the black perspective. Black actors, be they contraband property, cooks, or servants in the army, remained but extras without speaking roles, at best bit players, in this white man's drama. At times they caught Edmund Newsome's attention.[66] In his war journal he noted the black presence but briefly. He had watched black soldiers fight valiantly. When captured, he had witnessed

Confederates take the white captive and kill the black. In prison camp, he observed slaves conducting their own resistance by aiding prisoners' escape. These anecdotes were all marginal to his story. While witnessing black people knowingly face the Confederates' murderous intent to give no quarter and subvert prison camp rules, he could not imagine reason for exploring the black political perspective. Not unlike Newsome, Reese evinced little interest in the black meaning of the war. These self-liberating slaves became instruments for a white victory.

With the peace, white opponents of slavery worried as African Americans became something other than contraband property, something more than freed slaves. One-time slaves were reaching for the full rights of citizenship. Whites who had proclaimed their hatred of slavery and who felt their consciences absolved with the destruction of the slavocracy now awakened to deeply engrained images of their republic as a white one now compromised. The semblance of common cause based on opposition to slavery began to evaporate.

The impulses to erase the memory of a crusade against slavery and the black contribution to victory grew. During the war, black troops had marched into Vicksburg and later into Charleston, the symbolic core of rebellion. At the war's end, however, they were excluded from marching in the Grand Review in the nation's capital. In Jackson County, black veterans were denied admission to the Grand Army of the Republic and formed a separate "colored" post. Whites imagined their world would disintegrate as the black population grew. In response, local governments, following the pattern of segregation among the churches, created school systems, contrary to state law, that kept the races separate.[67] White spokesmen expected black citizens to be grateful to their "Republican liberators" and then to be quiet. They grew nervous at the emergence of black leaders, especially when they raised disquieting memories of the war's egalitarian promise. Jackson County's African Americans met in caucus and agreed to withhold support for any candidate "who will not pledge himself to administer the law to all men irrespective of race, color or previous condition of servitude."[68] And whites could not but recognize the threat when black political activists gathered in a statewide convention and attended to speakers who argued that their vote, though small, carried the balance in closely contested elections and that they would be wise to establish an independent bargaining position between the two major parties.

While reporting the Springfield conference, the Carbondale newspaper editor assured his readers that local black leaders had exercised prudent restraint by not attending. By the editor's conventional measure, black behavior was judged by the ability to curb innate antisocial tendencies. Thus, he watched Emancipation Day festivities and spoke for his white subscribers: "We must compliment the colored people on their behavior." Anticipating innate white fears, he noted that "not an angry or profane word was heard during the day." Freedmen were expected to vote Republican and little more. When a black man ran for office, white Republican voters defected. When African Americans seemed restive with their lot, the newspaper counseled that no matter the wrongs suffered they must remain patient and vote for Mr. Lincoln's party. If they forsook the party, they were accused of disloyalty and ingratitude. In turn, Democrats jeered that freedmen had exchanged their former servitude for another—this time one devised by their self-styled liberators.[69]

Speaking for his readers, Carbondale's Republican newspaper editor bluntly dismissed black assertiveness, in particular the incessant discussion of rights: he and his readers were "sick and tired of the Negro business." The nation seemed to be moving in that direction. If a white GAR post opened its doors to black veterans, it did so because its own membership was dwindling rapidly. But the war as liberation was being forgotten. Emancipation Day became a black holiday. According to the Carbondale newspaper, the day of liberation was irrelevant, its significance and meaning forgotten. It was a "commemoration of some event, though exactly what we do not know."[70]

At Carbondale the new university president helped his white neighbors forget "the Negro business." In the winter of 1884, the nation learned that Wendell Phillips, the uncompromising abolitionist, had died. In delivering his eulogy, Robert Allyn made clear his ambivalence on the reformer's egalitarianism. As an orator, none could compare with Phillips. But like many New Englanders who were quick to declare their disgust with slavery, Allyn distanced himself from abolition. For many who sought to maintain the moral order, the abolitionist seemed dangerous for advocating rights not only for black people but also for women. Moreover, Phillips, unlike many abolitionists who thought their work with emancipation was done, continued the crusade for securing black rights. While eulogizing Phillips, Allyn offered his warning on the freed slave's role in society. "We are still in doubt about this matter. . . . How many thousands are yet uncertain whether the freedmen have . . . been given the ballot too soon?"[71]

* * *

IN ITS AFTERMATH, the war lingered in memories as a time of waiting— waiting for the soldier's return, waiting for word that he had survived, waiting while listening to the word that a neighbor had been killed, waiting in vain. It lingered with the returning soldier who carried pictures in his mind of frightful deaths. Wives and parents lived in the war's shadow as they watched the veteran scarred in body or mind. Neighbors heard the laborer coughing. They watched the farmer limping. The war lingered in the silences and the absences—the veteran withdrawn and unable to make his private feelings public, the veteran who disappeared. Yet the lingering silences required words. When people gathered to pull words out from the silences, they fumbled, glossed over, and forgot.

While many veterans disappeared into the shadows, others assumed their places in public. With the growth of GAR membership, regimental reunions were organized. The veterans of the Eighteenth Illinois Infantry gathered on May 28, 1886—the anniversary of the regiment's creation. Survivors of the Battle of Belmont reunited annually. In 1897 over a hundred of General Logan's men marched in Chicago at the dedication of their commander's statue.[72] With each reunion, veterans attended to the reading of the names of comrades who had died over the last year. As their numbers dwindled visibly, they felt an urgency to preserve a record for posterity. First the Thirty-First Infantry, then the Eighteenth, organized the publication of a regimental history.[73]

Three veterans agreed to write the history of the Thirty-First. The narrative moved from the first encampment in August 1861 to the successive campaigns against Fort Donelson and Vicksburg, the march with General Sherman against Atlanta and then to the sea, the occupation of South Carolina, and finally the Grand Review in Washington. The text served as a monument in concept like the marble memorials erected in public places with the names of soldiers and the campaigns. A roster of the men who served appeared at the book's end. The authors collected photographs interlaced through the preceding narrative. Their account of the campaigns was an elaboration of what might be found in spirit on a marble column.

What had been bloody charges against the enemy were drained in the telling of the immediate experience. On occasion, passing reference was made to the "bloody and mangled bodies" strewn across a battlefield. Nameless men fell. The horror of the assault on Vicksburg's defenses on May 22 was glossed over: "The attack failed; by mistake, it was renewed, with the result of increasing the list of the dead and wounded."[74]

The authors boasted of the "hardy endurance" of the men who cut through Georgia and then pressed northward. These soldiers had become "immune to suffering" and the "privations" of war. Napoleon's famous march through the Alps paled in comparison. Like a marble monument the book remained silent on the war's larger meaning. With a passing nod to Sherman's critics, the authors assured the reader that the army had conducted itself in a "lawful" manner "justified by the law of nations." But why the war had been fought and so many had died fell beyond the purpose of the memorial. "Our government," the authors assured the reader, "stands vindicated before the world." The issue of slavery evaporated. Black people appeared as anecdotes: one was blown into the air at Vicksburg and survived; "refugees" in North Carolina appeared as a temporary impediment to the army's advance and then were removed.[75]

How the war fit into the history of the county had become a subject best unexamined. A decade after the war's end, James Brownlee had undertaken to write the first county history. He knew the war as a private in the Tenth Illinois Infantry and had joined the Carbondale post of the GAR. Yet he glided over the subject with assurances that "we may well be proud" of the county's contribution to the effort. The soldiers served gallantly. Many "cheerfully laid down their promising young lives" for the nation. While honoring them for fighting for "their principles," Brownlee did not pause to explore what those principles were or how principles divided neighbors. Lest the reader forget the names, Brownlee offered a "full list" of the soldiers in an appendix. Nothing more need be discussed. "We repeat it," he asserted, "Jackson has reason to be proud of the conduct of her sons in the hour of danger."[76]

Beneath the memories of the dead lurked persistent questions and possible meanings that seemed best kept private. Public exploration of the war's causes threatened to reawaken memories of deep, unresolved antagonisms. In southern Illinois the differences over slavery and race and cultural divisions between southern and northern immigrants remained. Memories flooded public life at election time. Republican stalwarts resorted to the Union. Veterans who had entered the war as Democrats—men like John A. Logan—had converted to Lincoln's party. John Dillinger recounted his conversion. A Democrat, he had marched with Logan to Vicksburg and returned home without an arm, and, like Logan, he also returned a confirmed Republican. Elections were hotly contested, and, notwithstanding Republican rhetoric, Democrats carried the county, albeit by narrow margins. During the two decades after the war, they prevailed in presidential and congressional races with the exception of the 1872 contest. Even when favorite son John A. Logan ran for vice president in 1884, he was able to tilt the balance in favor of the Republicans, but only slightly.[77]

While memories were kept alive at GAR post meetings and regimental reunions, the erection of public memorials seemed too difficult for southern Illinois communities. So Ezekiel Ingersoll, captain in the Seventy-Third Infantry, concluded. Concerned about memory, he displayed mementos of the war in his store window. When he traveled the country, he encountered communities—both North and South—that were erecting monuments before courthouses, public libraries, or on town commons in the soldiers' memory. In the North, convention was to purchase a marble statue of the soldier standing guard with rifle ready as if in defense of the Union. While touring the South, he was impressed that communities, though impoverished by war, had erected monuments. But the southernmost communities of Illinois seemed incapable of uniting behind such a project.[78]

Out of the evasions, words were being crafted so that the issues might be forgotten. North and South stumbled toward reconciliation by recognizing common race prejudices and by each honoring the valor of the other. The task required both erecting memorials to Abraham Lincoln and forgetting his warning that a house divided on slavery could not long endure. Healing required that the injuries of slavery be washed from memory and that the current southern reign of terror directed at the freed slave be accepted. In short, the trajectory of the war that led soldiers like Reese and Logan in their own ways to move from Union to slavery was reversed. Now both sides would be honored for their bravery no matter their convictions.[79]

In 1906, North and South came together at Vicksburg, this time for reconciliation. The state of Illinois had erected a magnificent memorial at the new battlefield park. For the dedication ceremonies, the Illinois Central scheduled special trains for dignitaries, bands, and national guardsmen. Two veterans of the Eighty-First Illinois—Francis Batson and Henry Hagler—joined the trip; George Washington Smith, history professor at the university, accompanied them. The ceremonies were carefully orchestrated to frame memories of the war. Most conspicuous by their absence were the black veterans. Indeed, they would not receive recognition at Vicksburg for nearly a century.[80]

The program included Vicksburg's schoolchildren—all white—singing "Illinois," "Dixie," and "The Star-Spangled Banner." Illinois governor Charles Deneen and Mississippi governor James Vardaman each saluted the courage of the men of both sides and spoke to the theme of national unity. Neither directly addressed emancipation as the war's great achievement. Deneen came close when he recognized that Federal victory achieved not only unity but "a full realization of the truths which our Declaration of Independence declared to be self-evident." But he refrained from making specific mention of black emancipation. Vardaman, however, cut closer to the core. After conceding that the right of secession, whatever its intrinsic merits, had been finally defeated by force of arms, he turned to the egalitarian principles in the Declaration of Independence. He had won elections by vicious race bating and later by calling for the repeal of the Fourteenth and Fifteenth Amendments. All men were not created equal, he declared. Instead, equal rights should be reserved for "all Caucasians and all Anglo Saxons."[81]

Vicksburg, so retold, became part of local memory. Readers of the Carbondale newspaper discovered advertisements enticing them to take the train to the battlefield. The Illinois Central published a lavish pamphlet replete with photographs and descriptions of the town, the battlefield, and the memorials.[82] Agreeing with Vardaman on race, Professor Smith opposed black admissions to the university unless they were of light complexion thus assuring him that some Caucasian blood ran through their veins. When lecturing on the battle and the park, he too framed the story within the emerging convention that erased slavery and black soldiers from the telling. While black citizens in Carbondale celebrated Emancipation Day, the white community was extending the principle of segregation from the schools to housing.[83]

The story was shifting in tone. Speakers at the veterans' reunions honored the soldiers and embraced a strident militarism that grew more vocal in the wake of the war against Spain. While Theodore Roosevelt spearheaded the building of the Panama Canal, senators and congressmen assured

Carbondale audiences that the nation's spectacular progress and its rise to world power stemmed from the energies unleashed by war. The nation now enjoys "a proud position . . . in the counsels of the great world powers." The present generation enjoyed a peace based on its military prowess: "no nation in the world is in the slightest degree disposed to pick war with us." Captain Ingersoll nurtured pride in the courage and endurance of his comrades. He fixed on the slaughter he had witnessed and compiled a notebook on the "The Magnitude of the Civil War." While many called it the "Civil or Great War," he preferred "the War for the Preservation of the Union." He counted the deaths in battle and boasted that no war could match his war. In late 1914, while reading reports of war in Europe, he advised an audience of veterans and neighbors: "Do not believe the Old Worlds' [sic] great war now raging will produce a parallel."[84]

The words employed to render meaning were chosen with audiences in mind. While the vocabulary to honor courage and sacrifice was transformed into militarism, the rites of memory also suppressed other voices, not only those of African Americans but also those of grieving parents and widows. A decade after the war's end, Daniel Brush rose to speak in honor of the "noble dead" in Woodlawn Cemetery and the "unknown" lying elsewhere in "unmarked" graves. He spoke for the "loving" friends and families whose "yearning souls desire to know" that "resting place" where they might lay a "flower." Brush assured his listeners that "no greater glory" can be imagined than to die for the "fatherland." And so he turned to the "mothers, wives, sisters" who bade farewell to "husband, brother, son." These women must be remembered and honored too as they enjoined the departing soldier, "as did the Spartan mother to her son 'Wear your shield, returned or on it.'"[85]

Quietly widow Laura McCullough kept her husband's diary so that one day she might give it to her son. Quietly mothers like Julia Bower folded up their sons' last letter and kept it.

* * *

THE WAGING OF the Civil War undermined the white settler narrative. The black presence could no longer be kept at the margins on ideological grounds; civil discord erupted within the county especially as the white citizenry met escaped slaves and black soldiers. If generations of frontier conflict had inured citizens to violence, the scale of bloodletting and the ensuing trauma left deep scars. Slowly through the era of Reconstruction and after, leading white spokesmen and pastkeepers found the means to repair the inherited narrative by forgetting the race issues that provoked the conflict and the black veterans in their midst and by covering the trauma with a renewed militarism and spread-eagle nationalism. In doing so, they found fulfillment in a county history populated by successful and self-satisfied white men posing before their Victorian homes surrounded by white picket fences.

CHAPTER FIVE

GILDING THE PAST

HE HAD MADE the land his property. He had staked out his town and named it Carbondale. He had laid out the streets, named them, and had drawn his blueprint for a Yankee utopia on the tracks of the Illinois Central Railroad. With property titles in his pocket, Daniel Brush yearned for Benningsen Boon's reputation as pastkeeper. When he read Boon's "Sketches," his town was scarcely a decade old. Rain dissolved the streets to swampland, well water stank, business lots facing the depot remained vacant, chocked with weeds. And he began to sketch his history. He kept a manuscript close by in a desk drawer alongside the draft of his regimental history. Perhaps uncertain of himself, he laid the manuscript history aside. But he took it out on occasion and imagined a time when it would appear in print. Whatever his hesitation, he felt fulfillment confirmed with the invitation to address the Old Folks Association.[1]

Brush, the aspiring pastkeeper, composed his thoughts around images of an agrarian order marked by simplicity and virtue. While reminiscing on an idyllic past derived from memories of his Vermont childhood, his thoughts were jerked to the present by bells clanging and whistles shrieking to announce another locomotive's arrival. Present clashed with past confirming him in his faith that the times were changing for the better. So he believed. With middle-class Americans in this Gilded Age, Brush looked to the republic's centennial birthday, especially the reports of the Philadelphia Exposition with its hall of machinery and immense steam engine boasting the nation's progress. The exhibit halls that re-created an earlier, simpler time, with the colonial kitchen, rendered perspective on the present. At once Americans cheered their sooty progress and held tightly to a green, quiet agrarian world. Together the contrasting images of the kitchen hearth and steam engine represented society's rapid transformation and its rootedness in the past. Out of that bygone world had emerged the character traits of virtue and industry that powered the national advance.[2]

Brush wrote this story of uplift into his autobiography and fixed it to his Yankee origins. His successes were dividends drawn from the habits of character that he accumulated at the family hearth and in the company of Vermonters. Piety and self-sufficiency, integrity and perseverance—these traits were intertwined. His parents both observed the Sabbath faithfully. In the same breath he recalled his father Elkanah as "moral and discreet . . . a good provider . . . true to the fulfillment of his duties" and "industrious." He was remembered as "economical, with no bad habits," in short a model for a young man to emulate. And his mother Lucretia instilled in her children the virtues of self-sufficiency. Shortly after the family's move west, Elkanah died. The son recalled his mother's "utter despair" and her gritty resolve to turn to God. "Only one resource was open to her in her agony. That was the widow's and the orphan's God in whom she had long trusted, and He did not fail her now." And so, "resolved to remain steadfast in her faith," she did "the best she could for her children." When relatives beseeched her to return home to Vermont, "the noble and heroic woman answered them *no*, saying that should she go back she and her little ones would be dependent upon their relatives, while if she raised them up in this new country they need not be dependent upon anybody, having the whole wide unsettled West to make a living in."[3]

Traditional virtues rooted in an agrarian age guided Brush and his generation in their ventures into a frontier and forward into a machine-driven world.[4] While extolling a society he had left behind, he built his new Carbondale home in the style of the Gothic Revival. The fashion in domestic architecture appealed to middle-class Americans who were both creating an industrial world and simultaneously clinging to a quiet traditional domesticity as refuge from the future they envisioned. Brush laid out plans for spacious symmetrical gardens in an English style. The house would sit sheltered among shade trees and set off from the street by a picket fence. He built just three blocks from the train tracks, an easy walk to the depot, where he assumed his duties as station agent. The railroad was the heart of the town, the sole reason for its existence and the principal source of its well-being. As if to put its stamp on the land, the Illinois Central ran its tracks at a diagonal, cutting across the gridworks devised by Mr. Jefferson for an agrarian republicanism and by Brush for his model community.

The railroad engine moved history forward. Naturally, as Brush sketched his town history, he began with the railroad, the surveying and laying of track, and the arrival of the first locomotive. The train came on the Fourth of July, 1854. Brush recounted the preparations. He had purchased fireworks. People came "from all the country around—men, women, children and dogs—and kept coming until at least two thousand were on the ground, most of whom had never seen a railroad or an engine or a car." As the train approached the depot, the crowd "shouted . . . all in surprise."[5] The engine of progress also brought unsightly elements that Brush wished to erase from his story. The laborers who had laid the tracks seemed a rowdy lot of immigrants, many Irish and conspicuously Roman Catholic. Brush, like many Yankees, winced at the prospect of these unruly classes besmirching his ideal community. Liquor signified the problem. While Protestant Yankees enjoyed a refreshing sip of homemade cider, they knew the virtues of restraint. But Brush worried that these intruders drank to excess. Their saloon represented vice and profligacy.[6] Moreover, the railroad brought civic unrest. While the captains of industry drew the nation forward, the self-serving lazy workers disrupted the workplace, sometimes violently, with their demands for higher wages and shorter working hours.[7]

In Brush's historical imagination the frontier represented opportunity and unfolding progress, and it unleashed the forces of social disorganization. Living with southern immigrant majorities at Brownsville and Murphysboro had reinforced his Yankee identity and confirmed him in his adherence to the Whig Party. For men like Brush, the Whigs had stood as bulwarks against license, as defenders of institutional restraint against individualism run rampant, as exemplars of piety and self-discipline against frontier abandon and religious enthusiasm. Orderly economic growth and prosperity depended on Yankee industry. By contrast, southern frontier culture nurtured slothfulness. Rather than engendering self-sufficiency, it encouraged dependence on bonded labor. Brush had watched the slavehounds in Murphysboro and, when in the South, witnessed vast natural resources lie undeveloped for the lack of "Northern industry and intelligent culture."[8] The saloon and gambling house flourished. He had witnessed such decay in Brownsville, where people drank to excess, commonly brawled, and raced horses.[9] He had observed the same in the Logans' Murphysboro and vowed to make his town an island of civic virtue.

A hedge was needed to protect this Yankee utopia from history's disintegrating forces. Once a gridwork of streets had been laid out, Brush and the town's leading investors began constructing the institutions necessary for well-ordered development. Lots in each of the town's quadrants were reserved for churches, and Brush raised subscriptions for the first school. An active Presbyterian, he resolved to put his denomination's stamp on his fledgling community. On discovering that the building fund fell short, he paid for the completion of the structure. By Brush's measure his town was an example against which to judge Murphysboro. The Presbyterian church was a pillar of transplanted New England culture. While living in Logan's town, he had watched a righteous few struggle to build a Presbyterian church but fail. The half-completed building was converted into a "Concert Hall," and the disgusted minister had removed to Carbondale. Guided by this vision, Brush met with the Presbyterian synod to plan for the creation of a college.[10]

Brush's vision emerged from nostalgia for a bygone New England village now transplanted to the Midwest.[11] Those who did not visit the Philadelphia Exposition and the restored colonial kitchen might have found similar exhibits at St. Louis or read evocative descriptions of Yankee village life in the popular periodicals. New Englanders were constructing an idyllic past as antidote to the shock of industrialization. While focused on the village common, the well-manicured streets, the freshly painted colonial houses, and the white church as symbols of stability, they strained to screen out the unsightliness of industry, laboring classes, and recent immigrants.

Though New Englanders were scarce in the region, Brush found allies. Robert Allyn, the new president of Southern Illinois Normal University, had spent his career promoting the virtues of his native land. The one-time commissioner of Rhode Island public education had progressed westward to take a series of positions at Ohio University and McKendree College in Lebanon, Illinois. Although a Methodist, he shared Brush's sense of New England's mission. It was, he reminded his audiences, "sturdy morality, diligent industry, and prudent economy" that made "New England so thriving a home and so highly respected abroad." He peppered his speeches with quotations from New England's sages such as Emerson and Whittier.[12]

Brush and his associates stamped a program of moral legislation on their "embryo city." They scrutinized the stranger. The industrious were welcomed and the shiftless sent packing: any able worker living idly, begging, or found "being of vicious character and depraved habits" was subject to fine and imprisonment. Peddlers were required to apply for a license. Keepers of houses of prostitution, of course, were subject to stiff penalties. The prospective proprietor of a billiard hall was expected to apply for a license and, if approved, was required to post bond as surety for his conduct. Gambling was prohibited. And for the sake of public decorum, authorities fined residents who "indecently exhibit any stud horse, bull, jackass . . . except in some enclosed place, out of public view." Moreover, "any female dog running at large . . . while in heat" was declared a nuisance to be shot by the city marshal.[13]

By comparison with neighboring towns, Carbondale's catalog of misdemeanors was extraordinary for its length. Most conspicuously, Carbondale stepped beyond local conventions on the matter of liquor. While other towns established licensing procedures, Brush had insisted from the outset that his Carbondale be dry. In an early meeting with the town's founders he "proposed that the sale of spirituous liquors as a beverage should be forever prohibited." Local authorities were empowered on complaint by a "competent witness" to obtain warrants for searching "any house, building, cellar or place within the city limits or one mile beyond" where a person might be keeping liquor "for the purpose of selling, bartering or giving away." Violators would lose title to their land.[14]

With care, this railroad town would become a clean and green community set in arboreal peace. Ordinances required property owners to keep the sidewalks swept, weeds cut, snow removed promptly, and unsightly rubbish cleared. The town planners encouraged the laying of brick sidewalks according to strict specifications and subject to inspection and envisioned public squares shaded with trees. Trees were planted and the government provided for their protection. Residents along Cherry, West Main, and Oak Streets were erecting spacious homes in the Italianate and later the Queen Anne style and, like Daniel Brush, were planting trees and gardens. "Ornamental and shade trees" were secured by law from "willful or accidental injury."[15]

Brush imagined his town as the embodiment of Republican ideals pervasive in the middle class. As a project to curb the excesses of American individualism when liberty turned to squalid licentiousness and to nurture the character traits of self-discipline and self-sufficiency, his vision was a utopian effort to channel the energies that contributed to progressive economic development. This emergent city, resting on solid "religious, educational and commercial" foundations, became a beacon of light for the people of southern Illinois.[16] By blending Protestant Christianity with learning and business

Daniel Brush house, Carbondale. *Map of Jackson County, Illinois* (Olney, IL: J. B. Westbrook, 1874).

into a seamless fabric, Brush and his associates were crafting their egalitarian principles out of the fragments left by civil war. Equality meant opportunity for men of character to strive for self-improvement within a well-ordered world. Slavery, they were satisfied, had not only imposed artificial restraint on freedom but also sapped the energies of the otherwise industrious and self-reliant. And while they had condemned slavery and the "Negro Whippers," they shied from excesses espoused by the abolitionist. Thus men like Brush had roundly condemned slavery as an institution, its advocates as immoral, and slave catchers as degenerate. Without embarrassment, even after the war, Brush owned that he had not voted for Lincoln in 1860 and had chosen instead the well-tempered platform of the Constitutional Unionist.[17]

In becoming Republican, such men forgot the party's original radical elements and embraced the captains of industry as exemplars of Yankee character and advance agents of progress. They were appalled when economically strapped farmers sought relief by supporting proposals to shift the basis of money from gold to paper currency. Demagoguery and outright theft threatened the republic. Equally subversive were labor's calls for higher pay and shorter hours.[18] Education, religion, temperance remained the foundations, agreed Brush and Allyn. And Sabbath keeping tied these verities together. This truth Brush learned from "my good mother." Not only is it "commanded by the Omnipotent and all-wise Ruler of the Universe," it is also "profitable to man." "In a worldly and business point of view the rest is needed to keep one's ability to work up to the right point, and . . . to meet with renewed relish the labor of the ensuing week."[19]

Brush's labors to pin his imaginary world to the ground required glossing over the presence of sweated labor and thereby denying vital elements of the historical forces he embraced. While maintaining this community as an island of stability, he attached it to a railroad that brought both prosperity and subversion. The town's attempts to regulate locomotives' sounds and speeds seemed to illustrate the tension. The railroad tied communities like Carbondale to market forces from outside in a bond of dependency. Periodically the president of the Illinois Central rode his train from Chicago to Carbondale and stayed at the Newell House. While inspecting the operations of his company, he scanned the landscape and its agricultural produce for future markets. From his railroad car, he converted the verdant landscape into commodities for transport and profit. One July he reported with satisfaction that "all the crops on the Main Line look well and promise as good a yield on the average as shown in any year in the past history of Road."[20] Simultaneously he was manipulating shipping rates to be charged local merchants and farmers. And by making themselves subject to rates dictated by the Chicago office, the people of Jackson County placed themselves in a dependent status.[21]

Carbondale's citizens could do little to control either the intrusive noises from passing locomotives or the tables of shipping rates set in Chicago. Nor could they control the social scene as they might desire. While Brush and his neighbors sought to create a community populated by industrious middle-class Protestants, the railroad leaders were forever looking for cheap workers incompatible with that ideal. In their calculations of labor costs, they looked to Irish and Catholic workers to lay and maintain the tracks. While writing his town history, Brush scrubbed these people from his account. But the Illinois Central continually recruited them to maintain rail yards. And to cut costs, the company was ever eager to find cheaper workers. If present employees insisted too strongly on a living wage, executives agreed to look to the South and to black labor. "It is in the interest of capital to accept labor," observed one executive, without regard to "race or color."[22]

Brush, the aspiring pastkeeper, felt challenged. In the mid-1870s a pack of salesmen descended on the town with a scheme to buy and sell the county's past. Commissioned by Wesley Raymond Brink, recently arrived from the East, they came to sell a plan to publish a handsome book-length county history. Throughout the nation, communities like Jackson County's seemed seized by a new fascination with the past. The republic was celebrating its centennial of independence, and Congress had summoned the citizenry to gather in their communities and preserve their own histories. As if in response, publishing entrepreneurs like Brink awoke to a new market.[23]

Publishers and their agents descended upon these communities with blueprints for manufacturing local histories efficiently and inexpensively. Before arriving they had created a template for organizing the project that made it possible to divide the labor among several authors. And so they came to recruit authors and to sell subscriptions. Anyone with the cash could buy a place in history. Salesmen ferreted out widows, proposing that for a fee they would insert a biography of their husbands into the book. The premium biography included an engraved picture of the family home. Buyers were assured that any unsightly piles of rubbish would not appear. If they wished, they could insert future improvements. Consider posterity, the salesman advised the patriarch. After he died, his children might divide the estate and sell the home. Children will lose their beloved birthplace. The picture ensured that the memories would not be lost.[24]

Brink had made Jackson County his first target in Illinois. A one-time lawyer, he had entered the history business in the early 1870s. When he and his agents arrived in Carbondale, they had rehearsed their pitch: this was a "golden opportunity" sure to bring "more real satisfaction in after life than has been afforded you by any other investment you ever made."[25] The organization was emerging with a cursory review of "The Aborigines" followed by chapters on the "Pioneers and Early Settlers," political organization, geography, minerals, agricultural resources, schools, and churches. The second half was devoted to histories of towns and townships.

Authors were needed to fill the empty spaces with words. Brink's agents looked to Carbondale's new normal university, doubtless expecting that the faculty offered the talents for producing the core of the book. At once they sought out President Allyn. A stranger to this community, Allyn had hardly unpacked his bags, and he was living in a rented house. Nonetheless Brink was satisfied that Allyn's literary skills would suffice. Allyn agreed to oversee the project and contribute sections on "the aborigines" and on wildlife. For the major portion of the writing he proposed his young colleague James Brownlee, whom he had brought from McKendree College to teach rhetoric and physical education. Though a stranger to the county, Brownlee agreed. For the sections on the several townships, Brink's men invited established residents or ministers to contribute what they knew about their communities. Brush was ignored. As an afterthought, he was invited to contribute a history of his Presbyterian Church.

Brink's salesmen had found their Carbondale historian. John Marten was not yet twenty. His father, a Prussian immigrant, had appeared in town on the eve of the Civil War, opened a cobbler's shop, and enrolled John in the new university. The student quickly won the attention of Cyrus Thomas and George French for his proclivity for scientific observation. Thomas, after joining the Smithsonian Institute, commissioned Marten to study Rocky Mountain locusts.[26] But even before that expedition, this bug collector had been appointed to write the history of Brush's town.

Brush had been elbowed aside. While he was revising his manuscript history of the town for publication, Brink's agents came peddling their subscriptions. Ever the self-promoter, Brush might have felt tempted to buy space for his biography. He had bought a piece of the 1874 county atlas that included a picture of his home on West Main Street. But he shut the doors on the salesmen. He would write the church history but contribute nothing more. The published history added to the injury. Young Marten made brief mention of Brush—as a storeowner—but credited others for founding the town.[27]

Newcomers, almost strangers, bought themselves into the history. Of the nine Carbondale biographies, the subjects of four had arrived since the Civil War. After opening a drug store, Francis Prickett "thought he would try his fortune west," moved to Kansas, and a year later returned. George O'Hara of New York had ventured his luck in several Illinois towns before settling on Carbondale. He bought four paragraphs in the history and soon after moved to the state capital. Eighty-four residents who did not buy a place in the text bought subscriptions, and of this lot nearly half had arrived since the beginning of the Civil War (40 percent), and of those twenty-eight (33 percent) arrived since the war's end.[28]

George Kennedy, an Irish immigrant, had arrived in Murphysboro after the war and joined Martin Ross, a transplanted New Englander, to establish a dry goods store. Kennedy bought a subscription to the county history as well as a business notice where he advertised the sale of groceries, kitchenware, farm machinery, and sewing machines. He and his partner were, the advertisement assured the reader, "gentlemen." Kennedy also wrote the town history. A third of the Murphysboro subscribers (twenty-four of seventy) had arrived since the war's outbreak. Of the twenty-nine who purchased biographical sketches, thirteen had come after the war. William Rogers advertised himself as a "traveling man." He enumerated his enterprises: he had managed a dry goods store in Cincinnati, then a Chicago hotel, and later hit the road as traveling salesman for a St. Louis lock company. In 1876, he appeared in Murphysboro offering his plans for renovating the county courthouse. He did not win the contract but did court and marry Annie, the daughter of Dr. Logan and owner of the town's principal hotel. Rogers appointed himself the proprietor of the Logan House and bought a piece of the county history. His biographical sketch might have been posted with the history's business notices. He assured his readers that his experience on the road made him especially suited to appreciate the "wants and desires of the traveling public." Moreover, his "social qualities and his natural and acquired abilities" were sure to "make his business a success."[29]

Only five purchasers of biographical sketches had been present at the town's founding in 1843. Although General Logan owned a full-page biography complete with portrait, he had moved to Chicago. In contrast to the Murphysboro and Carbondale historians, Ora Township's George Washington Holliday introduced himself as the "oldest resident" born in the county. But few others could claim anything resembling pioneer status. Michael Swortzkope had come from Pennsylvania by a circuitous route through Ohio, Indiana, and Missouri before landing in Grand Tower Township in 1850. He wrote the Grand Tower history.[30]

Whatever Daniel Brush's reasons for refusing a subscription, they did not stem from objections to the project's historical perspective. Indeed, Brink's *History of Jackson County* elaborated on the essential message of Brush's manuscript history, and both reflected the genius of the age. Designing their product against what they deemed to be prevailing market trends, Brink's crew knocked on doors, assuring subscribers that they would proudly display the published history on parlor tables. Success depended on the same principles of production that brought cheaply produced commodities to the dry goods stores. Standardization was the key. Just as clothing manufactures had devised a system of shirt and shoe sizes that fit the market, so too Brink devised a set of templates that could be altered easily and stamped on other counties such as Fayette, Edwards, and Shelby. Local history appeared within the standard formula. Whenever possible, texts written for one county were clipped and inserted into another. Timetables for production dictated the process. Authors need not come to the task with intimate knowledge of the subject, and research was not allowed to affect publishing schedules.[31]

Like the mass manufactured art of the Gilded Age, Brink's histories looked alike in size and design, format, and even in text. The histories were introduced often with the same words explaining the value of this project. Jackson County's volume began with the explanation that "few studies are more profitable to mankind than that of the past experiences, deeds, thoughts and trials of the human race." And so began the later Macoupin County history. Both explained that "by a knowledge" of "the families whose ancestors were early on the ground, and whose members have made the county what it is," "the present generation will be instructed, and the future will be guided." The chapter on Jackson County's "Pioneers and Early Settlers" opened with the same text as would Washington County's history.[32]

Manufacturing a local history required little more immediate knowledge of the subject than Brink's salesmen's. James Brownlee agreed to write the main body of the text, but he was unfamiliar with and unattached to Jackson County. Born in Indiana, Jackson County's new historian had moved first to Kansas and then to Illinois, where he joined the faculty at McKendree College before following Allyn to Carbondale in 1874. After teaching rhetoric for a decade, he moved to the University of Illinois, drifted back to Carbondale, and then set out for Oklahoma. Perhaps he felt the historian's task a daunting one. While written records were scarce, he assured his reader that he had sifted through "all available sources" and listened attentively to the elder keepers of oral memory. Brink's timetable dictated that he forego exhaustive research. The author need only write enough words to fill in the established template.

Following the publisher's instructions, Brownlee opened his account of "Pioneers and Early Settlers" with apologies that while "no labor has been spared to make the narrative both interesting and complete," the finished product remained "defective" and the lacunae obvious. "Many events and anecdotes worthy of insertion here have faded from the memories of the living." To fill his allotted space, he resorted to broad, vaporous evocations of a past, of the pioneers' "privations and distresses, of their heavy sorrows and simple joys, of their free-hearted hospitality, of their courage," but without the gritty detail of specific names and places. Undaunted by the lack of local color, he stuffed his pages with quotations and verbiage imported from elsewhere. When gesturing to a landscape that lacked local detail, he pasted into his text verses from poets, such as William Coggeshall of Ohio, New York's Washington Irving, New England's John Greenleaf Whittier, Ohio's William Gallagher, and Scotland's own Robert Burns, who had never set foot in this county.[33]

Standing at the location of old Brownsville, Brownlee stared into empty space. He could discern only the "few, faint traces that have survived the lapse of time." While some graybeards could recall this place, it is "scarcely known to have had an existence by the present generation." Undeterred, the historian took this opportunity to demonstrate his learning. He imported the "well-remembered lines" from Oliver Goldsmith's "The Deserted Village." Someday, he hoped, another poet would "embalm recollections of this deserted village." Meanwhile readers could indulge their fancies with nearly a half page of verse from eighteenth-century England.[34]

Brownlee and his coworkers, be they writing in Jackson or St. Clair County, represented the genius of the age. Together they stamped a narrative line onto their project that appealed to broad segments of middle-class markets no matter their specific locale. Echoing Daniel Brush, Brownlee invited his readers to "gaze backward into the 'beautiful land of the past.'" He resorted to conventions that extolled the character of the pioneer families, their courage, their openheartedness. When a newcomer arrived, neighbors gathered from miles to help cut the logs and construct the small, snug, "Indian proof" house. Furniture was "simple, and framed with no tools but an auger and axe"; "dishes were few and usually of pewter." Brownlee sketched the scene broadly; it may have applied to any place in the old Northwest Territory. Thus his words were easily pasted into other county histories. Though these early settlers have "passed from among us to the narrow house appointed for all the living," the fruits of their industry were manifest to the present. Frontier hardships had been overcome. Instead, today's reader, wrote Brownlee, sees a lovely landscape tamed and civilized: "[F]air towns and pleasant villages have gathered their happy populations, and resound with the 'hum of men.' Railroads run as great arteries though hill and across dale, while telegraph wires have woven a net-work over the land."[35]

The history pointed to an ever more bounteous tomorrow. By design it served as advertisement of the county's resources that would entice men with gumption and capital. Brownlee and his crew wrote a sequence of chapters on geography and soil resources, on mineral products, and on the animals and plants—each assessing potentials for development. "Agricultural pursuits" promised "rich returns" and would "attract strangers and reward all." The land with its vast reserves of coal and sandstone already yielded great profit. "No spot is more favored, and none is more full of promises of future growth and influence."[36]

While noting the landscape's beauty, the history returned to the profits to be gained. Robert Allyn wrote the chapter on the plants and animals, both "useful and annoying." Animal species had vanished, unable like the American Indian to endure civilization's relentless advance. Prairie grasses were vanishing to be replaced by orchards: "No business is more promising, and none has absorbed so much capital." If insect pests threatened the fruit, "scientific men should be alert to destroy these enemies of the race." Birds that preyed on these pests "should be protected, and such as destroy insects and larvae should be artificially bred." Taking his cue from a recent report published by the state horticultural society, Allyn catalogued the birds according to their utility. Bluebirds and swallows were of "the greatest value to the fruit-growers, in destroying noxious insects." Some woodpeckers were valuable and should be protected, but not all, in particular the sapsucker. Robins and crows were "birds of doubtful utility" that might be tolerated. In his third list, he identified those to be exterminated "by all, whenever opportunity offers": in addition to the sapsucker, he pointed to the oriole, the cedar waxwing, hawks, and some owls.[37]

The organization and historical perspective elaborated on prevailing opinion. A decade earlier a Carbondale resident had written a brief outline history for the local newspaper. Though Carbondale seemed "too young . . . to have a history," he wrote to advertise the town to the world. The article might have passed as a first draft of Brink's book. No other town in all the region offered investors a "better advantage." Coal resources were abundant. "We have gathered together" an inventory of raw materials and potential fields for investment. Business was growing. The list of dry goods stores, drug stores, jewelers, milliners, and hardware stores confirmed faith in the future. Railroad traffic increased steadily. The catalog of schools and churches and of newspapers and fraternal societies documented the emergence of a thriving community. This was an early exercise in town boosterism in which past and present achievement pointed to a glowing future.[38]

Prosperity's history seemed best told with biographical sketches. Men with gumption and grit who had paid for their places in the history offered their stories as models to inspire. William H. Davis, the son of a Welsh immigrant, had been a "poor boy" in Indiana. After serving as a blacksmith's apprentice, he began his wanderings in quest for wealth. After a short stay in Kentucky failed to pan out, he tested several Illinois towns before appearing in Brownsville. "His funds were low" and he worked for a farmer. "Firmness of purpose, and good resolves" soon paid off. He acquired two farms and a general store, which he boasted brought in $16,000 a year. "Opposite his name in every enterprise, social, moral or financial, may be written the unfailing word—success."[39]

Poverty "has given to the world the men of most brilliant intellect, uncontrollable ambition, and tireless energy." Fontaine E. Albright bragged that he was fortunate to be born poor, an "awkward and illiterate country lad" with "few or no opportunities." Poverty "has given to the world the men of most brilliant intellect, uncontrollable ambition, and tireless energy." While toiling behind the plow, he had stolen "every spare moment" to improve his mind and to study the law. After moving to Murphysboro, he hung out his shingle and soon after won election to the state legislature.[40] Thomas Logan, the general's brother, informed the reader that as a youth he enjoyed few "advantages," worked on a farm, and "occasionally attend[ed] school in a log cabin." His story concluded with the picture of his handsome two-story house and barn. A train steamed by his house, thus associating him with the dynamics of economic progress. He had become a successful horse breeder and owned "some of the finest blooded horses in southern Illinois." Below the picture of his house, he included images of six of his prize horses. "Mr. Logan," the biography concluded, "is one of those energetic and progressive men, who have done so much for the advancement of the agricultural interests of this state."[41]

Through their moral example, these men offered the reader guidance and advice, sometimes captured in pithy precepts: "[M]ankind may, primarily, be classed in two grand divisions: workers and drones." With the sketches, some bought space to display their homes as confirmation of their success. Some homes were modest, others substantial. All were well groomed with

Detail of Thomas Logan estate. *History of Jackson County, Illinois* (Philadelphia: J. L. McDonough, 1878) f. 72.

straight fences, well-ordered gardens, and shrubbery planted in rows. In the foreground the owner posed, well dressed, sometimes riding in a handsome carriage.

President Allyn used his position to elaborate on this worldview in print, at commencement addresses, and before civic groups. The study of history "reveals enough to show God every where." He summoned the skeptics to review the nation's remarkable emergence from wilderness to civilization. Look to the development of farm implements and steam power, to the advances in manufacturing efficiency and in transportation, to improvements in livestock breeding, and to the "multiplication of comforts in homes, clothing, foods." The dynamo driving history forward was lodged in citizens possessed of sound character, education, and religion. But such individuals found encouragement to strive for improvement because they lived in a free market where the rights of property were protected from arbitrary political whim. Thus, the age realized itself in the emerging large corporations. The large "capitalist" had become the advance agent in this divine scheme. With his great riches, he had gathered the resources and energies for improving commerce and transportation and for "uniting laborers into societies for mutual protection and education." "Take courage," he exhorted his audiences: "the better day is coming."[42]

Allyn delivered his message with certainty. While schools promoted the three Rs—"reading, riting, and rithamtic"—they could not guarantee progress without a fourth R—righteousness. He spoke and wrote in absolutes. But beneath his strenuous arguments lay doubts. He worried over the newspaper accounts of labor unrest and crimes against property. While sitting in a train station, he observed workers drinking and swearing. Crime seemed to be rising. The postwar years brought uncertainty. How, he wondered, could the former slave who appeared in his own community fit into his world? And what of the women demanding the franchise? Could his moral order accommodate the challenges of race and gender?

No matter its buoyant, self-congratulatory rhetoric, Gilded Age Republicanism remained haunted by the memories of an original egalitarianism. By the time of James Garfield's election, Republicans like Allyn came together in celebrating the coming industrial age and in pushing the race question into the background. While the sections stumbled down a path toward reconciliation by abandoning the freed slave, the aging agitators still pressed to resuscitate the memory of a commitment to integrate African Americans into this republican experiment. But men like Allyn did not listen.

The war had brought the subject to the foreground.[43] With the repeal of Logan's black code, the wardens of the moral order were no longer empowered to keep the community white. Simultaneously, the demand for labor that had drawn freedmen to the county during the war continued. A temporary boom in cotton production, the growth of coal mining, and the expansion of the railroad led to an expanded market for workers that drew freed slaves to the county. The numbers increased from 995 in 1870 to 1,528 in 1880. The largest concentration was in Allyn's Carbondale, where one in three residents was black.

Measured by his standard, many African Americans fit Allyn's model citizen. They came and stayed to raise families. They built churches—a half dozen in the county by the 1870s. They owned property and farmed their land. Some bought space in the county history. But white people worried that Illinois, as one lawmaker had once put it, would become "Africanized." They glimpsed the elements of a new narrative. Former slaves were eager to send their children to public schools, and the new state constitution provided for universal public education in principle. In response, communities like Carbondale moved toward school segregation. The county's spokesman at the state's 1870 constitutional convention asserted that the "African race" was not intelligent enough to vote responsibly and argued for the same reason against "mixed schools." The county superintendent of education echoed his white neighbors when he dismissed the integration of the races as "repugnant."[44]

Allyn returned to the question: how could his African American neighbor fit within his idea of a white republic? His answer was less than direct but revealing. On learning that President Garfield had been assassinated, the community joined the nation in mourning and invited Allyn to speak. On rising to address his neighbors, he invited them to consider that "the world itself stops" in "sincerest concern and sorrow." The center of Allyn's world was white. Thus, even "canibbal Fiji and Zululand" felt this loss. The hierarchy of races guided his thoughts on African Americans as well as on the indigenous peoples. Accordingly, he doubted the emancipated slave's ability to participate in his democracy.[45]

Allyn also stumbled over the woman question, a historical one: did the principles in the Declaration of Independence make equal rights for women necessary for the republic's integrity? Many said so, even among Allyn's fellow Republicans. Promises had been made that once slaves had received their inherent rights of freedom, the same should be extended to women. Had the time come? For party stalwarts the question was uncomfortable. Allyn spoke to the debate professing open-mindedness. But while gesturing to egalitarian principles, he could not let go his belief in a hierarchical order based on both gender and race. Expressing himself with the authority of his position—with learning and with measured judgment—he queried as if the answer were a self-evident truth: "Where would work for men be?"[46]

Keeping this moral order based on hierarchies of race and gender remained a worrisome responsibility for men like Allyn. As African Americans increased, they made their presence felt at the polls. While some Republicans had supported extending the franchise, they needed assurance that the new voters would show the "utmost respect to the white people." These new voters, like their white counterparts, seemed to constitute a self-conscious voting bloc capable of influencing an election's outcome. They were important enough for Democrats to compete for their support.[47]

Such worries did not appear in the county history except by a conspicuous silence. As the authors of the Brink history were gathering their materials, white people organized to discipline their black neighbors by terror. Throughout the nation, the rate of racial violence was increasing. Just four years before the history's completion, a mob had lynched a black man on the banks of the Big Muddy. Yet the historians kept silent.[48]

Readers of the county history found women safely tucked in the margins. They appeared in the accounts of pioneer days as nameless figures. Brownlee invited his readers to look back with nostalgia to a day when women dressed simply and were unaware of the finery found in modern dry-goods stores. "It is refreshing to know that the ladies of that ancient day considered six yards an extravagant amount to put into one dress." Today's woman commonly wears a dress made of "twenty-five and thirty yards." Some subscribers to the history bought space for their wives' portrait. Thomas Logan allowed as much space to his wife Sallie as he bought for his prize horses.[49]

The unfolding story of progress gilded over ever-present reminders of social discord as harbinger of a second civil war. While the county's worthies celebrated the ascendance of the large corporation, others spoke and acted in protest. Throughout the nation, labor challenged the power of capital. The National Labor Union, the Knights of Labor, and the Brotherhood of Locomotive Engineers gained recruits to protect wages and advance the eight-hour day. Meanwhile, rural communities rallied around the Patrons of Husbandry or the Grange to control railroad freight rates. Economic depression exacerbated tensions between capital and workers who grew the crops and operated the factories. The self-styled advance agents of progress who put their biographical sketches in the county histories were transformed into apologists for an emerging tyranny. A counternarrative emerged. Progress, contrary to conventional wisdom, brought poverty. So wrote Henry George. Many Americans nodded in agreement.[50]

Americans encountered the down-and-out, men without the means to support themselves, often dressed in tatters, drifting from one town to the next or wandering the rural byways.[51] They were called vagrants, hobos, and their numbers grew. Governments branded them a public menace. The guardians of public order wrote laws empowering police to cleanse their communities of this unsightly presence. Local governments established homes for the poor, at first for the orphan and widow, for the "lame, the halt and the blind." The wandering poor were admitted as well. Jackson County authorities reported that "there is almost an army of tramps who manage to get into the Poor House each winter."[52]

Tramps stole rides on the railroad.[53] Carbondale's worthies spotted them riding the rods beneath the freights. They appeared in the railroad yards, glancing furtively about for the railroad police, the tough railroad dicks. They were found dead along the tracks sometimes in bloody, mangled pieces. Some were thrown overboard by the fearsome dicks. Living with the Illinois Central raised discomforting images and questions: Were these men poor due to deficient character? Did the corporation attend to the welfare of the worker? Injuries and fatalities rose. Farmers recounted stories of the neighbor who was struck by a speeding train while driving his wagon into town. Questions rose whether Chicago's magnates should be held responsible.

The prevailing narrative, no matter how often invoked by men of prestige, could not satisfy the experience of many. With a shift in perspective, the builders of prosperity were transformed into destroyers. By one telling, William Ackerman, the president of the Illinois Central Railroad, was the future's architect. Men in towns along his line depended on his company for their wages; doctors and lawyers were kept on continuing retainer. What profited the company profited Jackson County, or so went the story. Ackerman agreed. But he and his Chicago cohorts could hear the agitators.[54]

In July 1877 Ackerman had completed his regularly scheduled tour of southern Illinois and returned to his Chicago office amid reports of a railroad strike sweeping toward the Midwest.[55] Beginning in Pittsburg, workers enraged by wage cuts were shutting down the railroads. Railyards were destroyed. Workers clashed with police and militia. The strike spread. Entire communities rose against the railroads. Meanwhile, coal miners joined. While tensions mounted in Chicago, Ackerman read the frantic dispatches from stations south along his tracks. "Lawless mobs" had shut down traffic at Mattoon, Effingham, Decatur, and Carbondale too.[56]

Ackerman wired the governor urging him to call out the militia. Meanwhile Carbondale's leading citizens braced themselves for the deluge. "Lawless Men have invaded our City, obstructed the Rail Roads," and forced "laboring Men" of the community to "cease work." The mayor was authorized to recruit law-abiding citizens for "suppressing any disorderly conduct, and to arrest" agitators who came to town intending to "interfere with work" or with the railroad. Already a large crowd—"two hundred miners and tramps," according to a local newspaper—gathered at the railroad station. Disgruntled miners in Murphysboro had torn up tracks, others had marched on Carbondale. Trains were stopped. Some were charged with "conspiracy to murder." And the troubles subsided.[57]

President Ackerman boasted that his workers had remained loyal—even while, in fact, he was devising new measures to cut their wages. Outsiders, he assured himself, had ignited the troubles in Chicago and down his railroad line. While Ackerman perpetuated this interpretation in his *Historical Sketch of the Illinois Central Railroad*, Brownlee and his colleagues simply erased this and other episodes of labor trouble from their accounts. Perhaps their history was completed before the strike. Five years later Edmund Newsome was composing his *Historical Sketches of Jackson County*. He too ignored the disturbance so incompatible with the conventional story. Nor would later historians break the silence.[58]

Brownlee looked past the seething conflict. He and his peers could celebrate progress without imagining its connection to poverty. Nor could they imagine that the capitalists who engineered this world were by their deeds provoking deep resentments. So immersed was Brownlee in the culture that spawned his narrative that he could not hear, even while he quoted from Oliver Goldsmith, the poet's bitter cry of social criticism in "The Deserted Village."[59] What Brownlee took for the Englishman's simple nostalgia for a bygone world was an anguished cry of outrage directed at the powerful who in their lust for wealth had laid waste to that world. Instead of heeding that voice, he appropriated those portions of the poem that might be used to evoke sweet and wistful thoughts. Brownsville's counterpart to Goldsmith's schoolmaster had long since gone: "[P]ast is all his fame. The very spot/ Where many a time he triumphed, is forgot." The sound of voices—of "grey-beard mirth" and of "village statesmen" pondering the latest news— that once set the tone of life had now grown silent.

Looking wistfully backward to his "Sweet Auburn, loveliest village of the plain," Goldsmith protested the men who had ravaged the land. Repeatedly he pointed to the "men of wealth and pride," the "tyrant's power," "the spoiler's hand." Perhaps an American reader would confine that lament to an English context, thereby dissociating it from the immediate scene. While the visible signs of hereditary privilege that dominated the English landscape did not apply to America, voices warned that the patterns of predatory European privilege were emerging. They echoed Goldsmith that "wealth accumulates" and that "trade's unfeeling train Usurp the land." The descendants of Goldsmith's dispossessed poor could be found along the railroad tracks and on the rural byways.

Yet Brownlee's cohorts scanned their chosen landscape through a different lens. The marketplace was part of the natural order. To tamper with its workings was to risk disaster. The poor were poor not due to Goldsmith's callous hand of the powerful but because of weaknesses of character. Thus readers like Brownlee read past Goldsmith's dire warnings of "trade's broad empire." Throughout the poem, they read over the stark warnings: "Ill fares the land, to hastening ills a prey,/ Where wealth accumulates, and men decay." Without reflection, almost as if by instinct, they turned "The Deserted Village" into an accompaniment to a Currier and Ives print.

Edmund Newsome captured the essence of this historiographical tradition in his *Historical Sketches*. In recounting the gritty details of the transition from frontier days to the age of steam he centered his story on the entrepreneurs who surveyed the land with a keen eye for resources, who built small communities, and who then abandoned them. He knew the hidden places on forested ridges where rotting timbers and rusting equipment marked the spot adventurous miners had once tried their luck. He could tell the story of community growth as well as decay, of ventures conceived with high expectations, and of enterprises that flourished as well as those that foundered.

When Newsome began to write, he had lived in the county for over three decades. An English immigrant, he had first settled in Murphysboro and then followed Brush to Carbondale. A one-time surveyor, he had ridden the land and knew it better than newcomer Brownlee. He had walked the ridges and the forests, the bottomlands and the prairies. He had sat with founding pioneers like Henry Dillinger and Benningsen Boon and had listened to their stories. Newsome absorbed his neighbors' perspective without criticism. He simply offered younger readers a "view of the past" that in its detail might prove "interesting." Hopefully they might "understand the present."[60]

Newsome began with the land and its topography. Succinctly sketching the "physical divisions"—the level bottomlands on the western side and the upper "rolling land" on the east—he guided the reader across the county, describing each township, its specific terrain, its streams and plant life. He named the creeks and plotted their meandering courses. He had followed the Big Muddy as it snaked its way through the ridges toward the Mississippi River, through that bend where the water "strikes a high wall of rock and turns at an acute angle to the south." The rock was named "Swallow Rock" for the countless nests "stuck on the face of the rocky wall." He recalled riding the "high lands" where the horizon opened northward to the next county and distant Pinckneyville. He knew the great hills and ridges abruptly jutting from the bottomlands (one was named "Devil's Backbone," another "Devil's Oven") and wondered what "convulsion of nature" had lifted these jagged masses from the earth.[61]

Nature's beauty did not distract him from the resources waiting to be exploited. Like the county's first surveyors, Newsome identified the lands fit and unfit for cultivation, the grasslands making for "excellent natural pasture," and the timberlands. With a keen eye for mineral deposits, he pointed to the richest coalfield—"five feet in thickness" near Murphysboro and "nine feet in thickness" in Williamson County. Sandstone in the north proved useful for construction; the limestone to the south would "bear a high polish" and would one day be exploited.[62]

Rather than attempt an account of pioneer days, Newsome picked up the remnants of Boon's history and, with a minimum of stylistic revisions and corrections, let the manuscript stand without comment. Thus, he was able to move past the frontier period, pick up where Boon had concluded on the eve of Andrew Jackson's election, and bring the story into the modern world.[63]

While Boon, the aging pioneer, looked backward to a simple frontier society, Newsome told the story of rugged, daring entrepreneurs and of the social changes that came with the driving power of steam, first with the riverboat and then the railroad. He returned to the Big Muddy, this time as an artery for navigation. In detail he listed the hazards challenging the river pilots: the twists and turns, the treacherous shoals at the Worthen farm and at Rattlesnake Creek. The *Walk on the Water* began the shipment of coal to the Mississippi and to markets in St. Louis. Soon Big Muddy coal earned the reputation "as the best coal west of Pittsburg."[64]

With the arrival of the steam-driven locomotive, Newsome's story shifted from the river to a series of "historical sketches of the cities and towns" on railroad lines. He enumerated the smallest points on the map, flag stations like Perry with a few houses and a store or Muddy Valley with a solitary store, mine shaft, and a few rude miners' shacks. These places sprang up on the Cairo and St. Louis, the Illinois Central, the Carbondale and Shawnee-town, the Chicago and Texas, and the Mobile and Ohio Railroads. Towns like Sato and Carbondale existed largely because of the railroad.[65] Without critical comment, Newsome recounted stories that despite his intent revealed rampant speculation and greed, rivalries between would-be town builders, success and failure.

While the "cross-roads" village of Bradley expected a railroad station to be built, a nearby entrepreneur successfully employed his money and influence to have the station placed at his town of Campbell Hill. "One of the store houses at Bradley was rolled up on two flatcars and, by the aid of mules, was moved to the new village." While Campbell Hill "became a prosperous little town," Bradley fell into the earth and has since been "forgotten."[66] Once Boskydell had shown promise. A quarry supplied building materials for the Illinois Central and later the normal school in Carbondale. Its owner "laid off town lots" anticipating boom times. A sawmill was established near the railroad track, houses were built, and some families came. But Newsome assessed a bleak future: at present Boskydell was "scarcely to be considered a town," and it was "not likely to be much of a town."[67]

The town stories often turned on coal. Mines around Murphysboro, Harrison, and Mt. Carbon became a prospering "center of the coal industry," with Murphysboro emerging as "one of the large cities" in the region. And, Newsome observed, the town "is still growing."[68] Carbondale "well earned its name." While a few mines had been tried in the area, the town thrived as a center for shipping coal northward to Chicago.[69]

Failed enterprises littered Newsome's landscape. Dorchester illustrated a recurring pattern of growth and decay within "only about seven years": it was "one of the towns that *was and is not.*" The houses for miners had disappeared already. Only the scars on the earth and the stories told by a few elder residents served as reminders. Eltham was a "prosperous little village" built around a sawmill and railroad depot. But after a fire consumed the principal structures, the "town was abandoned to its original solitude." Hope for rebirth was sparked when another railroad proposed laying track to the town. A surveyor came to prepare the ground, but then the project was forsaken. Eltham, Newsome concluded, is now "finally abandoned." Soon the traces where "considerable grading" had been undertaken would vanish.[70]

The rapid and repeating cycles of boom and bust were, in fact, integral to life in Jackson County. Newsome wondered whether Grand Tower's prospects pointed downward. Its location on the Mississippi River had once enticed developers who laid out a gridwork of streets and avenues. They watched as newcomers filled in the lots on Front Street with stores and hotels.

"As if by magic" this obscure landing "sprang into a young city." Then came stagnation: merchants left, industry slackened, "the town had passed its period of prosperity."[71]

Newsome had surveyed the rubble—the abandoned furnaces at Grand Tower, the moldering timbers that once were Brownsville, the rusting metal rails that once hauled coal from abandoned mines—that testified to enterprise failed. But like community boosters throughout Gilded Age America, he looked through the dismal wreckage toward a bright and ever-expanding future. If the dream for Grand Tower's future "has only been fulfilled in part," he promised his readers that "the time is yet to come to bring its entire accomplishment."[72] Men with virtue and industry provided the energies for filling the landscape with prosperous village centers. Once, not long ago, life at Ava revolved around a saloon and attracted men of vicious character. Shootings were common. When the railroad came, "rowdies" derailed trains. But businessmen with "wealth and industry" banded together, "built up the town," and "gradually diffused intelligence and purified the community." Churches were erected. "And now Ava is quite a flourishing and organized town."[73]

Such men of "wealth and industry"—builders of churches, businesses, and hotels—directed the county's progress. Corporations had names. Their employees remained faceless and nameless, only emerging momentarily from the story as undisciplined, ignorant ruffians. Miners appeared for fleeting moments and disappeared without comment. At times Newsome fixed place to ethnicity. The community at the Harrison mines was known to neighbors as "Italy." The mining settlement at Dorchester was called "Scotch Town." It became "a good market for what produce the farmers had to sell." "As usual," Newsome reminded his readers, miners were a "rowdy set, especially when they were drunk."[74]

Race was implicit in Newsome's history. Though witness to black contributions to Union victory, he returned home unaffected. He noted that the steady increase of the black population in Carbondale during in the 1880s from 20 to 25 percent but kept that story at the margins.[75] By his lights, white men with property made history. Like himself, they traced their genealogies to England. Industry—"pluck," his neighbors called it—and moral purpose guided these men who gathered on a stretch of land where the Illinois Central planned to lay track, laid out the streets and lots, and began to build in preparation for the railroad. The story lay embedded in property titles and their owners. Newsome, like Boon before him, recorded the lot numbers, the buildings, and the occupants. John Dunn built a log house on lot 104 and later added a larger frame structure. Daniel Brush built a store on lot 17; after his death the building became David Brown's shoe store. The first church was constructed on lot 99 in 1856.[76]

Newsome's *Sketches* was the realization of what Brush had attempted. Both projects worked to sustain an image of community by erasure. Newsome recounted the arrival of the railroad track from Cairo and the celebrations. Some had worried about possible accident, but "all passed off pleasantly." On the edges lurked unsightly challenges to the story. Like Brush, Newsome made no mention of the work gangs who graded the track beds and laid the rails. The railroad brought cultural differences to this Yankee community that translated into politics. Restrictions on billiard halls rankled some, but more volatile was the debate over alcohol. Simmering below the surface were deep divisions rooted in the Civil War. Those who called for the relaxation of liquor laws—the "whisky party"—challenged the "Black Republicans," gained seats in the town council, and though repeatedly outvoted, continued to press their cause. While briefly giving notice to the dissidents, Newsome reassured his readers that churches were being built. In 1868 the Christian church was completed on lot 114, followed by the Baptist church on lot 74. Meanwhile two "colored" congregations were gathering.[77]

Newsome concluded his history of moral uplift by recounting how the "friends of education," notably clergymen, rallied around a proposal to build a normal university. Church leaders from the region joined to petition the legislature for a charter. The first building was erected but then burned to the ground. Undaunted, civic leaders rallied to rebuild against "considerable opposition" from rival towns. Carbondale's champions prevailed in Springfield, and funds were appropriated. When the news was telegraphed to town, church bells rang, cannons boomed, and the people gathered that evening to enjoy the fireworks. Newsome was satisfied with his conclusion: "The educational interests and the absence of saloons are the chief glory and honor and sources of prosperity of this young city; may it long so continue."[78]

With Newsome's history, the work of Boon, Brush, Allyn, and Brownlee seemed to achieve synthesis. If Brush were able to lay aside disappointment that Newsome gave him scant attention, he would have found that its tone echoed what he had sought to accomplish. Perhaps Brush might have devoted more attention to the pioneer years, as he did when addressing the Old

Folks reunion. But the difference was one of emphasis. Both men, Newsome by Boon's proxy and Brush himself, looked backward to the hardy pioneers who by strength of character had laid the foundations. Newcomer Brownlee employed similar vocabulary. All looked to the present and future through similar lenses. Theirs was a story of the people who owned the land. In the current stage of human progress, capital moved the course of history forward. It was the large corporation, as Allyn reminded his audiences, that brought worker and investor together for mutual benefit and social uplift.[79] With this emphasis on men of substance, workers—be they railroad track crews, Irish and African Americans, or women—drifted through, always in the shadows. The story was populated by Englishmen of property. Whatever the cultural differences over liquor, they agreed that the essentials were railroads, education, and religion.

* * *

THE NINETEENTH-CENTURY'S tradition of pastkeeping in Jackson County came to fruition in George Washington Smith's *History of Southern Illinois.* Appearing in 1912, the three weighty volumes with their seventeen hundred pages rested on published histories of the thirty-five southernmost counties and interviews with eyewitnesses to a vanishing past.[80] Its authority rested on a settler narrative first expressed by Benningsen Boon and elaborated by his successors. The story was implicit in the county's founding survey map and the assumption that this was a place for settlers to achieve property. With this narrative, Smith inherited the habits of forgetting: that settlement was colored white and domesticating a wilderness entailed dispossessing American Indians and excluding African Americans, that domestication was itself violent, that settlement proved a waystation for transients both propertied and propertyless, and that labor and capital collided. Moreover, it enabled the pastkeeper to remain deaf to voices of contradiction. So powerful was this habit of forgetting that it enabled historians like Smith at the end of the century to extend their narrative into the Progressive Era of the early twentieth century and beyond.

Like the earlier county history, the success of this project depended on pleasing or convention. It depended on subscriptions of prominent businessmen, farmers, and professionals who bought space for their biographical sketches. Smith followed the tested formula. Even while aspiring to give greater attention to ordinary people, he could not free himself from the conventional mold that shaped the past into a narrative of explorers, warriors, institution builders, political leaders, and successful entrepreneurs. His discussion of the ancient mound builders echoed Robert Allyn's dismissive summary of the "aborigines," his portrait of the sturdy frontiersmen was an embellishment on Boon's memoirs, and his story of the growth of towns and civic improvements confirmed earlier boosters like Daniel Brush. While he extended his chronology into the Civil War and the Gilded Age, he studiously smoothed over the rough edges: the passions of the war quickly passed; disputes with labor were settled judiciously. The century ended with Illinoisans flocking to the Chicago World's Fair and marveling at the "White City by the lake."[81]

Smith innovated by opening with geologic time but did so without refashioning the conventional framework. After quickly leading his reader through the eons from the Archeozoic era to the Cenezoic and pointing to the evidence left in local rock formations, he assured his reader that this earth science enriched understanding of the history of "social, intellectual, and spiritual life" as well as economic development. Thus, he turned to the resources—the fertile soil, the timber, the coal, the "rich" reserves of "stone, oil, and gas" lying untapped below the earth—"which a wise Creator has placed within the reach of the human race."[82] Smith offered his reader a synthesis of the geological sciences with the science of race. What God had bestowed on the region waited undeveloped until a fit race had arrived. Echoing Allyn, he dismissed "the Indian race" as a brutal, intellectually benighted, "indolent, thriftless people." Because French men had children with Indian women, their offspring "lowered the tone of the social life." With the arrival of the Anglo-Saxon the resources of the land were improved, and according to God's providences civilization sprang from the raw wilderness.[83]

Progress—it became manifest in the study of human history. While reading the record of economic development through this lens, Smith blithely passed over the evidences of human spoilage. Frontiersmen had squandered the natural bounty. They had used the soil recklessly and had denuded the land of its forests. Though witness to his neighbors' "methods of waste," he remained unshaken in his confidence in the ingenuity of white people. Timber resources had diminished, but human ingenuity had responded. Railroads depending on timber for laying track might have faced a crisis of scarcity if it had not been for the development of a "scientific process" for treating and preserving wooden timbers. Construction design relied increasingly on concrete and steel. Meanwhile public-minded citizens had organized an annual Arbor Day for the planting of trees and flowers. Finally, Smith assured his reader that scientific surveys had concluded that although "the total area of timber has decreased," "the total leaf surface" is enough to ensure that "its beneficial influences" on "climate, water supply, etc. has suffered no loss."[84]

Smith's history amplified Allyn's confidence in the scientific management of land. While noting the frontiersman's mismanagement of the earth's bounty, he confidently looked to government-supported scientists for opening an ever more profitable era of agricultural improvement. The state government had established "experimental stations" in several counties that were undertaking the systematic survey of soil reserves and crops and were offering courses of instruction to local farmers. It had sponsored drainage districts to improve lands for cultivation. Smith's own university had created a department of agriculture to sponsor what he heralded as a "revolution in methods of farming."[85]

Smith deplored conventional emphasis on "political movements" that distracted the public from understanding "the march of progress in the social life of our people." The written record, he confided to his reader, was inadequate, thus requiring him to seek out oral testimonies. So wedded, however, to the principles of progress and racial hierarchies, Smith was unable to ferret out people on the margins. For example, he discussed slavery as an issue that pitted white people against one another but saw no reason to recognize the African American as historical actor. Nor were the new immigrants from eastern and southern Europe contributors to the advancement of society. Indeed, he worried that their vote undermined the purity of American democracy.[86]

Smith's chapter on Jackson County was a distillation of the earlier county history with brief reference to recent economic development.[87] His story of improvements and progress was told by way of biographical sketches in the following two volumes. Carbondale's Joseph Bundy, a farm boy born in a rude log cabin, worked and saved to pay tuition at the normal school, taught school, and won appointment as district supervisor. Not one to let opportunity slip by, he hitched his ambitions to the new telephone and power companies and ventured into the hardware business. Murphysboro's "flourishing condition industrially and commercially" depended on civic-minded entrepreneurs like John L. Schmidgall, who owned and operated a milling company and a coal mine that employed fifty workers and who served the community as mayor. In keeping with the tone of his history, separate sketches of banks appeared alongside biographies of bankers.[88]

When Smith retired during the New Deal years, he could feel confident that he had stamped his history onto local historical consciousness. He lectured generations of students who took careful notes as he revealed the verities guiding humanity's advance from the Greeks to the creation of the republic. When he attended meetings of a new regional historical society, he heard nothing to suggest that the habits of forgetting were unravelling or that voices so long kept at the margins were heard. The forgotten were kept safely forgotten.

* * *

IN THE WAKE of the challenges accompanying the Civil War and Reconstruction, local historians succeeded in restoring the inherited white settler narrative in a renewed and polished synthesis. Accordingly, the Jeffersonian promise inlaid in the original land survey had been fulfilled. Settlement and prosperity had been carved from a wilderness. And so, race, violence, class, dispossession had been forgotten. Yet that synthesis remained ever fragile in the face of experience. There were the drifters, not just the indigent but the respectables. The children of the pastkeepers themselves abandoned their homes. While community leaders grasped the ideal of an autonomous community—a later historian would call it the "island community"—dependence on outside capital raised doubts. And always there was the black presence—most notably the descendants of slaves who grew in numbers and sought what they believed to be the Jeffersonian legacy. The dominant narrative, while persisting into the next century, struggled to forget those ever-present, nagging contradictions.

PART TWO
HABITS KEPT, HABITS QUESTIONED

George Washington Smith felt secure in his rendering of the local past. If he were to peruse local histories in the Midwest, he would have discovered resounding confirmation of his white settler narrative. The national historical narrative, though different in content, followed the same trajectory of settlement and progress. That history was so embedded in imaginations that it seemed impervious to conflicting experience and voices of dissent. Local became national and national local. Throughout the nineteenth century local historians lived in an environment where class and race affected local experience. At times they included anecdotes that signified those phenomena, yet they remained enmeshed in inherited methods of pastkeeping even while they heard dissenting voices in the neighborhood. The synthesis remained useful for nurturing a sense of community identity. So powerful was that synthesis that it endured largely unquestioned into the twentieth century.

Thus, the writers who claimed ownership of the past looked beyond the workers in mining camps and in railyards who were essential to the community's well-being. If they attended to them, they dismissed them as ignorant, rowdy, slothful, and irresponsible. While focusing on the local dignitary, they did not allow the voices of protest to reshape their narrative. Nor could they imagine the significance of the local dignitary's dependence on distant, even faceless, financial magnates.

So, too, the essence of the original white settler narrative seemed impervious to the black presence. Possibility of reconstructing that story with the Civil War was tucked safely away, even while black voices became ever more noticeable in the twentieth century.

CHAPTER SIX

PASSERSBY, RICH AND PENNILESS

VIEWED FROM THE railroad depot, history seemed to be a story of progress. Trains loaded with coal and farm produce passed through, population increased, civic institutions—churches, schools, banks—flourished. So it seemed to the historian. With the angle of vision shifted but slightly, the story turned to the grimy faces of workers, to strangers who visited infrequently and who held the welfare of the community in their grasp, to the dead bodies scattered along the tracks, to the clashes between capital and labor. When read, the one history seemed self-congratulatory. The other, if written, might have provoked questions about how progress and poverty became partners.

* * *

FOR SEVERAL DAYS Rosario Panebiango had been living in a boxcar at the edge of Carbondale.[1] He had been moving slowly southward from Chicago with a crew of three dozen Italian immigrants hired to maintain the Illinois Central tracks. Provided lodging in boxcars fitted with bunks, stoves, and cooking utensils, they stopped for a few days on a siding at the edge of a community while they inspected and repaired the railbeds. Panebiango would dig a makeshift oven from a nearby embankment where he baked bread and idly watched the farmers driving their wagons into town. Sometimes he walked to the town square with his fellow workers to buy supplies. Across the square at the depot, he watched the finely dressed gentlemen escorting their wives and daughters to the train with their trunks and hatboxes.

Carbondale, like the other towns, seemed remote and foreign. Panebiango did not speak English well and relied on his foreman, Frank Simeone, to communicate with the bosses and, when needed, with the townspeople. He was part of a transient community. Workmates dropped from sight. Hobos drifted by. While attending to his loaves, Panebiango kept a vigilant eye on the tracks and the trains that roared past. In contrast to the nearby town and its semblance of tranquility, his world was perilous. Workers were cut in two by speeding trains. For a few days he watched the townspeople, these distant and unapproachable strangers, and then his crew moved southward, stopping briefly at Mounds and Cairo before crossing the Ohio River.

On the town square, businessmen met and exchanged pleasantries at the doors to the Jackson State Bank; with Theodore Roosevelt in the White House their world seemed secure; they noted the passing trains as signs of prosperity but glanced only briefly at the strange Italians. Neighbors who gathered at the popular Old Reliable for an ice cream soda were momentarily diverted from their gossip by the oddly dressed foreigners. A shopper may have bumped into one of Panebiango's friends and noted the man fumbling with his broken English to purchase flour. The Italians were a familiar part of the social scene. Trainloads of work crews passed through regularly. The townspeople became accustomed to, indeed looked forward to, the "strolling Italians" who appeared at the depot to entertain them with dances and tricks.[2] They called them Dagos and knew not their names.

The townspeople who met at the bank front or at the ice cream parlor attended to other names and faces arriving at the depot, such as visiting railroad executives from Chicago. From their private cars they looked across the wheat fields and calculated hefty profits.[3] Orchard harvests south of Carbondale convinced them to extend a spur line into the heart of the fruit country. Townspeople understood that these passersby who arrived with fat wallets and booked rooms at the Newell House and who then moved on brought the energies necessary for fueling the community's prosperity. Good times become better with the construction of a new roundhouse and freight building. The newspaper carried a regular column titled "Railroad Notes." Harry Walkup had been advanced to assistant chief clerk at the Illinois Central Chicago office. Anderson Proctor of Cape Girardeau, Missouri, was moving to the Carbondale offices.[4] And construction of the new depot was progressing.

These passersby, both the nameless and the named, played crucial roles in the town's development. Together their sweated labor and their capital fueled the economy; in contrast and sometimes in conflict they set the tone for community life. Each carried a competing narrative that explained the life of this community around the depot. According to one account, corporate leaders had brought the resources of capital and the energies of labor together and, with their genius for enterprise, had worked a dazzling transformation of prairies into thriving commercial centers. But for their initiative, places like Carbondale would not exist.

While the first narrative was trumpeted in the banquet halls of Chicago's Gold Coast and sustained down the tracks in the public press in towns like Carbondale, a competing story was offered by laborers huddled around campfires along those same tracks. Be they workers, hangers-on, or vagrants, they explained their lives in terms of a simple moral drama: that the celebrated captains of industry were, instead of civic improvers, predators rending the social fabric. While these powerful men were at once celebrating the virtues of enterprise and individualism, of competition and struggle, they were exploiting and oppressing their neighbors. In song and story these workers put their times in historical perspective. Labor unions such as the Knights of Labor and later the United Mine Workers told and retold the tale. One Chicago poet asked, "Who Owns America?" and then recounted the story of the government granting lands to the railroads, the subsequent profits, and the growing rate of social inequality and poverty in this Gilded Age.[5]

Although these passersby, both the privileged and the poor, set the tone and temper of life in this railroad town, they remained obscure characters in the local history books. Indeed, their absence revealed the nature of that narrative. Historian George Washington Smith sold space in his magnum opus to the men who both resided in the community and owned property. Thus, those who served and were dependent on Chicago capital appeared in print. Only a dozen years before Smith's history appeared, Henry Clay Curtis had come to town to operate a grain mill and elevator. Doctor Henry Clay Mitchell and attorney William Willis Barr had been on retainer with the Illinois Central. James Jones, venturer in mines, presented himself as the representative of his age. He had forsaken his father's "orthodox . . . spiritual beliefs" in favor of a straightforward faith in Darwinism. "The survival of the fittest" had become his maxim. "Whatever a man produces by his own skill or by his own capital is yielded to him for his own enjoyment and no human legislation should attempt to deprive him of its use." Finding socialism "a mild form of anarchy," he made it his life's purpose to "stifle the spirit of unrest in the ranks of labor and place the whole business fabric of the country upon a sound and healthy basis."[6]

* * *

PROFESSOR SMITH HAD perpetuated Edmund Newsome's model for history writing. While attending to the process of economic development that changed the physical and social landscape of Jackson County, Newsome had compiled a catalogue of mines—such as the Jackson County Coal Company and the Mt. Carbon Coal Company—of railroads and their growth, and of iron furnaces. As local history, his story centered on the county, as if it were an autonomous community, without attending to the sources of capital that, in fact, determined his story's direction. He glossed over the possibility that his enterprises operated on the frontiers of a network of investment houses in Chicago, St. Louis, New York, and Boston. Good times and bad depended on decisions made hundreds of miles away by investors who never came to this place.[7]

If Newsome had looked deeper, he might have noted that the outsider investor-speculators had been scouring the county as early as the days of Benningsen Boon's father.[8] While some mines were owned by local businessmen, many were operated by agents of distant capital. The land where William Boon had scratched out a few boatloads of coal for the New Orleans market eventually fell into the hands of investors in St. Louis and as far afield as Boston and New York.[9] Boston's John Tappan appeared on numerous deeds as principal shareholder in a network including Massachusetts men Lyman Coleman of Andover and James B. Thompson of Nantucket, as well as Forrest Shepherd of New Haven, Connecticut, and Walter Bidwell of Philadelphia.

After the Civil War the Gartside Mining Company, on exhausting coal reserves in the St. Louis area, ventured into the Illinois coalfields nearby Murphysboro. The Big Muddy Coal Company depended on St. Louis investors.[10] Other mines existed as part of large financial consortia such as the St. Louis Ore and Steel Company and the St. Louis Iron Mountain and Southern Railway Company. Regional mine owners and managers met in St. Louis to set prices and wages. In Chicago, New York, and Boston speculators purchased shares in the Muddy Valley Mining Company and the Union Colliery. The railroad's interest in the area was crucial. On the eve of the Civil War the Chicago office of the Illinois Central had sent surveyors to discover the best route between Murphysboro mines and the Mississippi River. In turn, the company's growth and stability became dependent on investors and markets as far afield as London.

Grange and Populist dissenters who wrestled with the national corporations and the threat they posed to local autonomy confronted these historical forces. Newsome did not. While identifying the wildcat speculations, the cycles of boom and bust, and the wreckage scattered across the land, he chose to embed that material within a dynamic narrative of economic expansion. In his *Historical Sketches* the distant actors affecting the cycles remained shadowy presences, and the products of their ventures were the mischances of the market's invisible hand. Following the model, later historians turned the likes of Daniel Harmon Brush and his family into single-handed agents of progress. A doctor or an attorney on the railroad's retainer earned that recognition.[11]

Speculators who never came created communities of laborers. In the 1840s the Dorchester mine, under the supervision of Edward Holden, recruited sixteen households, fourteen of which had recently arrived from Great Britain by way of New Orleans.[12] Eight families were headed by Scots. James and Violet Stoddard migrated with three children under ten years; Alexander and Mary Campbel stopped first in Missouri where their daughter Ann was born and then crossed the river. Four families were Welsh. Thomas and Mary Picton came to Missouri with four children and shortly after appeared at the Dorchester site with a newborn. A handful of unattached miners found beds at Susannah Willis's house. Willis, divorced with children, rented to three miners, including one listed as "mulatto" in the census.[13] When Holden, who preferred to live in Murphysboro, left town, this tiny community evaporated.

So, too, in 1900 outside capital had built housing on the edge of Murphysboro for immigrant miners, principally from Italy. Some had been recruited to break strikes and drive down wages. Samuel Congiardi and his wife Josephine were two years married and with an infant daughter when they left Italy. Samuel's family followed in 1898. While brother Tony lived with Samuel, Frank found a bed next door with five renters. Both brothers married. A community had sprung up with rows of houses, all whitewashed and ready for rent. Italian was the common language; English-speaking miners lived apart. As if instantly, this community became a market for local farmers. Some immigrants scraped their resources together to open a grocery store or butcher shop. But the mining town, like that of Dorchester, did not endure long. Some were seeking opportunity elsewhere, as far as Chicago or in nearby coal towns to the east in Williamson County. The exodus accelerated with declining rates of production and management's decision to cease operations.[14]

Meanwhile the Illinois Central had decided to make Carbondale a major hub of commerce.[15] With the construction of a roundhouse at the north end of town in 1898 traffic increased markedly; some counted as many as a hundred trains a day. The Chicago office designated the town a district office center and ordered the erection of a large two-story administration building north of the depot. Construction brought a wave of temporary workers to town. And the permanent population grew substantially—from 3,000 in 1900 to more than half again as many five years later. The Illinois Central listed 150 residents as its employees. The number was higher if road crews and transients like Panebiango were counted. Moreover the Ayer and Lord lumber processing company had installed a railroad tie manufacturing plant north of town that soon became a major supplier to the region. Middle-class merchants, attorneys, and physicians thrived. And real estate developers devised plans for new neighborhoods on the town's outskirts.[16]

In 1900, John Edmundson crossed the Mississippi River from Missouri with his wife Nellie. Twenty-one and strong, he found employment shoveling coal on the engines. Walking the tracks below, John McEwen kept account of the trains, their location, their switching positions, and their dispatching. Above both men was superintendent Daniel Foley, who had been working for the Illinois Central for twenty-five years. Together the three men represented Carbondale life. Foley, born in Massachusetts, the son of Irish immigrants, had stayed with the railroad since the great strike of 1877. Married for twenty years, he raised a family of five children. His son Louis was a stenographer in the railroad offices. Like his father, Louis would remain with the Illinois Central, having climbed to a superintendent's post by retirement. Edmundson was promoted to railroad engineer and was living in his own home, free of mortgage, with three children by 1920. And McEwen had earned a rapid series of appointments from conductor to district superintendent.[17]

These lives, however modest their success, captured the tone of Carbondale life as its leaders imagined. There were others, however, whose names appeared with Foley on the Illinois Central employment records but only briefly. The company's roster of employees with terms of seniority revealed the town as a waystation for transients. In 1903, two in three employees on the lists worked for the railroad for five years or less. Some moved on for better positions. Laborers like William Bridges, John McGuire, and George Nelson were employed for only a year and vanished without leaving a trace. These transients had, like the carpenter Frank Blankenship and Richard Maher, taken rooms in a boarding house. Whatever their reasons for coming or going, their presence, however fleeting, signified another submerged facet of local life.

One in five employees had been with the Illinois Central between six and ten years. In 1903, Edward Eisfelder had worked with the railroad for six years. Although he and his family stayed in Carbondale briefly, he persisted with the railroad all his working life. J. A. Dickens, train dispatcher at the Carbondale depot, had worked for the Illinois Central for seven years, left town with his family, and took employment with another railroad in Nebraska. Others drifted away. Joe Robertson, foreman, moved his family to take employment in the coalfields at nearby Sparta. Others vanished.

And 13 percent had been employed for more than ten years. With the exception of boiler-washer Hickam, they were clerks, dispatchers, and superintendents. They were road masters who oversaw the inspection and maintenance of tracks in the district. And unlike Hickam they were likely to move up in rank. J. F. Porterfield had been with the Illinois Central for more than fifteen years when he came to Carbondale. A native of Pulaski, Illinois, he began work on the rails during the summer and returned to school in the winter. After learning telegraphy, he gained steady employment and was advanced to office clerk. He proved himself a man on the make who did not allow himself to sink roots too deeply lest he lose an opportunity. He moved from New Orleans to Chicago and then to Fort Dodge before coming to Carbondale. He had hardly unpacked his trunk before moving to the Vicksburg offices. Again he returned to Carbondale for a short stint before returning to New Orleans as division superintendent.[18]

The depot and the rail yards set life's rhythms. And while townspeople may not have recognized transients like Rosario Panebiango or even the new switchman Oscar Henderson, they knew individual locomotives by name. Engines 356 and 71 were visible personalities. They killed. People felt the trains roaring past often in defiance of speed limits. At the tracks, contrasting worlds opened to them. Women, wives and daughters, finely dressed, waited at the platform preparing to board with porters attending. When watching a freight rumble past, they might have spied smudged faces peering out from between the tender and baggage car. During the winter months the transients became more visible as they drifted into town in search of shelter.[19]

Passenger trains with their sleeping and dining cars opened new worlds of tourism for the well-to-do. Carbondale newspaper advertisements lured readers to purchase excursion tickets north to Chicago or south to Hot Springs, New Orleans, Jacksonville, and Tampa. Connections might be booked for Cuba and Mexico or for New York and Europe.[20] Jessie Shryock, the wife of the university president, lectured the Women's Club on life aboard an ocean liner. Miss Pierce delivered a talk on her trip to Italy and her visit to Pompeii. Bessie Smith returned from Holland to recount her impressions of Dutch food and costume. And the members congratulated themselves that they were "becoming world travelers."[21]

Meanwhile the coroner witnessed the rhythms along the tracks. On January 24, 1903, E. E. Knauer recorded the death of Barry Morais: "run over by some engine and train on IC tracks at Carbondale." Personal property was noted: "nothing but his clothing." The recording continued down the ledger's pages. On February 14, Byron Baldwin was struck dead by southbound Engine 51. A month later Charles Craig was found "crushed between 2 cars" in the north yards. In June an "unknown negro" was struck by a passenger train; his possessions amounted to "nothing." On the same day William Crow was "run over by an ICR Freight train going north on west rail of main track of north yard." Several railroads ran through Jackson County, and sixteen men were killed in that year—one in Pomona, three in Murphysboro, two in Elkville, and the remaining ten in Carbondale.[22]

Railroad executives cultivated an image of themselves as instruments of economic prosperity and benefactors of their workers. In turn, their employees were grateful and loyal. So they had told themselves. And while this image was reflected among the company's retainers in small towns like Carbondale, the gritty experience of life on the tracks provoked questions. Neighbors shared stories of injuries and damages inflicted. Burning coals flew from passing engines and set fire to fields and buildings. Railroad construction blocked waterways and flooded property; school buildings suffered damages from nearby traffic; smoke and cinders drove customers from shopping districts. Eight-year old Elmer Jernigan was struck by a train backing through Murphysboro; his leg was crushed and later amputated. Trains sped past the normal school in Carbondale, sometimes at twenty miles an hour, a rate noticeably in excess of the city's six-mile-an-hour limit. Austin Bolin was driving his wagon across the tracks in town when a speeding train slammed into his wagon and threw him forward under his horses.[23]

Juries routinely assembling in the county courthouse to hear cases against the Illinois Central might not have been surprised by the reports compiled in the state capital.[24] Between 1888 and 1894, 350 employees were killed on the Illinois Central. In 1894, 51 were killed. Twenty-two injuries led to amputations. And in 1903, 57 employees of the Illinois Central were killed in the state. If the ten passengers and the deaths the railroad commission dumped into a miscellaneous box called "others" were added to that figure, the count for the Illinois Central was 171, or one in five of all statewide railroad fatalities.

Work around the trains was lethal. Brakeman Byron Baldwin rode a freight coasting through the Carbondale yards when he was struck dead by a pipe used for watering engines. His wife Bessie sued for negligence.[25] Sometimes the railroad dismissed an accident as "slight"—for example, when a fireman received broken ribs, was cut in the head, and fell into a state of shock. The Illinois Central's reputation was affected by its opposition to legislation requiring air brakes. Corporation managers were loath to install "telltales" on the tracks that warned workers atop moving cars that they were approaching low bridges. Four Illinois Central employees were killed by overhead obstructions in 1903. Legal opinion was turning with public sentiment. Once the Illinois Central had found shelter from suits under the fellow servant doctrine that established that if one worker were injured or killed due to the negligence of another worker, the company itself was not liable. But no longer. The courts were finding companies liable for injuries and death. Until then, company executives liked to assume a paternalistic role toward their employees and would pay money out of their pockets to an injured worker or his family. As the courts reversed themselves, executives grew disinclined to be so benevolent.[26]

Rosario Panebiango may have heard how Byron Baldwin had been killed. Perhaps the two men had passed one another in the rail yards. If not, such accidents were commonplace. But because the Italian's stay was uneventful, no one—neither the coroner nor a newspaper reporter—had reason to record his presence. Two months later, Panebiango was with his work gang

HABITS KEPT, HABITS QUESTIONED

in Newbern, Tennessee. One day—it was February 13, 1904—he was baking bread alongside the track.[27] As was company practice, the door on one side of his boxcar had been nailed shut, thus requiring him to crawl back and forth beneath the car while tending to his baking. A locomotive backing into that train of cars caught Panebiango beneath the boxcar, severed his left leg in two just below the hip, and cut off three or four toes. The accident might have happened in Carbondale.

Panebiango sued. The company's attorney argued that he was not working on the day of the accident and that the doors on both sides of the boxcar were open for his safe passage. The judge and jury, however, were not satisfied with either argument and awarded Panebiango $5,000. The Illinois Central appealed but was unable to reverse the judgment.

Similar cases that came before the Jackson County court reminded the citizenry of the hazards posed by the railroad. Near midnight on March 16, 1899, the Carbondale-Carterville train was pulling into the switchyard. As it backed slowly through, brakeman James Jones jumped from the engine and was walking down the tracks to attend to the coupling of some freight cars when he was struck dead by a speeding train. The court found in favor of the family to the sum of $3,000. Four years later readers of the Carbondale newspaper learned how the same train killed fireman Fred Harfler: on falling between two cars "his head was severed from his body, his leg badly mashed and other injuries sustained." The coroner found the cause of death to be a "defective coupling."[28]

George Atwell had moved to Carbondale to take employment as a section hand. After living in town for a year, he understood how dangerous the work was. If he were to pick up the *Daily Free Press*, he would encounter stories on the front page of a brakeman cut in half in the switching yards, a fireman falling between cars to be mangled terribly, or a laborer being struck by a southbound train. Atwell had been assigned to a night crew.[29] On February 8, 1901, foreman Martin Marlow learned that a switch on the tracks north of town required repair. He took six men, including Atwell. After a quick inspection, the foreman ordered his crew to take the handcar to a storage shed to collect the tools and a replacement rail. One of the crew cautioned that a northbound passenger train was late and that the handcar should not be left exposed on the track. The foreman dismissed the worrier. With three men at each end of the rail, the crew was carrying the unwieldy burden to the handcar when suddenly the foreman shouted orders: "Come, boys, take

146

the car off quick; there is a train coming." Instantly the men dropped the rail and raced to the tracks. Three reached the handcar first, but with the train bearing down on them they jumped clear. Somehow, however, Atwell erred and stepped into the oncoming train. The train had been traveling at a rate of thirty-five miles an hour, twenty-five miles in excess of city limits, and knocked him thirty feet.

Later that day the public read how Engine 356 had ended Atwell's life. He left a widow, Laura, and five children. Soon after, his widow brought suit. The Jackson County jury listened to her attorney demonstrate the railroad's negligence and awarded her $5,000 damages. The railroad attorneys, frustrated by a local attorney's ability to appeal to a jury's sentiment, took the case to the appellate courts, but to no avail. The higher court listened to the Illinois Central with impatience. The evidence was clear: with the obstruction lying across the tracks, "the lives of the passengers and crew of the coming train were in immediate peril"; testimonies confirmed that the railroad had acted without regard for human life; and Atwell had responded to imminent danger to others in a responsible manner.

Newspaper readers awakened to other stories. Early Sunday evening of April 19, 1903, the crew of a northbound train alerted the Carbondale station master that they had seen a man lying by the side of the tracks just south of town and near the normal school.[30] He appeared to be either dead or injured. C. H. Hall and Steve Costigan walked back along the tracks with the train crew to investigate. The body was cut in half. Costigan could still recognize that it was his brother Urban. Urban Costigan had been working as a brakeman on the southbound freight—engine number 71. Somehow, shortly after the train had pulled out of town, he had fallen between the railroad cars. The coroner also noted that he had broken his wrist.

Death became commonplace, often not worthy of attention. There was C. B. Farmer, killed by freight. The coroner simply noted that his clothes were delivered to his wife. Some remained anonymous. And there was the mute record in the coroner's ledger of the "unknown Negro" who had been struck dead by a speeding southbound train.[31] Bodies littered along the tracks were a common sight. The stories seeped into community awareness. Workers as well as residents in town sued the corporation, which in turn brought countersuits and prolonged litigation. While town and state governments struggled to invent the means to regulate the railroad, questions arose: were workers simply irresponsible or careless as the corporate attorney argued, or should responsibility shift to the corporation for its negligence? Beneath these individual mishaps, questions were asked whether a systemic antagonism existed between capital and labor. In this context wages rose to the forefront of discussion.[32]

The snippets in coroners' records, in court cases, and in newspaper notices informed imaginations. While the anecdotes provided material for a local history that turned on conflicting interests, that narrative seemed incapable of challenging dominant beliefs that were replicated and preserved in the gilt-covered histories found on parlor tables. The Chicago magnates and their retainers adamantly argued for their story. After the strike of 1877, they went about their business without regard for the disaster and congratulated themselves that their employees were loyal. Railroad workers also recounted lifetimes of colorful stories devoid of conflict. The romance prevailed. When labor organizers protested loudly enough to be heard, they were dismissed as irresponsible spokesmen of the "dangerous classes."[33]

Nonetheless, the counternarrative remained at the edges, demanding attention. The Knights of Labor and the Patrons of Husbandry, brotherhoods of brakemen and of carpenters, later Populists and socialists were speaking to experiences that chipped at prevailing Gilded Age rhetoric. Conflict seemed imminent. The transients, ragged and strange, whom citizens encountered tramping the country roads and lurking on the railroad sidings, sparked imaginations, even doubts. In 1886, a great strike rising in the west began to sweep eastward from one rail hub to the next toward Illinois. At the same time, Illinois miners were demanding a fair share of the fruits of their labor. Strikes hit St. Louis, spread across the river to East St. Louis, and then erupted in Cairo. News flashed northward from Cairo that the Knights of Labor were organizing—four hundred strong. In Chicago authorities braced themselves. The police had trained a special force to meet an uprising; a cavalry unit of the state national guard was publicly drilling. In nearby Murphysboro strikers gave notice that trains would be stopped. And in Carbondale the mayor was alerted that work on the university's new main building had been interrupted when "5 col[o]r[e]d Men and one white struck for 175 [sic] per day." Acting promptly, he ordered their discharge and squelched possible conflict.[34]

Though Carbondale escaped open confrontation, memories of 1877 and then Chicago's Haymarket Riot of 1886 had sunk into public awareness. A generation later, readers of the newspaper read accounts of labor conflict that were placed in context of those events. The county sat in the midst of coalfields linked together and, in turn, joined with larger markets by a network of railroads.[35] Mine and railroad workers clashed with management sporadically and sometimes violently. Owners who routinely planned strategies to drive wages down exploited ethnic differences to break labor solidarity. In neighboring Williamson County they imported black workers from the South to replace white labor. In Murphysboro they recruited Italian immigrants to the same ends. Violence seething below the surface erupted sporadically, most dramatically in the 1890s and the 1920s. Meanwhile the United Mine Workers grew in strength.

The Brush family found itself entangled in the conflict. Daniel Brush had staked his town's and his family's fortunes on railroads and coal. Soon after the Civil War his Carbon Hill Coal Company was digging south of town. Along the tracks to the immediate north other investors followed his example. For two generations the Brush family clung to this formula even while the Murphysboro mines prospered and their venture dwindled in production. Before Brush's death in 1890, his adopted son Samuel T. had ordered the mine closed. Meanwhile, the family watched the rail lines extend eastward into Williamson County and the mines at Carterville and Herrin. In the 1890s Williamson's production exceeded Jackson County's, surpassing it a decade later by seven times. Carbondale had become a hub for coal traffic and prospered.[36] And Samuel remained fixated on coal.

Samuel T. Brush presented himself, much as Daniel had, as the epitome of American character and enterprise.[37] According to his own telling, he began life as a "helpless orphan." While acknowledging his uncle for taking him in and providing a "comfortable home," he was "ambitious . . . to be doing something for himself." At age twelve, he was hawking newspapers on the Illinois Central. After two years on the road, he returned to work for his uncle first in his store and then his bank. Eager to improve his prospects, he trained to become a telegraph operator. When the Civil War began, he joined his uncle's company where his skills in telegraphy were at once recognized. Though a "boy in years," he proved himself a "man in spirit." Quickly he earned the confidence of his superiors. At war's end, he had proved his organizational skills as assistant to the adjutant general. On return, he assisted his uncle in opening the Carbon Hill Mine, ventured into lumbering, and oversaw the operations of a company specializing in preserving fruit.

A self-conscious exemplar of his age's ideals of rugged individualism, Samuel fashioned himself into a guardian of the community. Always eager to promote the "moral well being" of Carbondale, he joined the Presbyterian Church and, following his uncle's example, oversaw its growth. As president of the Anti-saloon League, he could boast that no liquor was dispensed in town. Samuel felt rooted in Carbondale—he counted himself the only resident to live there continuously since its founding. He was, he congratulated himself, a go-getter with the eye and imagination of a civic improver. In 1903, when he undertook to develop a new neighborhood on the northeast side of town, he directed that clean sidewalks be laid before any lots were sold and that a new school and church be ready for prospective residents.[38]

On exhausting the vein at Carbon Hill, Samuel scanned the landscape for new ventures. In 1890, he found investors in St. Louis, Cincinnati, and Indianapolis to begin operation of the St. Louis and Big Muddy Coal Company. Under his management, the company sank its first shaft in nearby Carterville. The venture proved rewarding. In two years production ranked sixth in the state, and tonnage continued to rise. Stock was sold in New York.[39]

Local venture was again intertwined with a national system of finance. Accordingly, the prevailing conflicts between capital and labor came home to Brush's community. In the 1890s, economic depression and falling coal prices prodded mine operators to cut wages. Protesting miners were heeding the call for union organization. The strike seemed their only recourse. In 1894, a poorly organized workforce closed the mines but could not hold the line for long. Three years later, a stronger union called again for a strike. Although the United Mine Workers could count a meager statewide membership of 228, a majority of the state's 38,000 miners walked off the job. Union membership soared to 30,000.

Samuel and the other Illinois operators weathered the first strike, but they could not so easily resist the second. Within months, the owners capitulated to the union's demand for higher wages. Samuel, however, did not need to make concessions. While calculating the losses from a strike, he speculated on the advantages of being first to heed the workers' demands. If he were to stay open, while other operators produced little for the market, he would reap the profit. So he proposed to raise his workers' pay in exchange for assurance they would continue to dig coal and not join the union. They agreed, and Samuel profited. Equally significant, he earned the distinction of operating the only nonunion mine in the state.

The stratagem appeared to some as a model of statesmanship. Samuel, who always liked to see himself as a benevolent employer, felt confirmed. While refusing to bargain with a union, he assured himself that he was able to treat his workers with fairness.[40] At once he expressed support for labor's call for an eight-hour day and remained obdurate that this offer was his alone to make and that it could not be construed as a concession to a union. He satisfied himself that he knew his workers: paying them more did not improve their lot; most were content with their earnings. If he raised wages, they simply worked less. While he believed that necessity nudged the "ambitious man who wants to go ahead and make all he can," his records proved that worker a rarity. Indeed, he testified to a government commission, men paid thirty cents a ton earned, in fact, less than those paid twenty-six cents a ton. His miners were happy not to join a union. They trusted him: "[T]here is no difference between me and my men."

When the state's mine operators agreed to negotiate collectively with the United Mine Workers, Samuel declined to participate. When settlement was reached on a pay rate of thirty-six cents a ton, Samuel responded that he was not bound by the agreement. When he raised his rate from twenty-six to thirty cents, his workers walked out on strike. If they did not return, he threatened to hire black labor from Tennessee in their stead. The strikers stood firm and, within days, watched carloads of African Americans arrive. White strikers armed themselves. Samuel appealed to the governor to send the militia but was rebuffed. The conflict, he was told, was of his making alone and would be averted by accepting the statewide agreement. Local authorities responded by supplying as many as five hundred deputies to protect the mine and the scabs. Samuel hired guards and armed them.

For the next year Samuel refused to recognize the union. Still the caring patriarch, he offered higher pay. But the strikers remained obstinate. Meanwhile, Samuel and his cohorts worried over reports from central Illinois mining towns that strikers and mine guards were killing each other. In June 1899 Samuel's son had recruited more black workers.[41] When a special train carrying forty strikebreakers and their families approached the Carterville mine, strikers were lying in ambush and began shooting. Samuel Brush was on the train and joined in the exchange of fire. The sheriff telegraphed the governor that he was "powerless" to maintain order; the strikers were poised "to wipe out [the] Brush mine" unless the militia was dispatched. Samuel echoed the appeal: the miners and their families under his protection were "terrorized"; they "have not eaten or slept"; their safety required that the militia be sent "immediately." The governor complied and dispatched two companies, one from Carbondale, to the battle scene.

The troops secured the peace, though an uneasy one. If Brush had been applauded in the press, his intransigence tested public patience and roused resentments. Weeks after the troops arrived, Samuel visited Murphysboro to attend to legal affairs. On completing his business, he was walking to the train depot to return home when suddenly Ezekiel Morgan and Roy Bowman set upon him with clubs. Both were miners, and Bowman was a local prizefighter.[42] Though beaten severely, Samuel recovered and hired a Carbondale neighbor as his bodyguard.[43]

Weeks later the troops went home, and within days strikers and scabs were shooting each other. That Samuel had imported black workers to break the strike exacerbated resentments. White miners exchanged shots with black workers near the Carterville station; five strikebreakers were killed, and the wounded retreated to the mining camp. Again the two militia companies were ordered to the scene, and a third was added. While order was restored, opinion remained bitterly divided. Carterville's residents were sympathetic with their striking neighbors and grew resentful toward Samuel Brush. In Carbondale, opinion divided with a significant portion of the community sympathetic with Samuel. When a dozen strikers were indicted for murder, the court ruled that local opinion prevented a fair trial and the proceedings be moved to a neighboring county.

Samuel, determined to see the strikers punished and justice done for his black employees, hired five attorneys to assist the prosecution and took rooms near the courthouse in Vienna to oversee the trial. Each day he took notes and in the evenings conferred on strategy with his prosecution team. His reputation was on trial. When the jury returned with a verdict of not guilty, the defense attorney spoke to cheering crowds celebrating that Samuel had been defeated and that, despite his money, his attempts to malign "law-abiding and good citizens" had failed.

Samuel had entered the crisis fortified with strong conviction that dismissed unions as detriments to the public welfare. Moreover he had gambled that his stand would put him at competitive advantage with other mines that had bowed to the strikers. But he had lost. His reputation tarnished, he needed to employ guards to protect his mines. And production had declined by a third. Meanwhile, the union mines boasted ever higher rates of production. Within a year of the labor crisis, Samuel closed his mine. He might have followed his competitors' example and begun talks with the union. But, as a friend remembered, Brush "had fought the union because of principle, not because of money. . . . He thought he was right."[44]

The St. Louis and Big Muddy Coal Company fell into receivership and was managed by a Peoria businessman. Samuel watched as other mines that had followed his example closed. Outside capital was salvaging the damages. New York speculators had bought a neighboring mine once owned and operated by local investors. In 1900, Brush regained control on condition that "all differences" with "its former employees" would be brought to "amicable settlement." He stuck to his principles, however, and struggled to keep out the union. Five years later, he bowed to pressure and sold the mine to operators who recognized the union.[45]

Broken, Samuel packed his bags and moved to live with his son in Boulder, Colorado.

* * *

THE RAILROAD AND coal drove Carbondale's history. Its residents witnessed these forces when they watched the soot belching from the engines and the freight cars in their endless trains piled high with coal. That history also turned on dependency and transiency, represented by the strangers who visited long enough to invest and then left and by the workers who stopped and then moved on. By keeping these faces nameless and at the edges, a town history might still be written without recognizing the forces and consequences of such dependency.[46]

While Samuel T. Brush was struggling against his workers, and while the Illinois Central was adding tracks and switches, the Chicago-based timber processing company of Ayer and Lord was devising plans to build a plant in Carbondale.[47] Railroads needed wooden ties that resisted decay. And as the miles of track grew longer, so did the demand for pressure-treated lumber. Profits from the plant in Somerville, Texas, encouraged company executives to expand operations at strategic locations along the Illinois Central at Grenada, Mississippi, at a connecting line to Argenta, Arkansas, and at Carbondale. At Argenta the company created a factory town complete with hotel, company store, and barracks for its principally black workers. As a bustling railroad town, Carbondale seemed promising. If local forest reserves were nearly exhausted, Ayer and Lord expected easy access to timber supplied from Tennessee and Kentucky, Missouri and Arkansas. Moreover, it applied its practice of recruiting cheap and black labor from the South.[48]

In 1901 John B. Lord dispatched agents from his Chicago offices to promote the project with Carbondale's business leaders. The strangers bedazzled their audience with their project to build the largest processing plant in the world—one capable of producing four million ties in a year, a million more than the Texas plant. Buildings and equipment would cost $150,000. In addition, the company had entered into a cooperative venture with the government in Washington to create an "experimental plant" for improving techniques for wood preservation. The company's superintendent of operations predicted that the plant would hire between 150 and 200 workers. William Schwartz, organizer and president of three Carbondale banks, listened as the company explained that the project depended upon the acquisition of 200 acres of land near the juncture of the southbound tracks and the spur running to Paducah, Kentucky. When Ayer and Lord proposed that the town's business community acquire that land, Schwartz readily agreed to promote the purchase.

The deal, gushed the *Daily Free Press*, was "Carbondale's Christmas Present."[49] The business community was abuzz with enthusiasm. The project confirmed faith in scientific progress. The newspaper explained the method to force sap from wood by steam and then infuse a compound of zinc and chlorine under pressure of one hundred pounds per square inch. J. S. Baker, the supervisor of equipment in all the company's operations, explained that soon the technique would be improved by substituting creosote for the zinc compound. Meanwhile business leaders awakened to new opportunities. The influx of workers meant a boom for real estate and construction interests. Moreover, the Illinois Central could be expected to bring more workers to town for the construction of additional track. In six months Schwartz announced that the land had been acquired and turned over to Ayer and Lord. A decade later, readers of the *Daily News* were asked: "What business was not benefitted many times over the amount of cost" for the land?[50]

Although the president of Ayer and Lord visibly altered the physical and social scene, local historians looked past his presence but, true to convention, accorded place to William Schwartz. Plant managers from Chicago oversaw the recruitment of workers with offers of weekly wages as high as seventy-five dollars. The cheapest employee was the tie carrier, who by company policy was black. While managers drew laborers from the South, they recruited skilled workers and office personnel from the immediate neighborhood.

Once the plant opened, John Willoughby left the railroad for Ayer and Lord and soon was promoted to chief engineer. The newspaper announced in early 1903 that three employees were leaving the Illinois Central for Ayer and Lord: Harry Walkup moved to the Chicago office, Don Bailey to the Grenada office, and E. G. Cooper to the Carbondale office staff.

The tie plant became a booming enterprise. Townspeople gawked at the new smokestack as it rose upward; the newspaper boasted to its readers that it was the tallest in the region.[51] Payrolls passed two hundred, and real estate and construction interests leaped at new opportunities. Surveyors laid out a subdivision with new streets and house lots, all within easy walking distance of the factory. Tie Plant Place included space for two hundred new inexpensive houses. New laborers, principally black southerners, arrived. Due to Ayer and Lord, the black population had doubled (from 586 to 1,140) between 1900 and 1910. One in five Carbondale residents were black. And the lines of segregation became clear with the concentration of these new-comers in the northeast corner of town.[52]

As it had in the South, Ayer and Lord assigned black labor to the most menial positions. But unlike previous practice of relying on single males, the Carbondale plant attracted families. They came from Tennessee, Kentucky, Arkansas, and Mississippi. Lorenzo Fletcher and his wife Marina, both born in Mississippi in the 1880s and married for more than twenty years, began their migration northward with four children, first to Missouri and then Illinois. When they rented a house on East Sycamore Street, the couple had seven children. The eldest son Thomas had joined his father at the tie plant. Next door lived Robert and Della Mathews with their three children. A few houses down the street lived the Silas family from Tennessee. John and Eura had been married thirty years. With his income at the tie plant and hers as a domestic servant, the couple had bought a modest home. One daughter worked as a cook in a restaurant, and a son joined his father at the tie plant. Another daughter, her husband who also worked at the plant, and their thirteen-year-old daughter lived in the same household. One block north on East Larch Street lived Burt Flippin, his wife Lucy, and their three children. Burt and Lucy had migrated from Tennessee, as had their neighbors Robert and Elnora Thornton and their son Robert.

While Ayer and Lord had stimulated the growth of a black community, it had brought invisible health risks. The preservation process consumed vast amounts of water, second only to the railroad, and in turn dumped large quantities of refuse into nearby water systems.[53] With the plant's opening, fish began dying in Crab Orchard Creek. The alarm prodded the newspaper to respond, assuring readers that the zinc treatment was not toxic to wildlife and cautioning that the plant was preparing to increase production. The welfare of the community depended on the "successful and uninterrupted operation of this vast industry."

A decade later Ayer and Lord had converted to a creosote treatment system. Thousands of fish in the Big Muddy River were dying, and the local game warden pointed to a "stream of poisonous creosote" draining from the plant. Company spokesmen insisted that science had not demonstrated any lethal effects from the chemicals. Residents on the northeast side of town discovered pools of water in the fields nearby the plant that were clogged with an ugly tarry substance. On a dare, one young man dove into a pool and emerged with a sticky substance clinging to his body. His friends never forgot that sight. A portion of the plant erupted into fire and explosions that dramatically confirmed fears regarding the materials employed by Ayer and Lord. Cattle were dying as well.

Meanwhile the business community reminded the public that it had discovered the formula for continued growth and prosperity. The town's welfare was dependent on outside capital. The newspaper understood: while dismissing reports of health risks around the tie plant as detrimental to economic expansion, it kept its readers informed of transitions in ownership of the company and its eventual purchase by Koppers of Pittsburg. On the eve of the Great Depression, the town awoke to the possibility that a new clothing factory might begin production in town if the right incentives were offered. The town leaders delivered a short history lesson: by purchasing land for Ayer and Lord, the community had benefited beyond expectations. Bankers and businessmen did not forget. When representatives of the Good Luck Glove Company visited in search of a prospective branch site, the same community leaders mustered the funds ($45,000) to acquire the land and build a factory alongside the railroad tracks. When the factory opened, the newspaper congratulated the town's financial elite. The "benefits to the community" were manifest. Though the company paid low wages to young women, these jobs ensured that they would remain in town rather than move elsewhere. "Households and relatives have been kept together."[54]

The journalist slipped past another part of local life that made for an alternative history of this railroad town—one that moved from the wealthy strangers who held Carbondale's well-being in their grasp to the homeless strangers lurking near the rail yards. These nameless people were reminders of the people who had stopped to earn a living and moved on, or of Jackson County's children who calculated no alternative but to go on the road. With the Great Depression, the drifters became more apparent. President Franklin Roosevelt had acknowledged the presence of "the forgotten man at the bottom of the economic pyramid." Always a common part of life in this railroad town, the hobos increased. Townspeople encountered them at the rail yards, in back alleys, and at their own back doors begging for a "handout."[55] They stood at the roadsides hitchhiking. Residents talked about a camp at the outskirts of town where these unemployed drifters congregated, pooled their meager resources, concocted a "banquet," and shared information about train schedules and railroad dicks.

The newspaper informed readers of the deaths: two "from drinking poisonous alcohol," another struck by a train. Meanwhile, the hobo began a transformation from the misfit whose lack of character had led to personal misfortune to a desperate soul who for no fault of his own had fallen on hard times.[56] A newspaper journalist stopped to listen to hitchhikers on the edge of town: out of sheer desperation they had left wives and children in search of employment. They were the farmers who had lost their farms, the women on the road picking fruit, the lumberjack now unemployed and on the road to a brother's farm in Mississippi. The reporter walked away reflecting that these people looked for the right to work that an economic order could no longer provide.

While recognizing the plight of these people cut loose from their homes by abrupt economic disruption, these Carbondale residents glimpsed a history of their locale that turned on dependency and transiency. Eventually the closing of the Koppers plant and the Good Luck Glove Factory pointed to that history. The fundamental question arose that had been lurking for generations: What is local history? Can it be contained within political borders without distorting the social life of that locale?

* * *

STILL, THROUGH THE transitions from horsepower, to steam, to gasoline, the local historical imagination remained pinned to the original surveyor's map and the accompanying settlers' narrative. The cast of actors remained those who acquired their niches of property within the squares. So, too, historical imaginations were so confined by the squares designating county boundaries and the accompanying illusion of a self-contained county narrative that the significance of outside actor-investors in the local economy were given short shrift. Thus, local record keepers—coroners and census takers—and attorneys collected and recorded the material for a counter-story that included both transient laborers and distant investors without pausing to reconsider the dominant history. And so while today's national histories seek to portray the past from the bottom up—the railroad workers and miners—and appreciate the web of finance capital that shapes society, local pastkeepers have yet to absorb this perspective.

CHAPTER 7

RECONSTRUCTION AND RACE

AT ITS CREATION, Jackson County history was imagined to turn on two themes: the fulfillment of egalitarian ideals and the exclusion of both native peoples and African arrivals. While white pastkeepers believed they had largely succeeded in wiping their history clean of the American Indian presence, African Americans persisted, grew in number, and kept a consciousness of themselves as historical actors. If heard, their voices challenged the dominant narrative with memories of violence and aspirations grounded in egalitarian principle.

* * *

BY THEIR ARRIVAL and then by their deeds, African Americans promised to work a reconstruction of Jackson County society. During the Civil War they had liberated themselves, escaped north, and fallen into the shadowy status of contraband property.[1] Even while legally recognized as something other than slave but something less than citizen, they confirmed fears among the white majority that the war, regardless of assurances to the contrary, was waged for their freedom and for mixing of the races. When the legislature in Springfield approved the Thirteenth Amendment abolishing slavery and repealed the black codes for keeping Illinois white, African Americans claimed equal rights of citizenship. The black population grew rapidly. From 1870 to 1880, Carbondale's had doubled from 283 to 597; Murphysboro's grew from 125 to 234. And the county's total had increased to 7 percent.[2]

They came aware of themselves as actors in a history that looked backward to slave pasts and forward toward the promise of self-determining futures. The history was immediate, made palpable by parents telling children the stories of the dark times—of humiliations that accompanied bondage, of whippings, and of siblings and spouses broken apart by sale. They relived the times when Union forces approached and they evaded the slave patrols in their flight to freedom. They remembered the black regiments they joined and their comrades who risked their lives. At war's end, they quickly recognized that peace and freedom did not bring security. Southern whites, seeking revenge for defeat, let loose a terror against the freed slave. Families once broken by sale desperately sought reconnection in preparation for flight north. Children listened to the veterans recount their return to old homes in search of wives and their exodus to Illinois. Within a decade of the war's end, African Americans were making themselves into self-sufficient, propertied farmers. Families grew and communities flourished. But for color, they represented the Jeffersonian ideal of the self-determining agrarian citizen. They stepped into public life. They built churches, voted, created political networks, and ran for office. They made public celebration of their struggle for equality. Some had elbowed their way into the county history to be listed as subscribers, and a handful bought space for their biographies.

Many came as laborers in search of work at the Grand Tower iron furnaces.[3] Others found employment as farmhands. And like their white counterparts, they drifted away. Others like the Bosticks planted themselves in Jackson County. Soon after the war's end, this extended family from Williamson County, Tennessee, began to gather south of Murphysboro. Five—Burton, Dudley, Hardin, Stephen, and William—had been young men at the war's outbreak. The slave's fear of the owner's power to break the family apart had come true, as one branch of the master's household inherited these men and marched them to Arkansas to clear new lands for cotton production. As the war progressed, they overheard their masters discuss the advance of Union troops toward Vicksburg. In December 1862, they plotted to break loose together. In early January the fugitives met Union naval forces on the Mississippi River and were enlisted. All five were assigned to the USS *General Bragg*. For the next six months the ship patrolled the Mississippi in support of the Vicksburg siege and then moved south toward Confederate forces where it endured fierce enemy bombardment. Stephen Bostick received a bullet wound in the right shoulder, and William severely injured his leg while passing ammunition to the gun crews.

Stephen and William pointed to their scars while sharing their stories with their family. Both had been transferred to hospitals, and Stephen was discharged for his disabilities. The remaining Bosticks had been discharged at Mound City, Illinois, and began to make their way north toward Jackson County. Stephen, who had been living in Cincinnati, followed. Family bonds were tight. Some Bostick men returned to their Tennessee home in search of relatives. Stephen and Hardin found women they had once known in the old plantation community, brought them to Illinois, and married them. Old Tennessee neighbors joined this small settlement, bought lands, and raised families.

On the other side of the county near Elk Prairie, another cluster of black families was gathering.[4] Nathaniel, Reuben, Jerry, and John Williams told their children the family stories. Their parents, Nathaniel and Celia, were owned by a Mr. Short of Columbia County, Georgia. The sons were sold and separated several times over. They remembered their owners in succession and by name and temperament. Nathaniel told his children how he was working as a carpenter for his owner at the time, a Mr. Stanford, when General Sherman's army marched into Georgia. At once he freed himself. Reuben and Jerry were owned by a Mr. Burkhalter. Jerry had learned blacksmithing, while Reuben worked as a miller. John, while owned by another master, also became a blacksmith. At war's end the brothers, their wives, and their children first set out to Mississippi and then turned north to Illinois, where they acquired land and settled. James Jackson came with his wife Lucinda and their children from Florence, Alabama. For nearly four decades he had labored for his master while always praying for freedom until Mr. Lincoln's army arrived. After serving in the army as a teamster, he moved north to Cairo and then to Elk Prairie where he purchased land and prospered. Their stories became the foundation of a black settler narrative.

Soldiers who served and fought together followed each other. Henry Guy, Henry Grier, and William Berroman had enlisted in the Fifty-Sixth Colored Regiment. They recounted the bloody battle against a superior enemy at Wallace Ferry in Arkansas. They told the story of that critical moment when white troops were nearly overcome but were saved by this resolute black regiment. After serving on the *General Bragg*, Isaac Ingram and Isaac Morgan reunited with their Bostick shipmates. More came with similar service records and formed their own post of the Grand Army of the Republic, where they shared memories and compared their infirmities. They carried an intense group identity. Unlike the county's white posts, each of which included residents of a specific town, the black post, though grounded in Murphysboro, drew members scattered throughout the county.

Black newcomers were forming a memory community from the stories of bondage, of personal liberation, and of their bloody fight against slavery. Though many could scarcely read or write, they carried a sense of history's direction that their white and writing counterparts could not pause to consider. Soon after arriving, the county's black residents organized each summer to commemorate emancipation. By passing over an American date— such as the Emancipation Proclamation or the passage of the Thirteenth Amendment or the moment when slaves were freed in a state, such as June 13 in Texas—and by adopting instead the August anniversary of slavery's abolition in the British empire, they not only placed the moment in a larger international context but affirmed their independent sense of history.

Recalling past trials served as transition to current work and aspirations for the full rights of citizenship. When black leaders joined statewide networks to promote political participation, they bridled at white Republican leaders who lectured them on their debt to the party. Rankled by this familiar paternalism, the former slaves ventured to consider breaking from the party.

On a personal level Elk Prairie's Williams and Jackson families felt white expectations enclosing when they bought space for their biographical sketches in the county history.[5] Unable to write, they told their stories to a white author. Their progress from slave to free propertied farmer resembled numerous white biographies. In unison they closed by stressing that while denied the literacy necessary to assume full responsibilities of citizenship, they promised their children an education to "take an honorable position in society." Translating these words into his own presumptions, the interviewer praised the family's achievements and hoped that their lives would serve as "striking example[s] to all of their race." Credit was due for being "good, consistent Republicans." In light of their debt to their Republican benefactors, the author prayed that "they could be nothing else."

African Americans had learned to anticipate white expectations and deeply engrained predispositions to violence. When Bostick men visited their old plantation community in Tennessee, they heard stories of white rage.[6] During the war, white neighbors had driven slaves to a nearby river, lined them up against the water's edge, shot them, and tossed the bodies

162

into the current. On returning home defeated and embittered, Confederate veterans attacked their black neighbors on the public square of the county seat. A gun battle ensued with a local Bostick who had served in the Union army leading his neighbors. Black migrants from the South had witnessed the rise of the Ku Klux Klan. On crossing the Ohio River, they heard the familiar accents from slave days. And the Klan was riding the byways of Jackson County. So encircled, black arrivals bought land when they could in close proximity of one another and at safe distances from the white majority. The transient worker who lived in the midst of white majorities in towns like Murphysboro and Carbondale remained exposed.

One such black man fell to the racist rage in the winter of 1874.[7] News flashed throughout the county that a black male had sexually assaulted several white women, including a child, and had murdered one. While lawmen scoured the country, vigilantes patrolled the roadways. On learning that the sheriff had arrested a man in Cairo and had brought him to the Murphysboro jail, a mob broke into the jail, overpowered the guards, dragged the man to the bank of the Big Muddy River, and hanged him from a tree.

Hundreds of white people witnessed this black man twisting in agony as he was hoisted into the air; black neighbors attended to reports of the bloodletting from a safe distance. Decades later children listened to their elders recount the story. While the lynching riveted attentions, only a few scraps of newspaper reports remain. In time the story assumed different shapes as the ways of remembering and the habits of forgetting twined around the event and were guided always by race.

Three perspectives—one black and two white—framed the story. For black arrivals the spectacle raised memories of the promises of Reconstruction betrayed. Their family stories gave immediacy to the reports of the lynching and confirmed that such bloodletting was endemic to this society. Their white neighbors also acknowledged the pervasive violence but with an opposite understanding. Some accepted mob behavior as an instrument of justice. Others were embarrassed at what reminded them of rough-and-tumble frontier days and wrote to wipe that unseemly past from their histories. No matter their understanding, white people were indifferent to the black person at the rope's end.

How Jackson County's black residents responded to this lynching on the banks of the Big Muddy remains elusive. Other than the scraps of paper documenting military service, land owning, and community behavior, the evidence is scant. While urban African Americans, such as Ida B. Wells, expressed their indignation against the race terror in print, their rural counterparts like the residents of Bostick settlement might seem silent in comparison—their voices lost. Nonetheless, their celebration of Emancipation Day, the formation of their own GAR post, and their efforts at community building and political organization is sufficient evidence to appreciate their sense of themselves as actors in history. They recognized the meaning of their times as they saw the Ku Klux Klan appear in southern Illinois and as they listened to the reports of lynching not only in the South they fled but also in southern Illinois. They did not forget. If they failed to recall the lynched man's name, they remembered the significance of this and so many deaths. Later, their children would receive copies of the *Chicago Defender* and read its reports of black resistance to racial injustice with their parents' stories providing historical context.

Meanwhile, white Americans devised a variety of ways to gloss over the same pervasive predispositions to violence and, in doing so, to forget the subjects of savagery. When they remembered the lynching on the bank of the Big Muddy, they treated it as an event that stood alone, as if divorced from broader social traits—in short, as an anecdote of local color. In the same breath, they linked violence with justice and transformed brutality into maintenance of the community's moral core. Men who felt aggrieved by a neighbor sought justice by bloody retribution. Disputes between families turned to killings. Carbondale's residents watched the Bulliners and Hendersons of neighboring Williamson County shoot one another from ambush.[8] Friends and allies of each family joined the killing. Because George Sisney disputed the Bulliners' claim over a crop of oats and won in court, they attacked Sisney's home and forced him to seek refuge in Carbondale. One evening in December 1874, while he sat in his parlor, Sisney was wounded as an assassin fired a shotgun through the window. After recovering, he was shot to death through an open window, this time by Marshall Crain, whose family had joined in the Bulliners' blood feud. Crain was arrested and sentenced to death.

Neighbors, impatient with the courts, rose up to protect their moral order by exacting prompt punishments.[9] Hooded Klansmen were active in northern Jackson County around Vergennes and Ora. Thieves were apprehended and summarily whipped. Vagrants were sent packing. Despite appearances, the Klan, wrote one citizen, was neither "uncivilized" nor a mob but rather a keeper of public order. Neighbors were ever mindful of the "overwatching" unknown Klansmen: "those who have been hitherto noted for laziness have become the most industrious" citizens; "tyrannical husbands" have been visited at night by the hooded horsemen.[10]

By the lights of many white Americans, lynching became an expression of the democracy's desire for justice. Presidents from Andrew Jackson to Theodore Roosevelt, attorneys, even Supreme Court justices, gave the nod to lynching as necessary expedient and remedy for unreliable judicial systems.[11] White Americans recognized that the methods for seeking justice worked along a continuum of styles, from personal feud to vigilante lynching to legal executions. During the Civil War, Lindorf Ozburn and William Weaver, once comrades in the Thirty-First Regiment, clashed, and Weaver struck Ozburn dead with a brick. When Weaver was arrested, Ozburn's neighbors stormed the jail, dragged Weaver into the street, and beat him to death. In 1901 another mob gathered, this time outside the Carbondale jail. Thomas Moberly was charged with attempted rape of a little girl. Moberly was black and the girl white. When the crowd grew aggressive and leaders were brandishing a noose, the police quickly escorted their prisoner to a train and safety.[12]

Legal executions became rites of justice performed before large crowds and as religious exercises. By convention the court condemned the guilty for "not having the fear of God before his eyes but being moved and seduced by the instigations of the Devil."[13] Newspapers reported the preparations of the condemned. Days before his execution, Marshall Crain was escorted under armed guard to a mill pond where, clad in white robe, he was baptized and then taken to church. On the designated day, crowds gathered. Through his barred window, he shouted his confession: "[M]y soul is stained with blood, and my punishment is just." He had composed a poem that he read to the gathered throng. Then clad in his baptismal robe, he proceeded to the scaffold. A minister delivered a brief sermon and invited the crowd to join the condemned in the hymn "There Is a Fountain Filled with Blood." All prayed. Then Crain with hood over his head dropped to his knees over the trapdoor and once again confessed. The trapdoor was released. Once pronounced dead, his body was taken to the street for display.[14]

Not all the condemned climbed the gallows in baptismal robes. Nor did they all read a poem. But the minister preaching a short sermon and leading the crowd in hymn was expected. Religion mixed with commercialism. Photographers took pictures of the condemned on the scaffold over the trapdoor and sold copies as souvenirs. Days after John S. Jones's execution, the Fair, a Murphysboro store, sold a postcard-size photo of him on the scaffold moments before his death. At the bottom margin, customers were reminded that "It Pays to Trade at the Fair."[15]

Respectable citizens were embarrassed. These men—owners of land who had bought their places in the county history—presented themselves in a domesticated world of well-groomed homes with picket fences and gardens, striking dignified poses alongside their wives and livestock. The image of crowds gathered before a corpse dangling from a tree limb or gallows, the faces leering at the camera, did not comport with the pictures they had bought in the history book. Lynchings were reminders when they read the Chicago newspapers that they lived in a frontier world barely civilized. So, too, a hanging held in public, no matter the legal niceties, awakened in the spectators the base lusts that had degraded their recent pioneer forefathers. Thus the respectables called upon the governor to arm law-abiding citizens against violence associated with the Ku Klux Klan and family feuding and applauded legislation prohibiting executions in public. Accordingly, the history writers passed over such unseemly behavior as unworthy of remembrance.[16]

No matter their differences on violence, white people focused on what they deemed the welfare of their white community and ignored the race terror. The lynching on the bank of the Big Muddy became an incident of local color told and retold by neighbors. In the tellings the black man became a stage prop in the drama. The man's cries of innocence were forgotten, his agony lost from memory. His name seemed incidental. Was it Wyatt or White? Perhaps it was Twite. Some said that the man's wife had sold the body for five dollars, others heard that a doctor had kept parts of the body preserved as a souvenir. Where the man lived or where he lay buried seemed incidental to the story. Although local historians chose not to put it on paper, the story persisted as oral memory for generations well into the next century.

One telling of this savage act, while grating to the modern sensibility, illustrates the way the habits of forgetting and remembering intertwined with engrained racial attitudes to produce its horrifying effect.[17] In the early twentieth century, Murphysboro's white residents who frequented Joe Borgess's butcher shop listened to him recount the story. The principal character in his account, however, was not the black man at one end of the rope but a woman at the other end. While the mob dragged its victim to the river bank, the sheriff followed screaming his threats to prosecute.

The men hesitated. At that moment "Granny Patchett" elbowed her way through the men, seized the rope, sternly berated them for their weakness, and pulled the noose over the man's head. As she tightened the rope, the men felt shamed by her stern resolve and stirred themselves to action. At her command they tossed the rope over a limb, and, according to Borgess, she shouted, "Pull hard and tight."

Oblivious to the horror, the butcher transformed the act into testament to "good old Granny Patchett's" civic virtue. As a boy, he had recognized this small woman dressed in simple calico as a moral anchor of the mining community. Perhaps her English accent caught his attention. Though she spoke in a rough manner, people learned to recognize her tender intent. On encountering a miner staggering out of a saloon, too drunk to find his way, she took his arm and led him home. With stern voice she shamed a laborer from squandering his pay on drink. Wives and children were saved from starvation thanks to her. Butcher Borgess remembered her as "a terror to evildoers." She may have carried a gun; he was not sure. But she had a sword that people said had been her husband's. In framing the lynching as nostalgia, Borgess relegated the black man to the margins.

This scene with the local pastkeeper regaling neighbors with his reminiscences was reenacted openly without anticipation of critical comment. In this context storekeepers overtly sold picture postcards of lynchings, and white customers sent them through the mail without fear of censure. Both local and national historians paid no heed to race terror in their midst. Meanwhile, black voices were insisting that the violence be condemned publicly. While W. E. B. Du Bois and the National Association for the Advancement of Colored People were seeking to rouse the national conscience, porters on the Illinois Central Railroad were delivering packages of the *Chicago Defender* to young black men waiting at railroad depots who in turn distributed the newspaper. Black subscribers read grisly accounts of race riots in Tulsa, East St. Louis, and Chicago along with the editors' summons to confront this national disgrace.

Again, in 1915, Jackson County's black residents awakened to white rage.[18] News flashed through the county that a Carbondale black man had shot a town marshal. Days earlier a black laborer in Murphysboro had shot a union leader and then surrendered himself. But the Carbondale man had fled. Hundreds of white males from surrounding communities scoured the countryside, many publicly vowing to lynch the accused. Tensions had been mounting for weeks. In July, Elizabeth Martin had been brutally bludgeoned to death at her home. The black house servant Joe DeBerry, despite his protests of innocence, was promptly arrested. As an angry mob gathered at the jail, police drove the accused to safety in a neighboring county. But the news had traveled ahead, and that city's authorities declined to house the prisoner for fear of a lynching. Concerned that an inflamed mob would overpower the police if the prisoner were returned to Murphysboro for trial, authorities appealed to the governor for state militia.

Circumstances surrounding the murder were left dangling. Martin's husband, a prominent attorney, had suddenly skipped town and fled across the Indiana border to the resort at French Lick. It was said that he traveled with two women. Two days later he committed suicide. Meanwhile DeBerry continued to protest his innocence. Observers believed that he lacked the mental faculties to understand the situation. On the day of the trial he was escorted past a raging crowd shouting for his blood. Yet he smiled dumbly as if uncomprehending. When his attorney persuaded DeBerry to change his plea to guilty and beg for mercy, he agreed. Six hours later the judge sentenced DeBerry to be hanged.

While the crowd outside the courthouse was denied a lynching, citizens expected to witness an execution. The sheriff, mindful that the law forbade public executions but eager to placate his neighbors' thirst for blood, offered to appoint special deputies as witnesses—in short, as many as desired to attend. To expedite the application process he ordered the printing of special passes. On the eve of execution day, reporters and photographers gathered around DeBerry. Sheriff White hired a photographer to record the execution. Hundreds, perhaps a thousand or more, had come from the surrounding countryside.[19]

Perhaps some had not been able to attend, or they stood too far at the back of the crowd to see the prisoner drop through the trapdoor. To answer the disappointed, the newspaper provided a detailed account. DeBerry had been calm, smoked a cigar, and posed smiling for photographers. He walked to the gallows with "that queer smile that belonged to him alone." Some thought him crazy. The gallows had been expertly constructed. Readers learned that the rope was three-quarters of an inch thick and made from silk hemp. It was sixteen feet long and cost twenty-five dollars. Days later, Murphysboro learned that photographs of the execution would be shown at the local theater. Sheriff White who owned the town newspaper and the theater assured prospective customers that viewing Joe DeBerry's last moments was beneficial to community morality: "[M]any prominent citizens pronounce these pictures a great moral lesson." The spectacle awakened engrained habits of thought among white people. Respectables were embarrassed. Sensibilities had been pricked throughout the state and beyond. A St. Louis newspaper condemned the "uncivilized" spectacle and advised that missionaries should be "diverted to Murphysboro" instead of sent to foreign parts. The sheriff retorted that the criticisms were "false" and "slanderous attacks on Jackson County." In response to public outcry, the governor had ordered the postponement of an execution scheduled for the following week so that authorities might abide by the law. He pressed Sheriff White not to appoint so many special deputies for future executions. White shot back that he would appoint as many as he saw fit.[20]

While recalling the stories of white rage, black families had found affirmation in their own print medium. With each edition of the *Chicago Defender*, they read the descriptions of the gruesome carnival and, in turn, began to create a new association. They waited for the familiar porter at the depot, where they would either receive a bundle of newspapers or entrust their detailed reports of the local scene to be delivered to the Chicago editors. Illinois, "the home of our honored Lincoln," had disgraced itself. The editors asked whether DeBerry's fate would have been suffered by a white man. How many African Americans, deprived of education and opportunity, have fallen to deep habits of oppression in this society? "How many Joe DeBerrys are we going to convict tomorrow?" In response, local readers supplied the Chicago office with copies of the theater advertisements for the execution photographs. Jackson County's black families were not alone when they read the editors' letter to the governor protesting Sheriff White's "malfeasance" and demanding his removal, followed by their call for "united action" from "federated clubs of the state and every organization" to support legislation prohibiting future disgraces.

* * *

WHEN JOE DEBERRY was hanged, a second generation of African Americans had come of age. Though local history was written to obliterate their presence, they persisted with a sense of themselves as historical actors guided by memories and aspirations. In 1907, Stephen Bostick bought a place in the county atlas for his portrait. By doing so, the freedman now property owner, Union veteran now GAR member, reached to announce his life's achievement. However, his portrait did not appear amid the rows of other men, all white. Instead, it stood segregated on a single page framed by broad white margins.[21]

Parents kept the stories of slavery they had heard as children. For generations Carbondale's black youth had attended to Mandy Harris as she relived her childhood on a Mississippi plantation as a slave. They remembered her "hair-raising" tales of "paddy rollers" who patrolled local plantations at night and apprehended slaves who had slipped out without the master's permission. Harris vividly recounted the routine "whipping, beating, and sometimes killing." She remembered the field hands who succumbed to the heat,

Steven Bostick segregated in *Standard Atlas of Jackson County* (Chicago: G. A. Ogle, 1907), 73.

crying, "Water me! Water me!" Sometimes the overseer would relieve them. Sometimes he would beat them. Sometimes a slave would die after "gulping down water from his shoe." Then the overseer would order a hole to be dug by a fence post for the body to be buried. Black youth remembered the men who had fought for freedom—the battlefield stories, the limping gait caused by a rebel bullet, the persistent cough from the hardships of soldiering. The Bosticks kept the story of their parents' flight from the South. They had first made Kansas their destination. But on arriving in Jackson County, they chose to unpack their wagons and settle. As if to confirm their resolution, they built a church and a school and marked out a community cemetery.[22]

Some black residents had become independent entrepreneurs; they were barbers and blacksmiths. Henry Sims and William Smith of Carbondale farmed their own land. The descendants of the black farmers near Elk Prairie had also persisted. Many more were fleeing north with nothing. When crossing the Ohio River, they sank to their knees on Illinois soil and burst into songful jubilation. Unskilled and illiterate, most hired themselves as day laborers. While some came to the Grand Tower iron furnaces, many heard that the Illinois Central was hiring, and they drifted into Carbondale to work in the yards and on road crews. Employers enticed them to the mines at Mt. Carbon on the edge of Murphysboro and to the shafts at Hallidayboro just north of Carbondale.

What they discovered were variations of familiar patterns of exploitation and oppression. Employers pitted black workers against white to drive down wages.[23] Black laborers were recruited to break strikes. While they had escaped the vicious racist regime of Mississippi governor Vardaman, they encountered Jackson County's own Klan. The Springfield race riot of 1908 had devastated that city's black community. Months later a mob of thousands in nearby Cairo killed a black man. A postcard circulated with a picture of his burned head fixed to a pole. A Carbondale newspaper offered its front-page opinion: "Our idea is for the Negro to make himself as little of a problem as possible . . . and there is really no valid reason why the Negro, as a Negro, should upset the tranquility of his white neighbors or the equanimity of the nation."[24]

Like Stephen Bostick, African Americans persisted against race barriers. Reaching for full citizenship, they voted and organized in support of the Republican Party. Yet the party took the freedman's vote for granted. Attempts to organize and create an independent voting bloc came to naught.

The promise that Reconstruction would bring education and opportunity for self-improvement had been short-lived. Veteran teachers from the Freedman's Bureau had arrived after the Civil War to hold classes for the children of slaves, but they soon left. Schools were built, but within a countywide pattern of segregation that, like the national trend, denied comparable support for black education. Black candidates for school board elections were resoundingly defeated.

African Americans could measure the temper of the times when they watched their white neighbors flock to motion picture theaters to watch D. W. Griffith's *Birth of a Nation*. Appearing within months of the DeBerry execution, the film sensation turned the promise of emancipation into a nightmare and Reconstruction's egalitarian mission into anarchy and terror. White civilization lay prostate, ready to be ravaged by savage freedmen and evil white demagogues. Audiences cheered to see order restored and civilization rescued by the white knights of the Klan. Though white and black critics objected strenuously that Griffith had distorted the past to fan race hatred, white audiences jammed box offices to watch white America rescued from freedom-crazed African Americans. Those who could afford the trip took the train to St. Louis to view the film. When the film came to Carbondale and Murphysboro in 1917, it was shown in segregated theaters.[25]

African Americans like Alexander W. White were keeping another history—one of hope, betrayal, and persistence. Born a slave in Kentucky, White was fifteen when the war for freedom had ended. Since then, he had witnessed the rising terror and the indifference of his government. He and his wife Sarah had migrated north to safety and settled first in East St. Louis and then Carbondale. In the spring of 1917 East St. Louis had erupted in rioting directed at the black community. Perhaps Carbondale seemed safe. The county's black residents, several from Murphysboro, thought so, and they gradually moved there. But life remained precarious. Police refused to patrol black neighborhoods, while Klansmen and lynch mobs moved about with impunity. While White came with harrowing memories of race violence, his neighbors understood. They read the *Defender*'s account of East St. Louis, of "full grown men and women" rampaging the city streets, beating little girls and old men to death, and throwing babies into burning buildings.[26]

"Is this democracy?" the *Defender* asked its readers. "For two hundred and fifty years" the white man "has denied" the Negro "every means of advancement," has made "special laws to crush and debase him," and has "taken his life without fear or punishment." "This is the time to protest and protest vigorously." W. E. B. Du Bois came to East St. Louis to investigate. Two years later rioting in Chicago underscored the pervasive crisis. America, readers of the *Defender* were reminded, was "reaping the whirlwind." The battles of the Civil War still raged in the streets. The nation had become infected by "the color madness of the American white man" and had made itself into "the land of the lyncher and of the mobocrat." If an older generation of African Americans had sought refuge by passive acceptance, a younger generation was "awakening."[27]

Alexander White discovered others ready to heed the call. Both minister and merchant, White possessed a talent for organization and leadership. In July 1917 he invited his neighbors to form a local chapter of the National Association for the Advancement of Colored People. He was elected president with Frank B. Packson acting as secretary and O. G. Villard treasurer. While the East St. Louis rioting raged, the Carbondale branch gathered its meager resources and wrote to the national headquarters in appreciation of the "great work" the association was doing "for the Advancement of the Colored People." "And knowing also that you are at quite an expense in fighting the good cause," the group had emptied its treasury—$16.48—and sent it to the national office. "It is not so much but it is given with A sincerity" and in the hope "that you will be successful in your undertaking."[28]

Shared experience and historical perspective inspired collective action. The recently created Ancient United Knights and Daughters of Africa appealed to a common identity. But neither the NAACP nor the Knights and Daughters could attract more than a handful of members. With the NAACP, the cost of membership—one dollar a year—may have been too much. Moreover the founding members had left town before the decade's end. A decade later, twenty Carbondale residents came together to apply for recognition as a local branch. The national headquarters wrote its encouragement. But once again the local vanished from sight.[29]

Institutional fragility notwithstanding, a common history was not forgotten. The segregated school, while a symbol of rights denied, carried the name of Crispus Attucks as a reminder of black heroism in the cause of American liberty. Carbondale's African Americans had revived the celebration of Emancipation Day on August 1. Although the community had neglected to celebrate that date for a spell at the turn of the century, it had not forgotten. In the early 1920s, when readers were attending to the

Defender and imagining the creation of a chapter of the NAACP, they re-vived the holiday. The elders' memories of the day had remained vivid—so strong that the town followed their lead against prevailing convention. Most black communities in Illinois observed January 1, the date marking the abolition of the American slave trade in 1808. But Carbondale insisted that the community keep to August 1, the anniversary marking abolition in the British empire as prelude to a transatlantic movement culminating in the American abolition.[30]

Past and present struggles joined in the pages of the *Defender*. Its readers followed the stormy career of Marcus Garvey, his penetrating criticism of a white culture deeply, irretrievably enmeshed in racism. They attended to Du Bois as he tangled with Garvey in debate that cut to core issues of the black movement: To what degree could white culture be changed? What were the best measures for securing black rights? However Carbondale readers interpreted the national issues, they kept aware of the debates that remained invisible to readers of white newspapers. In turn, the *Defender*'s management was looking for ways to link with local readerships. To boost subscriptions, it recruited reliable correspondents in towns like Carbondale who would report news otherwise ignored by local white newspapers.

In the 1930s the Chicago office found its Carbondale correspondent in Viola Devers. She had come to town in 1926 with her husband Fred and set-tled in the northeast section on East Chestnut Street.[31] While Fred worked in the mines, Viola stayed home to raise thirteen children. When an agent from Chicago visited the family, Fred introduced him to local businesses to sell subscriptions. Meanwhile, the agent had cemented what became a long-term relationship with Viola, who agreed to send reports of local affairs on the northbound train. Devers informed readers of local social life: Viola Crim hosted a dinner in honor of her brother visiting from Chicago; Jesse Hays had returned to Nashville to "take up his position in a medical college."[32]

The black community was visibly gathering its energies. Emancipation Day drew larger crowds each year. Families organized reunions with relatives returning from as far as Detroit and New York. Memories were shared, and speakers put the moment in historical context. The summer of 1936 marked the fourteenth consecutive celebration.[33] In the weeks after Independence Day, while organizers prepared, the white newspaper took note. Amid the daily reports from Spain of the fascist insurrection and interspersed with accounts of "Negro" crime, readers were alerted that the crowds promised

to be uncommonly large. An amusement company arranged to offer enter-
tainments at Woods Park. Ruth Ellington, the sister of the "famous Negro
dance band leader," had agreed to bring her band.

William Pryor, a graduate of Attucks School and the university, opened
the celebration and introduced the mayor, who spoke briefly. A delegation
of Republican leaders, including the party's candidates for governor and
lieutenant governor and the "only colored national Republican committee-
man," came to revive allegiances to the party of Lincoln. Do not forget, the
two candidates lectured their audience, how much was owed their party.
The Roosevelt administration had made their issue simple: "the constitution
against communism." Now, "a despotic Democratic administration" pits
class against class. While it "lulls us with talk of security," it works to institute "a new enslavement." The candidates summoned the children of slaves
to remember that "the only perfect security was slavery." Unless voters awoke
to the looming crisis, there "will again be slavery such as existed in 1861."[34]

Pryor spoke on the history and meaning of Emancipation Day, but his
words were ignored by the Carbondale paper and were lost before they got
to the *Defender*'s offices.[35] While listening to Pryor, African Americans
turned to elders on the edges who still talked of their days in bondage and
their brutal masters. They were observing changes in society. Once black
people lived in all parts of town. But the black farmers who owned land on
the west side of town were dwindling in numbers. Black people seemed to be
pushed toward the northeast section. They talked about hooded Klansmen
disrupting Sunday church services. The Free Will Baptist church on the west
side of the tracks had been set afire. After the second fire, the congregation
moved across the tracks.

Meanwhile, the university promised opportunity for Pryor and a small
group of African Americans.[36] Born in Tennessee, Pryor had come to town
determined to advance himself. On entering the university, he took a room
in the home of Frank Bowers on Marion Street and supported himself as a
porter at the Roberts Hotel. Active in community theater while at Attucks,
he enrolled in the university as an English major and joined the Dunbar
Society, a club named in honor of the black poet Paul Laurence Dunbar. On
receiving his degree in 1931, he secured appointment to the Attucks faculty.

Like their white classmates, most black university students came from
the immediate region and had grown up in a world defined by segregation.
Like Pryor, they rented rooms in private homes in the northeast corner of

town. Some black families offered improvised dormitory accommodations. Students walked to campus through a segregated world past restaurants and lunch counters that denied them service. They lived with families who worked in kitchens and ate in the back alley. They passed the railroad depot where a separate car for black passengers was added to the southbound train. On campus they stayed on the margins. Their faces appeared in group photographs, such as those at the Dunbar Society, but because they were poor, many could not afford the price of an individual portrait. School dances were carefully monitored lest black and white students appear too intimate.

"We are moving slowly." In 1939 Emma Lewis reported to the national office of the NAACP that, after repeated attempts, the Carbondale branch had mustered the required fifty members to apply for charter status.[37] Her parents had migrated from Tennessee when she was a child and encouraged her to attend the university's program for certifying teachers.[38] After following her family to Chicago and marrying, she returned to Carbondale single before 1930. At times a teacher and at others a seamstress, she earned enough to own her own home on the northeast side of town. Meanwhile, Lewis won recognition for her civic-mindedness and her organizational talents. She was active in the Illinois State Association of Colored Women and was president of the association's local chapter. In 1935 she returned to the university to complete requirements for the baccalaureate.

Lewis's organizational abilities were crucial for reviving the local NAACP. Sporadically and ineffectively, a William Anderson had attempted to recruit membership. At the end of the decade, Lewis took the initiative by inviting leaders from the state organization to speak on its mission, its legal defense work, and the importance of local branches. At once, communication with the New York office became regular and productive. Within months, she had compiled a roster of dues-paying members—fifty-three in all and enough for chapter status. Regularly she requested literature, inquired about procedures, and discussed the details of Carbondale's contributions to the national and state organization. By the end of October she informed New York that an executive board had been named and committees, ranging from education and labor relations to publicity and entertainment, had been appointed.[39]

Lewis's talents and energies proved indispensable. Women who had worked with her in community affairs and their husbands were ready to join. While women represented half the membership, the association appealed to a small portion of the community. Laborers comprised the majority of black Carbondale. Perhaps membership dues of one dollar discouraged participation.[40] One miner joined and proved an active member, serving as vice president. Fifteen teachers and ministers comprised nearly a third the membership. One doctor, an undertaker, a mechanic, and a porter attended. Two worked for the railroad. Although the railroad tie plant on the north edge of town hired a significant number of black laborers, none appeared at meetings.

With Lewis's creative energies, the chapter could promote the NAACP mission "to ensure . . . equality of rights of all persons and to eliminate racial hatred and racial discrimination." No longer did the national office wonder about Carbondale's silence. Regularly she wrote to request information and application forms for recruiting. If new members failed to receive the *Crisis*, she promptly wrote the New York headquarters. Membership rose to seventy-five. While the members recognized Lewis for her education and abilities, convention led them to elect two males, clearly less educated, to serve as president and vice president. Keeping records and corresponding were imperatives that made Emma Lewis the obvious choice for secretary.[41]

As a teacher, Lewis was concerned that young people seemed indifferent to the NAACP; only one student had enrolled. On returning to the university, she resolved to awaken black students. She looked to the Dunbar Society, which was dedicated to self-improvement, in particular the "development of the intellectual, social, and athletic ability of its members." With a membership between fifty and seventy-five, the society was the most conspicuous black organization on campus. When it decided to stage its first dramatic production on campus, Lewis volunteered her services. Believing that the future depended on the young, she applied to NAACP headquarters for materials addressed to that audience.[42]

Emma Lewis wrestled with her academic work, in particular French, and after two years was asked to leave. Yet she remained on campus to raise awareness of the NAACP. With the war against global fascism, attentions turned to political action. Readers of the *Defender* awakened to the call for "Double Victory"—one against Hitler, the other against racism at home. A. Philip Randolph, head of the railway porters' union, had called for a march on Washington to demand redress as a condition for supporting the war effort. He came to Chicago and spoke to a crowd of twelve thousand: "Better that Negroes face extermination than a life of segregation with its degradation and bitter humiliation. Rather we die standing on our feet fighting for our rights than to exist on our knees begging for life." The crowd cheered. "Negroes are going to march and we don't give a damn what happens." The *Defender*'s readers learned that President Roosevelt had responded by addressing the need for eradicating discrimination and by creating a commission to ensure fair employment practices in defense work.[43]

Membership increased in the Carbondale NAACP. In the fall of 1941, two dozen students formed a "tentative organization" to raise funds to send two delegates, Wallace W. Price and Frank Owens, to the NAACP youth convention scheduled to meet in late October at the Hampton Institute. Again Lewis volunteered her talents and recruited three members from the Carbondale chapter to advise the students on fundraising. Price and Owens, both from East St. Louis, rented rooms on Marion Street. Both were active members of the Dunbar Society. They returned from the convention inspired by speeches delivered by such leaders as NAACP head Walter White. The student group grew to about two dozen members; Price and Owens had recruited two of their fellow lodgers. It earned recognition as a "junior branch" of the national organization with the stated purpose "to do away with any unnecessary social barriers existing on the campus."[44]

At war's end, however, the student branch had vanished. Veterans returning home saw that little had changed in town or on campus.[45] Across the street facing the train depot, the Hub diner served food to white customers only. Down the street, the manager of the Varsity Theater directed the black audience to a segregated balcony. At the entrance to the university campus, Carter's Cafe served white students only. Enrollments at the university rose rapidly, most noticeably with veterans on the GI Bill. While the university scrambled to meet a housing crisis, black students still settled for rooms in the northeast section. The city population was growing. Signs posted at the town borders displayed the numbers by white residents first and then by black. The school board responded to growing population and crowded classrooms by redrawing districts for white students but keeping black students confined to the old separate building.[46]

No matter the surface impressions, an awareness of the historic significance of the times roused dissatisfactions. The rhetoric of the war years—the "Double Victory," the president's affirmations of equal rights—had not been forgotten. Eleanor Roosevelt reminded the nation of the contradictions between professed principles and behavior. Leaders felt the pressure. President Truman spoke to the need for securing equal rights for all and appointed a commission to prepare recommendations for righting wrongs. Black veterans had returned carrying memories of insults that came with serving in a segregated army. When Warren St. James enrolled at the university, he reminded students that he had served in the South Pacific in the belief that the war would end racism at home. Frustration was mounting. Although Illinois had created an Inter-racial Commission and had enacted legislation to protect the rights of citizens, behavior had not been addressed. While St. James and other students witnessed injustice before them, the town newspaper focused attentions on the South—the lynchings and its defenders of white supremacy such as Mississippi senator Theodore G. Bilbo—as if the issue were somehow foreign to the community.

On campus, black students listened to leaders, all white, profess their sympathies by encouraging discussion of race. A member of the administration served on the state Inter-racial Commission. Faculty members expressed their support for Eleanor Roosevelt. Some delivered lectures on African American poetry, art, and music. They arranged a panel discussion on "the future of race problems," with Professor Louis Petroff and veteran Warren St. James sharing the stage. The university museum hosted a traveling exhibit of African art. The university observed a Brotherhood Week, where ministers spoke to the subject of race and students responded that segregation was pervasive at home.[47]

A few black students—Warren St. James and Joe Farmer—spoke boldly to the campus community and insisted on being heard. But they seemed the exception. Black students seemed quiet and easily overlooked by the white majority. Black athletes were rare on the intercollegiate teams. John Algee, a Carbondale native, had briefly attended Wilberforce University in Ohio, and on returning home he resumed his university studies.[48] At Attucks, he had been an outstanding athlete, lettering in football, basketball, and track. Black athletes, however, were not allowed to play on either the basketball or football teams for fear of body contact between the races. But a few appeared on the track teams, and Algee proved himself a star sprinter. No African American appeared on the staffs of the student newspaper or the yearbook.

Some white students were listening.[49] Inspired by the idealism of leaders like Eleanor Roosevelt, they expected to see the adoption of an expanded bill of rights embracing comprehensive social justice. Impatient with the president who seemed to speak to these ideals but achieve little, some supported progressives such as William O. Douglas and Henry Wallace for president. A few had turned to the one party that seemed consistent in its stand against Jim Crow—the American Communist Party—and arranged to meet party organizers from Chicago.

They came from conservative white communities that did not question conventions on race. Helen Mataya, the daughter of an immigrant coal miner, grew up in nearby Herrin. Arriving on campus, she joined a literary society, the yearbook staff, and the student newspaper, where she became an editor. She attended meetings of the Independent Student Union, recently created by students dissatisfied with the established student council and its indifference to minorities. Mataya was soon chosen president and worked with the Dunbar Society to organize Brotherhood Week. Franklin Hamilton came from nearby McLeansboro; unlike St. James he had not served in the army. Nor had he heard the *Defender*'s call for a "Double Victory" until arriving on campus. He began to listen to older students, such as Mataya, call for openly confronting the conventions of Jim Crow. He grew a beard, likely as a badge of independence and principle, read poetry and gave books of poetry to young women he admired, and appeared at gatherings of the Inter-racial Fellowship.

When Hamilton attended fellowship meetings at the Episcopal church, he mixed with students who were part of a biracial network committed to changing campus life. Robert Weingarner, a veteran who had returned home troubled by cruelties meted out to black soldiers in the war, had grown up in Carbondale with stories of his ancestors' opposition to slavery. Robert Brooks, a high school student and doctor's son, brought a natural affinity for radical causes. In the fall of 1946 the fellowship organized a public panel discussion on race relations. Brooks volunteered to participate and joined St. James and Nola Lanton, a black student from Carrier Mills.[50] Seventy members strong, the fellowship rallied behind the Independent Student Union.

Doubtless inspired by Eleanor Roosevelt's work at the United Nations, the Union drafted its own bill of rights for adoption by the student council. In the winter of 1947, Weingarner presented the statement of principle: all students, whatever their race or religion, be they veteran or not, fraternity or independent, male or female, must be guaranteed equal rights. The declaration proposed that race barriers on the athletic field be dropped, that students be guaranteed equal opportunity for employment on campus, that all be guaranteed reasonable food, housing, and medical care, and that black students be accorded equal treatment with their white peers in the classroom. In the event that they endured any act of discrimination, they must know they have the right to appeal to the student council for redress.[51]

Attentions were turning to action. Mataya and friends challenged the color line at the Varsity Theater and were thrown out. They had worked to desegregate homecoming in 1946 with the local police looking on nervously. As president of the Independent Student Union, Mataya campaigned to integrate student government and with her cohorts persuaded John Algee to stand for a seat on the student council. Though Algee fell short of election, Weingarner had been chosen. While the council considered Weingarner's proposal and the objections, his allies turned to the most conspicuous example of discrimination—Carter's Cafe.

Sitting directly opposite the main entrance to the campus, Carter's had become a center of social life.[52] The food was cheap: less than fifty cents got a burger, hash browns, and a "cup of joe." The food may have been bad (looking back, Franklin Hamilton guessed it would be considered a "greasy spoon"), but Carter's had a jukebox and a dance floor. And students were oblivious to the fact that their black peers would not be served. A handful of students, like Hamilton and St. James, negotiated with the management for a change in policy but were rebuffed. They filed petitions with the Illinois attorney general citing state law that "no person can be discriminated against in any public place because of race, creed, color, or national origin" but were ignored; they petitioned again, then telephoned the attorney general's office, later sent a telegram, and then drove to Springfield. But, as they recounted, "all these efforts were to no avail."

The issue assumed a momentum of its own. A handful of black students challenged Carter's directly. One day they walked in and occupied a booth. After some tense moments, they were ordered to leave. Soon after, Franklin Hamilton walked in and immediately sensed a strange silence in the air. "What happened?" he asked some friends. He was quickly told the story, with the addendum that once the students had left, the manager had made a conspicuous display of spraying the booth with insecticide.

Franklin Hamilton, Warren St. James, Robert Weingarner, Robert Brooks, John Algee, and Helen Mataya organized. They distributed an appeal to fellow students that recounted their attempts for over a year to "stop discrimination at Carter's Café against the colored students of this university." Now that appeals to the management and the government had failed, they turned to their peers "in the belief that you haven't forgotten that the men who left our campus to fight for democracy were of all races and creeds and now they are back seeking the rights they fought for." Now was the time to act—that is, to mount a boycott against the Carters "until their discriminatory practices are stopped."

While preparations were made during spring break, readers of the *Carbondale Free Press* would discover an occasional report of a lynching, but that happened in the South. White supremacist Senator Bilbo was in trouble for his financial dealings, but little was made of his blatantly racist remarks. Georgia politicians—all white—were squabbling over elections—also all white. Readers might have noted that Jackie Robinson played well for the minor league Montreal baseball team; the announcement of his move to the major leagues would come in weeks.

While Algee was training for track season, Mataya, St. James, and Hamilton created a brief handout summarizing the issue and calling on students to join the boycott. Hamilton was chosen picket captain. Signs were painted: "Do we have Bilbo in Carbondale?" "Did we destroy Naziism?" "John Algee (colored) track star can't Eat here."

On the morning of March 24, 1947, the picketers arrived. Standing in the rain with umbrella in one hand and placard in the other, they watched students walking past, pretending not to notice. At times the owner stood in the entryway, watching with an air of indifference. In time, a reporter from the newspaper arrived. When asked the purpose of this demonstration, Hamilton explained that the Carters were not only acting in "violation" of state law but were "opposed to the democratic ideals on which the nation has been founded." While one picketer walked by with a sign that read "Bill Keene, captain of the Cross-County Team, Can't Eat Here," Hamilton declared that it was a "disgrace to all of Southern Illinois that Negro students are refused service at this confectionary that serves other students at SINU." The picketers returned the next day. When asked by a reporter what had been accomplished, Robert Brooks explained that the boycott awakened "the student body and the general public." Since students were busy with classes, he explained that the demonstration would "discontinue" at noon. While a black woman was handing out flyers and students were entering the diner, he assured the reporter "a picket line would operate at some future date again."[53]

Debate continued. St. James, Hamilton, and their cohorts placed the picketing of Carter's within a national narrative that rested on founding principles of egalitarian possibility and ensuing discrepancies between ideals

Picketing Carter's Café. Courtesy of General Photograph Collection, Special Collections Research Center, Morris Library, Southern Illinois University Carbondale.

and practice. St. James reminded his peers that while he stood in the rain with picket in hand, his thoughts turned to the South Pacific and the "dark dreary" rainy nights he stood guard duty. He had served to protect democracy. But what had he found at this university was flagrant insult. And that was why he had carried a sign asking whether "Nazi-ism" had raised its head in Carbondale. Others, writing in support of a student bill of rights, echoed his protest.[54]

With judicious air, critics responded.[55] Surely, one contributor to the student newspaper noted, Randall Carter could not be considered a Nazi: had he been seen goose-stepping on the pavement before his diner? The Inter-racial Fellowship and the Independent Student Union were inflating issues and instigating needless turmoil on campus. Proposing a student bill of rights, one argued, was frivolous. Furthermore, it was written without regard to the rights of white students and thus was not intended to be universal. Black people, in fact, could find other places to eat on campus. For the moment, the self-proclaimed spokesmen of reason advised students to pay no heed to this "propaganda" based on private "gripe."[56]

In sum, the critics chose to avoid discussing the narrative of American history. If they did, they counseled restraint, patience, and responsible behavior and recommended faith in the nation's innate ability to address whatever wrongs lurked in the community. Put simply, the picketers pushed recklessly, too hard, and too fast. "To insist that the black man and the white are ready to live together on terms of complete equality is as obviously inaccurate as it would be for the average man to look at his hand and then declare he had six fingers upon it."[57]

St. James responded. Perhaps, he conceded, fixing the Nazi tag on the "Carter boys" was "meaningless." One could not expect, as his critic had noted, the Carters to give the Nazi salute in public. Yet, he reminded readers that many Americans have hidden behind the "shield of Democracy," harbored doctrines of "race superiority" not unlike the Nazis, and expected the minorities they despised to fight for this country. In their own way, the Carters expressed themselves when they "spray out booths where colored veterans had been sitting." For that action they "receive praise." As to those who professed as if self-evident truth that black and white people were not yet capable of living together, St. James retorted that "it is absolutely inaccurate to believe that we of the colored race are in agreement with the idea of waiting years to receive the equality that is rightfully due to us now."[58]

The editors printed St. James's letter and, in anticipation of readers' response, tacked a special notice assuring the public that "signed columns do not necessarily present the opinions of the Egyptian." The pickets did not return. The Carters noticed no slack in customers. Attentions seemed to turn elsewhere, and the issues raised that spring day seemed to have been forgotten. If the written record suggests that the habits of forgetting had prevailed, the picketers persisted in keeping the memory. One had saved newspaper articles, copies of handouts calling for a boycott, photographs of protestors standing in the rain, even a copy of the diner's menu. Years later John Algee was still telling the story to his family. And so was Helen Mataya. Nor had college administrators like Charles Tenney, who had encouraged programs to educate students on black culture, forgotten.

Jeanether Simon had been challenging the race policy of the Carbondale schools.[59] She and her husband Lit had come from Tennessee in 1940 and settled in the black section of town on East Oak Street. Determined to secure the best education for her children, she chafed at a system that recycled worn textbooks to black students and denied them access to courses of study offered to their white peers. She applied to the school board that her children be admitted to white schools, but the board rebuffed her. She wrote again. She made telephone calls repeatedly and to no avail. Undeterred, she walked her children to the white high school to register them. She was sent home. Undaunted still, she appealed to the state attorney general: Carbondale, she argued, violated Illinois law against discrimination. The Springfield office dodged the issue by advising that she return to the local school board. The school board felt discomfort. In special session with two of the five members absent, it turned to the "request of certain people for admission." No matter that the members had on occasion accepted applications from students outside the school district, they summarily ruled against Simon. "The majority of our classes were already overcrowded." Embarrassed by the board's terse response, the school superintendent wrote expressing his regrets and thanking Simon for discussing the "problem calmly and without antagonism or bitterness." The family kept the letter lest the story be lost.

A mother walking to school to register her children, a student standing in the rain with sign in hand, a church aflame, an elderly woman sitting with young students to give them council—these were moments that might be recalled as anecdotes peripheral to a community history. Or they might be brought to the center. There were choices to be made. Alternative narratives coexisted in the same space, the one slipping past the other, the other grating against an unexamined historical consciousness. Black and white people knew the national anthem. After President Truman's order to integrate the armed forces, soldiers served together regardless of race. While both knew to rise at "O say can you see," the black soldier remembered the "Negro National Anthem" that evoked memories of hard times and the promise of a brighter future. At the center, however, remained a story of development and progress that turned on white but not black entrepreneurs, on churches and organizations usually white, and that accorded scant attention to the northeast section.

In the summer of 1955 Emmett Till passed through Carbondale twice on the Illinois Central. The first time, he sat in a railroad car bound from Chicago to visit relatives in Money, Mississippi. When the train stopped in Carbondale, the town likely appeared dull to the city youth. The day was hot, with the temperature soaring into the nineties and humidity rising to the saturation point. From the coach window he saw few black faces. The *Defender* did not come that day, so Richard Hayes had not walked to the depot. Across the street was the Hub diner. If Till had stepped out for a bite to eat, he would have been curtly told to leave. Black locals his age were taught when walking on the sidewalk to step off the curb to make way for a white person. As the train began to roll forward, he might have noted the Varsity Theater: Betty Grable was on the screen flirting with Jack Lemmon. The proprietors drew audiences by advertising air conditioning and assuring white patrons that African Americans were assigned to the balcony.[60]

A week later Emmett Till was kidnapped. Days later he was found, viciously murdered, his body mangled by sadistic beating and riddled with bullet holes. After identification, he was placed in a wooden coffin and sent north in a baggage car. When his body passed through Carbondale, no one noticed. Days later Richard Hayes delivered the *Defender*, alerting its readers to the crime. Articles described the Chicago scene: crowds at the station, the grief-stricken mother, the "bruised and bullet ridden body." *Jet* magazine followed with photographs of the disfigured body. Till, the *Defender* announced, had become a "martyr" in the crusade for equality.[61] Black citizens who might have turned to the *Southern Illinoisan* would find no mention of the atrocity.

Two forms of historical consciousness met at the train depot. The Emmett Till murder raised memories. African Americans in Carbondale knew the land around Money, Mississippi; many visited relatives in that vicinity. Reading the *Defender* brought them back with reports of the murders of George Lee and Lamar Smith, who had tried to register black citizens to vote. One had been killed on the courthouse steps. Lee, Smith, and now Till were reminders of a long history from slavery, to the broken promises of equality, to race terror and Jim Crow. The newspaper told the familiar story without abandoning hope. The editors had rejoiced at the Supreme Court's ruling in *Brown v. Board of Education*. By "outlawing racial discrimination in public schools," the court had given the nation "the greatest human rights document in modern times." But Mississippi remained a bastion of white supremacy. Though cotton was no longer king, the state seemed to be "still fighting the civil war."[62]

The Carbondale newspaper gave expression to an alternative historical consciousness that had yet to grasp the significance of the murders. Lynching happened in the South. Deplorable as that practice might be, it was treated as a natural and integral part of that social system. Finally the wire services awakened the editors, and they began to make space for the trial of Till's murderers. At first, the story did not seem important enough for the front page. Emmett Till and his mother appeared as shadowy figures, Mamie

Elizabeth Till often simply as "a Negro." The murder was framed by explanations that this black youth had dared to whistle at a white woman.[63] So too, insults and scuffling occurred on the streets of Carbondale without notice.

From this perspective, a black presence and a discussion of universal rights slipped to the margins of history. The past worth remembering—one crafted by Daniel Brush—had been revived for public use in Carbondale's centennial celebrations in 1952. Civic leaders had organized festivities and a historical pageant celebrating a "Century of Progress," as told by the two spirits of past and progress.[64] Opening with George Brush and the founders, the production took its audience to the Civil War and General Logan, the founding of the university, and the flowering of a cultural life with the establishment of the Cosmopolitan Literary Club. The spirits of past and progress paused to wonder at the technological advances, such as the coming of a steam laundry and electric lights. A short town history had been cobbled together with a portrait of Brush in the frontispiece.[65] Echoing Brush, the story turned on pieces of property. Readers learned that the first bank was established in Daniel Brush's store. They read brief accounts of church building and the opening of the first opera house and of the establishment of the first electric plant. In keeping with the traditional model, little was made of a black presence. One unnamed black person appeared in a group photo.

Like Brush, the tellers of that story attended to the builders of commerce and community. If they had walked a few blocks east of the depot and north, they might have discovered another vital commercial life.[66] Charles Arnette, born in New Orleans, went to Attucks School and, after attending a barber school, opened his own shop that had become a thriving enterprise. Nearby was Kopp's Meat Market, Wood's Laundromat, the Carr Grocery, Edward's Cleaners, Russell's Grocery, the Holder Moving and Transfer Company, and the Algee Funeral Home. And at the corner of Washington and East Jackson Streets, a stone's throw from the railroad tracks, stood the Tuscan Lodge, the home of the African American Masons. Anyone looking east from the railroad depot could see the two-story brick building where this thriving black organization had been meeting, and which even opened its doors for state-wide gatherings of black Masons.[67]

People living in small communities remember their past by sharing stories of specific places on the street. In their tellings, time and space meet in vicarious walking tours of the neighborhoods with anecdotes related to the houses and their families, businesses and their proprietors. Elder keepers of the past enjoyed the status that came with reminiscing. Benningsen Boon had assumed that role of pastkeeper, and so did Joe Borgess while recounting life around Mt. Carbon. Carbondale had its pastkeepers, both black and white, who invited listeners to imagine a walk through the streets in time.[68] Elderly white women who remembered childhoods in town toured their past by house lots and the owners: they remembered neighbors who kept gardens, the "beautiful oak trees and trumpet vines with orange colored blossoms," and the spacious homes. They recalled the eccentrics, the Civil War veterans with their gray beards, the teachers and the students. They relived the summer evenings playing hide and seek; all the neighborhood was their playground. In similar fashion their black counterparts took listeners on walks through their neighborhood, stopping to relive childhood recollections of neighborhood shopkeepers who sold them candy and to recount family histories.

Though similar in form, white and black descriptions changed at the tracks. One white woman made passing mention of Attucks, "Carbondale's all negro school, grades through high school." It was across the street from Woodlawn Cemetery, where the town gathered on Memorial Day. She had not heard that slaves who had escaped during the Civil War were buried in that ground in unmarked graves. By contrast, African Americans who crossed the tracks to work at restaurants as cooks or dishwashers or in homes as servants told their own stories of segregation and insult. Cooks told their children stories that after preparing meals, they were ordered to eat on the steps in the back alley.

By 1960, the town seemed oblivious to growing tensions. Black families seemed to be confined in an ever-tighter circle in the northeast section. Housing prices were rising as the university grew in size. Real estate agents worked to keep white sections white. Water and sewage lines in the northeast section were, according to concerned observers, deficient in comparison to white neighborhoods. The black university student population was growing and was still confined to the northeast section. Black students, increasingly from Chicago, walked unawares into taverns in surrounding towns and were beaten. Carbondale was not literally a sundowner town, but neighboring towns were. In practice, however, police routinely ordered black residents to leave white neighborhoods after dark. And everyone saw the crosses burning in town.[69]

Carbondale's African Americans believed that city leaders remained oblivious to a national movement demanding equal rights. The NAACP was languishing, and school integration had yet to be achieved.[70] In turn, those who appeared unmoved by the issue could fall back on a historical perspective that counseled restraint. The history they had learned in school and was dramatically enacted in film confirmed that liberty for black people easily turned to licentiousness.[71] *The Birth of a Nation* had been remastered with a music soundtrack, and its trailer now included "The Star-Spangled Banner" complete with the marines raising the flag at Iwo Jima. In 1957 it was shown on campus. Four years later *Gone with the Wind* returned to theaters to mark the opening of the centennial of the Civil War. If the film seemed less offensive, it conveyed the same message that Reconstruction had been a social disaster. If the white-robed Klansman did not appear on screen, audiences recognized his presence behind the scenes. The older story of predatory Yankee carpetbaggers manipulating gullible and irresponsible freedmen and preying on a prostate South remained.

Black parents who wished for integrated schools might not have reflected on the history curriculum. The prevailing fashion in textbooks consigned them to the margins. When they appeared, they appeared as problems dividing white people against each other. Students studied an account of Reconstruction that reinforced the film dramatizations. They read that as an experiment in freedom, Reconstruction proved "unnatural." Faced with such "iniquitous government," the white South saw little recourse but to restore order by force. "The Ku Klux Klan," students learned, "took advantage of the Negroes' superstition and fear to force them back into a position of social and political obscurity." Reports of violence were "exaggerated," and the national government's attempts to suppress the Klan were folly. Finally, "home rule" was restored. The scars remained, however. But for the "bitter punishment meted out to them by the reconstruction acts," white Southerners would not have "cherished resentment for the defeat" of 1865. The story was powerful, impervious to correction. W. E. B. Du Bois's magisterial refutation was ignored by historians for decades, even during the first stages of the modern civil rights movement.[72]

By contrast, students at Attucks School gave voice to a black historical perspective on the times. While their counterparts in the white school performed on stage in blackface, the drama club across the tracks presented

Ethiopia at the Bar of Justice.[73] The Attucks students had selected Edward McCoo's play from several scripts created by black writers for black schools that deliberately confronted prevailing white understandings of African American abilities and history. In the Attucks performance of *Ethiopia*, Robert Crim played Justice, a character who listens to Ethiopia debate Opposition, who in justifying his oppressive behavior twists biblical authority, "efface[s] from History many a fact," and perverts public opinion to accept slavery and Jim Crow. Ruby Johnson as Ethiopia calls upon History to speak the truth: that Africans had built the monuments of ancient Egypt.

The First Slave, played by Philip Kendrik, enters and explains that though he lived in a "primitive home" in Africa, his "morals were pure." Turning to Opposition, he charges that he had been robbed of everything "but my faith in God." To the claim that African Americans have contributed nothing to the advance of civilization, Crispus Attucks enters and declares that "I fell as a martyr to the cause of civilization in the western world." The black patriot's declaration notwithstanding, the Slave of 1861 testifies that his people still labored to build the white man's southern society: "We felled his forests, we tilled his fields, we protected his home, we nursed his children" but received nothing in return. Thus, in 1861, the slave heard God

Attucks School drama club enacting *Ethiopia at the Bar of Justice.* Courtesy of Melvin L. Green Macklin.

190

call upon "His Moses Abraham Lincoln." The story continues with the Civil War Veteran declaring that "when civilization was about to fail in America, Ethiopia saved it." To those who say "that Ethiopia has done nothing for civilization," Veteran points to the "Two Hundred Thousand Strong" who fought for the Union.

Labor and Business each take the stage to remind Justice of their contributions. The early American colonies teetered on the brink of failure until the arrival of black workers; so, too, the South would have languished if not for uncompensated sweated labor. Business adds that black entrepreneurs toil upward toward success in the face of white trickery. Womanhood enters to indict the antebellum South: "[W]ith the door of hope shut in her face . . ., with the school house door bolted and barred against her," and "although debauched in body and mind," she has "brought forth a people who by their rapid strides have excited the wonder of the Twentieth Century."

The pageant presented a black Atlantic perspective that stretched from ancient Egypt to America, from Haiti to Liberia. Haiti, "proud and graceful," enters to the Haitian national anthem and declares that she has given the world Toussaint Louverture, the island's liberator. Liberia introduces herself as "a child of the American slave trade" who returned home, "established a government of, for, and by Ethiopia," and "is building schools and industries." Both bring their stories to the present: the United States sent marines to Haiti needlessly, and bankers "engineered . . . a scheme to crush the life out of Liberia."

One by one speakers step forward to read the precious documents in American history that both affirm and indict: the Declaration of Independence, the Thirteenth Amendment, followed by the Fourteenth, and the Fifteenth. The pageant invokes "the spirit of John Brown" with Louverture. It addresses Opposition's continued oppressions: poverty, prejudice, and terror. The character of Anti-Lynch Law cries that after facing scornful opposition in legislatures and the courts, "Justice has lost its sway." But Public Opinion steps forward to admit that it has been blinded and misled by a "one-sided press" and promises that it will change. Robert Crim as Justice decides that "Opposition will gradually fade away" and that Public Opinion will open its eyes.

In form, *Ethiopia at the Bar of Justice* resembled the town's centennial pageant "A Century of Progress," but in discordant voice. In closing, the cast came together to sing the "Hymn of the Race," "Lift Every Voice and Sing."

In contrast to "The Star-Spangled Banner's" military tone, James Weldon Johnson's anthem speaks to a "dark past."

> Bitter the chast'ning rod,
> Felt in the days when hope unborn had died
> . . .
> We have come, treading our path through the blood of
> the slaughtered

Yet Johnson's anthem echoed McCoo's closing line that foresaw a time coming when "Mercy, Love, and Justice are now [Ethiopia's] own."

> Sing a song full of the hope that the present has brought us,
> Facing the rising sun of our new day begun,
> Let us march on till victory is won.

The playwright had reminded his audience that the dominant history lesson on race had always been vulnerable to doubt and challenge. Even if the pickets at Carter's were forgotten, the action of those black and white students, all from this region, was symptomatic of a conscience, nagging and persistent. Black and white people were exploring ways to express themselves, sometimes in concert and sometimes separately. During World War II, David McIntosh, music teacher and folklorist, had joined with black male students to rent a house just north of campus and to create a "Negro co-operative." While Warren St. James and Franklin Hamilton were standing in the rain at Carters, Charles Tenney, then assistant to the university president, moved quietly to shut down Carter's. The diner had been purchased by the university in preparation for future expansion. Within weeks of the picket, he informed the Carters that their lease would not be renewed and that they were to leave at once. That fall, a lease agreement was offered to other proprietors on condition "that said premises shall be open to all students of the University."[74]

In the spring of 1954, Eleanor Roosevelt came to speak at the African Methodist Episcopal Church. The NAACP had sponsored the event to award her with a plaque recognizing her "continuous fight for human rights." Perhaps Roosevelt pricked sensibilities; she had used her reputation to summon the nation to attend to black rights. While the event was buried on the newspaper's third page, her presence served to acknowledge and affirm the issue of human rights.[75] Weeks later the supreme court ruled on *Brown v.*

Board of Education. In the wake of the ensuing crisis at Little Rock, three of the nine black students came to study at Southern Illinois University. The athletics program with Don Boydston in the lead was actively recruiting black students from the segregated South.[76]

Students, both near and far, added energy to a local civil rights movement. A Student Action Committee had begun in the winter of 1959 as an informal group of black students frustrated with race relations on campus. Willie Brown emerged as organizer and spokesman. Recruited from Memphis's Booker T. Washington High, Brown was an A student and captain of the football team. When he brought his concern to University President Delyte Morris, he was counseled to move slowly. Meanwhile, the black students he had recruited seemed to have lost interest; some had been strongly advised not to press hard. Undeterred, Brown kept a core of black and white allies together and turned attention to the town. At first the committee proposed that local businessmen meet to discuss race relations, but only a couple accepted the invitation.

The committee, through frustrated, decided to undertake a systematic survey of businesses with the intention of bringing its findings to the chamber of commerce and the town council. The report was detailed. All barbershops but one—Arnette's on the northeast side of town—refused to serve black customers. Yet two of these shops had black workers shining shoes. It named five restaurants that refused service to African Americans. The same applied to hotels and motels as well as real estate interests. "A Negro can't buy, rent or lease a house on the west side of town."[77]

In the winter of 1960, Brown presented his report to the city council. While a handful of businessmen seemed receptive, he and the Student Action Committee had already decided that moral suasion was not enough. The committee took its case to the state Commission on Civil Liberties, which in turn alerted the attorney general and the commission on human relations. While the students waited, they watched activists in Greensboro, North Carolina, take direction action against segregated lunch counters. The sit-ins captured imaginations. In the *Defender* Langston Hughes, who had once been invited to lecture on campus, praised the young people who bravely faced time in jail for their action.[78]

One day in April, three black student athletes walked into the Hub diner and seated themselves at the lunch counter.[79] They waited for service, but the proprietor walked past as if they were not there. Customers walked in and promptly left; they had read about the violence in Greensboro. The students returned the next day and the next. As they waited, they worried whether their standing in the university would be prejudiced. One knocked on Don Boydston's door. Boydston had recruited him and was ready to lend emotional support. He listened to the young man as he recounted the painful experience. As he unburdened himself, the student regained his composure and left vowing to continue. The demonstrators persevered for four days. People on the street were watching. The proprietor was losing business. Then, a waitress slid a glass of water across the counter to one of the three and poured a cup of coffee.

The protest had gained momentum. White and black students joined in support of integration. Black and white ministers from both sides of the tracks gave their endorsement. The Student Action Committee distributed flyers to black residents urging them to challenge segregation throughout the city and assuring them that state law confirmed their rights. If a merchant defied the law, the committee promised to take the case to the attorney general. Businesses quickly let go segregationist practice.

* * *

Within a decade the schools were desegregated. Black railroad engineers, once allowed to operate locomotives only in the yards at the edge of town, now appeared before the depot at the controls of passenger trains bound for Chicago. Teachers introduced students in integrated schools to black literature. As if to recognize the black presence and to mark the passing of an era, the town named a park and erected a monument in memory of Lenus Turley, a black champion of civil rights and pastor of Rock Hill Baptist Church.

Seemingly, two separate narratives moved toward reconciliation. But forgetting takes different forms. The Turley monument acknowledges a past. And its erection, significantly in the white section of town, can offer perspective on the past—namely that the past is past. Is it past? That is the question underlying the national debate over reparations. Or is the past present? Black voices query why the larger white community could not appreciate Turley's work while he lived. Is the past, though remembered, tucked away effectively though in a different manner than former forgetters of the past had imagined?

* * *

FOR TWO CENTURIES, whiteness colored the founding settler narrative and its later forms. Though illusory, that perspective seemed to succeed with the Indian. While it shaped early efforts to exclude the African American, it faced persistent contradiction. After the Civil War, black immigrants at first by their very presence and soon by their voices challenged the white narrative and lived a black settler counternarrative. Yet the original story would not be easily revised or discarded. Segregation shaped education and housing policy, access to public utilities, police protection, and the keeping and shaping of the past. Black history is kept in a separate museum and a separate genealogical society; it is consigned to a separate month. Yet slowly and inevitably it undermines that original white historical imagination.

CONCLUSION

IMAGINATION CONSPIRES AGAINST the habits of forgetting. The encounter may come as a fleeting moment. A walk on a country road ends abruptly with reservoir waters covering the way. What communities and stories lie submerged beneath? Neighbors remembering the county home for the poor hear that burials lie unmarked on that land. If there were tombstones, what stories would they recount? Illinois poet Carl Sandburg lingered longer to reflect: an immigrant laborer, not unlike Rosario Panebiango, "sits by the railroad track/ Eating a noon meal of bread and bologna" while the dining car "whirls by, and men and women at tables/ Alive with red roses" savor their "steaks running with brown gravy/ Strawberries and cream, eclairs and coffee." Forgotten lives lie beneath the printed pages of the traditional history. Edgar Lee Masters explored his Spoon River country to reflect on the black man unnoticed except as the object of heartless white practical jokesters, the son who died a disappointment to his parents, the Chinese youth struck dead on the playfield, and the "unknown" buried without marker.[1]

When John Allen came to the Southern Illinois University museum in the 1930s, he imagined a history of Jackson County and the region that would rescue the commons from neglect. He oversaw the creation of miniature dioramas depicting the life of hardy frontier families, collected relics of a bygone agrarian world, scoured attics for family papers, and recorded tales and beliefs of a passing generation. A founder of a regional historical society as well as a folklore society, writer of a newspaper column on the area's past, he had won the reputation as southern Illinois's foremost public historian. At the end of his career his columns were gathered into two books that can be found in bookstores today.[2]

No matter his intent, historical horizons remained within convention's confines. Allen collected farm tools and kitchen implements, notebooks crammed with folktales and stories, and boxes of research notes that added detail to but did not challenge the past presented in Benningsen Boon's "Sketches of the Early Settlement." Sessions at the historical society customarily attended to such subjects as "Grandfather's Old Clock" and ancestors who had migrated by way of the Cumberland Gap.[3] Always the speakers staked out a past devoid of ethnic and class complexity. Once, at a meeting of the folklore society that Allen attended, attentions were turned to a black past.[4] Grace Partridge Smith, doubtless the most accomplished folklorist in the group, had been listening to black elders and urged her peers to follow suit—but to no avail. When visitors to the university viewed a series of murals depicting the commons in the region's history, they met a past populated by hardy pioneers and prosperous farmers, all white. A solitary black man appeared in a painting of the famous Lincoln-Douglas debates. He sat at the bottom edge, listening silently as the politicians debated his fate.

At his career's end in the late 1960s, Allen felt assured that his historiography remained intact. An old color line still separated the northeast quarter from the remainder of the town. Although Carbondale was preparing for school desegregation, history itself remained segregated, with the black story appearing separate from the white. Senior members of the black community kept alive the memories of local banks rejecting their home mortgage applications. Until recently people suggested that any community history must include a chapter on the town's swimming pool. In the same breath they talked about segregated pools in nearby towns such as Cairo. A public pool did not exist in Carbondale until 2016.

But experience was pricking imaginations. Recently proposed plans to erect a solar energy park in the northeast corner of town on the site of the old tie plant were embraced by city councilors. While the greenness of the project signified a departure from traditional attitudes that propelled earlier generations to despoil the environment, people who had lived for generations atop creosote contamination reminded the larger community of its historic indifference to living conditions in their neighborhood. Why the sudden attention given to this land soaked in tarry ooze? Citizens who remembered neighbors falling sick and dying questioned whether assurances of the park's environmental purity were trustworthy. Homeowners pointed to lawns that could not grow grass and shook their heads in disbelief. And their voices could not be ignored, nor could their memories.

Reimagining community history can be at once wrenching and enlightening. Recognizing deeply embedded habits of both forgetting and thereby memory challenges what was once accepted as a useable history and sense of identity. But resolution comes slowly. The dominant story lingers and, thereby, filters dissonant experience. Even if Benningsen Boon's history is forgotten, the narrative of white settlement persists as foundation for explaining life in a modern century. No matter how demonstrably incomplete its claims, that historical perspective has a life of its own that remains integral to the life of community. It lingers as a powerful, though unspoken, part of imaginations. Its traits—no matter how distorting their influence—cannot be separated from the story of community. The black body hanging from a tree may be forgotten; the habit that allowed his name to be lost from memory persists. Yet, the horizons of imagination do expand. That white settler narrative that served a portion of the community is being laid aside. Voices telling another story cannot be silenced.

Each generation, one of John Allen's contemporaries reminds us, writes its own history to fit its experience.[5] While race intrudes into and undermines the traditional narrative, other elements of the story remain tucked beneath waiting to be examined. That the county's welfare is so dependent on a network of distant investors who regularly infuse and then withdraw their resources remains a story in plain sight waiting for the historian to pause, look deeply, and imagine another story. Other stories have remained until recently far below the surface, but they are emerging. The establishment of a nationally recognized Woman's Center in Carbondale, for example, signifies a shift in awareness that will open deep consideration of gender in this locale. And the debate over the solar park illustrates that no community can escape the consequences of economic behavior that has led to environmental degradation.

Such emerging concerns will inspire imaginations to create a usable past. I hope this project will assist readers who inquire into their own local pasts.

NOTES

BIBLIOGRAPHY

INDEX

NOTES

Introduction

1. For memory studies, Nora, *Realms of Memory*; Samuel, *Theatres of Memory*; Lowenthal, *Past Is a Foreign Country*; Hobsbawm and Ranger, *Invention of Tradition*. See the journal *History and Memory*. For specific applications, Slyomovics, *Object of Memory*; Gross, *Neighbors*; Trouillot, *Silencing the Past*; Hulbert, *Ghosts of Guerrilla Memory*; Batinski, *Pastkeepers*; Rice, *Creating Memorials*.

1. Dispossessing: Land and Past

1. *History of Jackson County*, 9–10.

2. For example: *History of Fayette County*; *Combined History of Randolph, Monroe, and Perry Counties*; *History of Marion and Clinton Counties*; *Combined History of Shelby and Moultrie Counties*.

3. Thomas, "Report on the Mound Explorations," 143–45; Thomas, *Catalogue of Prehistoric Works*, 59–60; Smithsonian Institution, *Annual Report of the Board of Regents*, 580–86.

4. Wagner, *Archaeology and Rock Art*, 31–34.

5. Smithsonian Institution, *Annual Report of the Board of Regents*, 580–86; Thomas, "Report on the Mound Explorations," 17–19, 141–47; Thomas, *Catalogue of Prehistoric Works*, 59–60.

6. Horsman, *Race and Manifest Destiny*, 190–207; Fitzpatrick, *History's Memory*, 13–50.

7. Allyn, "Wendell Phillips," "The Scholar's Inheritance and His Duties," "Progress," Robert Allyn Papers.

8. *History of Jackson County*, 9.

9. Sayre, "Mound Builders"; Silverberg, *Mound Builders*, 105–28.

10. Bieder, *Science Encounters the Indian*, 55–193.

11. McAdams, *Records of Ancient Races*, 111.

12. *History of Jackson County*, 9.

13. McAdams, *Records of Ancient Races*, 5.

14. Baring-Gould, *Annotated Mother-Goose*, 31–32, 36–37, 58–62.

15. Duncan, "Cosmology of the Osage"; J. Brown, "Regional Culture Signature"; Lankford, "Great Serpent."

16. Dorsey, "Osage Traditions."

17. La Flesche, "Osage Tribe," 274.

18. Pauketat, *Ascent of Chiefs*, 40–65.

19. J. Brown, "On the Identity"; Townsend, *Hero, Hawk, and Open Hand*, 105–47, 194–213.

20. Radin, "Winnebago Hero Cycles."

21. J. Brown, "On the Identity."

22. Lankford, "Path of Souls," 177–208; La Flesche, "Osage Tribe," 162–67; Dorsey, "Osage Tradition."

23. Lankford, "Path of Souls," 177–88.

24. Wagner et al., "Mississippian Cosmology."

25. Wagner, *Archaeology and Rock Art*, 107–8.

26. Shackelford, "Frontier in Pre-Columbian Illinois," 186–96.

27. Smith, *History of Southern Illinois*, 1:23–24, 27.

28. Southern Illinois University Carbondale, University Archives, ML, box IX, 1900.054, pp. 108–15, 1930.23, pp. 47, 62; Batinski, *Pastkeepers*, 121–53.

29. La Flesche, "Osage Tribe," 211, 285.

2. Squaring the Circles, Filling the Squares

1. Illinois Survey Field Notes, XXVII, 273.

2. Masthay, *Kaskaskia Illinois-to-French Dictionary*; Schoolcraft, *Travels*, 209–11.

3. Demos, *Circles and Lines*, 1–24, 57–66.

4. Nabokov, *Forest of Time*; Barr, *Boundaries between Us*.

5. Shackelford, "Illinois Indians."

6. Shackelford, "On a Crossroads," 352–53; Wagner, "Written in Stone," 57, 72; Beres, *Power and Gender*, 59–60.

7. D. J. Costa, "Miami-Illinois and Shawnee"; Dowd, *War under Heaven*, 12–19.

8. DuVal, *Native Ground*, 13–102.

9. Usner, *Indians, Settlers, and Slaves*, 13–104; Ethridge, "Introduction," 1–22; Weight, "Come Recently from Guinea."

10. Hinderaker, *Elusive Empires*, 1–186.

11. Morgan, *Land of Big Rivers*, 127–28.

12. Morrissey, *Empire by Collaboration*, 194–223; Dowd, *War under Heaven*, 114–212; Bowes, *Land Too Good*, 78–111, 260–62.

13. Bowes, *Land Too Good*, 12–15, 143–44; Ferguson, *Illinois*, 40–41, 119–20.

14. Feldman, *When the Mississippi*, 160–61.

15. Owens, "Jean Baptiste Ducoigne"; Owens, *Mr. Jefferson's Hammer*.

16. Jefferson to Jean Baptiste Ducoigne, June 1781, Jefferson, *Papers*, 6:60–64.

17. Kapller, *Indian Affairs*, 2:64–68, 165–66.

18. Ferguson, *Illinois*, 180–81.

19. The following depends on several essays in Lewis, *Cartographic Encounters*, in particular Barbara Belyea's "Inland Journeys, Native Maps," 135–55, and Pater Nabokov's "Orientations from Their Side: Dimensions of Native American Cartographic Discourse," 241–69; Bruckner, *Geographic Revolution*; Warhus, *Another America*.

20. Jefferson, *Notes on the State of Virginia* [London, 1787], in *Writings*, 123–32; Onuf, *Jefferson's Empire*; Pocock, *Machiavellian Moment*, 506–52.

21. Jefferson, "Report on Government for Western Territories," 1 March 1784, in Jefferson, *Writings*, 376–78. Onuf, *Statehood and Union*; Linklater, *Measuring America*, 29–132.

22. Jefferson to Ducoigne, June 1781, Jefferson, *Papers*, 6:60–64. Sheehan, *Seeds of Extinction*; Onuf, *Jefferson's Empire*.

23. Owens, *Mr. Jefferson's Hammer*, 64–66, 76–77.

24. Calloway, *Shawnees*, 138–44; Owens, *Mr. Jefferson's Hammer*, 122–23, 211–39.

25. Jennings, *Creation of America*, 275–314; Jennings, *Empire of Fortune*; Anderson, *Crucible of War*, 595–96; Slaughter, *Whiskey Rebellion*, 28–60; Kukla, *Wilderness so Immense*, 121–35, 161–67.

26. Russo, *Keepers of Our Past*, 9–108.

27. Leichtle and Carveth, *Crusade against Slavery*, 44–48, 64–65, 201.

28. Watts, *An American Colony*; essays in Cayton and Gray, *American Midwest*, in particular Eric Hinderacker's "Liberating Contrivances: Narrative and Identity in Midwestern Histories," 48–68, and Susan E. Gray's "Stories Written in the Blood: Race and Midwestern History," 123–39; Barnhart, "Common Feeling."

29. Barnhart, "Common Feeling," 52–54.

30. Barnhart, "Elegant and Useful Learning." Hall, *Western Monthly*, 576–88; Hall, *Letters*, 212–14.

31. Hall, *Seven Stories*, 32; Hall, *Notes on the Western States*, 150–213.

32. Hall, *Legends of the West*, 352, 388; Hall, *Letters*, 215–33.

33. Hall, *Western Monthly*, 576–77; Hall, "The French Village," in *Seven Stories*, 20–33.

34. Barnhart, "Common Feeling," 51.

35. Barnhart, "Elegant and Useful Learning," 15–17.

36. Dexter, *Bondage in Egypt*, 108–34, 443; Salafia, *Slavery's Borderland*; Jordan, *White over Black*, and Bradburn, *Citizenship Revolution*, 256–71.

37. Dexter, *Bondage in Egypt*; Simeone, *Democracy and Slavery*, 1–66; Phillips, *Rivers Ran Backward*, 15–77.

38. Dexter, *Bondage in Egypt*, 112–13.

39. Simeone, *Democracy and Slavery*, 21–23.

40. Leichtle and Carveth, *Crusade against Slavery*, 101–4; Dexter, *Bondage in Egypt*, 108–34, 180–92; Ress, *Governor Edward Coles*, 101–18.

41. Ecelbarger, *Black Jack Logan*, 9–31, 32–68; Dexter, *Bondage in Egypt*, 88–89, 287–88, 386–87, 512.

42. Ekberg, *French Roots*, 241–63; Morrissey, *Empire by Collaboration*, 63–138; Aron, *How the West*.

43. Weight, "Come Recently from Guinea"; McCorvie, "Archaeological Griots."

44. Darby, *Immigrant Guide*; Ford, *History of Illinois*, 1–55; John Reynolds, *Pioneer History of Illinois*, 23–24, 125–28; Ekberg, *French Roots*, 255–56.

3. Settlers and Transients

1. Boon, "Sketches," 2, 57–58; Feldman, *When the Mississippi*, 137–79.

2. Boon, "Sketches," 27–31; Whitney, *Black Hawk War*, 548–50.

3. Boon, "Sketches," 27–34.

4. Ibid., 63–70. Wagner, *Archaeological Survey*, 90–128; Mazrim, *Sangamo Frontier*, 95–170.

5. Fredrickson, *White Supremacy*, 136–79.

6. Boon, "Sketches," 25–26.

7. Ibid., 40–48, 51.

8. Ibid., 28, 71–75.

9. Newsome, *Historical Sketches*, 1–4; Benningsen Boon, vf, JCHS.

10. US House of Representatives, *Journal*, 26–27; Kammen, *Mystic Chords of Memory*, 49–56.

11. Boon, "Sketches," 28–30, 33–34; Patterson, *Early Society*, 6.

12. Jackson County Historical Society, *Jackson County, Illinois*, 27–47, 58–74. Billington, *America's Frontier Heritage*, 181–97; Thernstrom, *Other Bostonians*, 220–26, for comparative rates of persistence and transiency; Doyle, *Social Order*. Population mobility was examined by conducting a random sample of census lists with a confidence level at 95 percent.

13. Jackson County Historical Society, *Jackson County, Illinois*, 68–84; Gildehaus, *Annotated 1850 U.S. Census*; Dexter, *Bondage in Egypt*, 467–519. Ancestry.com is invaluable tool for the following discussion. In addition to census materials are related genealogical materials. The latter was used with caution.

14. Jackson County Historical Society, *Jackson County, Illinois*, 27, 75–84.

15. Ibid., 89–91. Dexter, *Bondage in Egypt*, 482, 492, 502.

16. Dexter, *Bondage in Egypt*, 168–69; Jackson County Historical Society, *Jackson County, Illinois*, 119–20.

NOTES TO PAGES 56–64

17. Jackson County Historical Society, *Jackson County, Illinois*, 33, 100, 120, *History of Jackson County*, 114; Newsome, *Historical Sketches*, 24; Bower vf, JCHS; Dillinger vf, JCHS.

18. Newsome, *Historical Sketches*, 153–54; Husband, *Old Brownsville Days*; Brush, *Growing Up*, 53–62; Sneed, *Ghost Towns*, 74–75.

19. Reynolds, *Pioneer History of Illinois*, 388; Ecelbarger, *Black Jack Logan*, 9–31.

20. Brush, *Growing Up*, 10–51.

21. Ibid., 111–25, 132.

22. Ibid., 132–36, 146.

23. Maycock, *Architectural History of Carbondale*, 1–26; Wright, *History of Early Carbondale*, 3–22.

24. Newsome, *Historical Sketches*, 159–60; Jackson County Historical Society, *Jackson County, Illinois*, 34–35; Allen, *Legends and Lore*, 344–50.

25. Lansden, *History*, 42–43, 97–98, 238–39.

26. Ecelbarger, *Black Jack Logan*, 21–31; J. P. Jones, *John A. Logan*, 59.

27. Jackson County Historical Society, *Jackson County, Illinois*, 102–4.

28. Newsome, *Historical Sketches*, 15–16, 121–26, 132–38, 176–77; Allen, *Legends and Lore*, 135–37; Grand Tower vf, JCHS; Sneed, *Ghost Towns*, 72–88.

29. Boon, "Sketches," 57–58; Dexter, *Bondage in Egypt*, 129–31.

30. Newsome, *Historical Sketches*, 102–5, 121–26. For the miners, see Gildehaus, *Annotated 1850 U.S. Census*, 206–7; for mobility of the miners, the 1850 census was compared with the 1840 census in Jackson County Historical Society, *Jackson County, Illinois*, 76–85, and Jackson County Historical Society, *Eighth Census of the United States*.

31. Hall, *Letters from the West*, 27; Silver, *Our Savage Neighbors*, 69, 98, 300.

32. Faragher, "'More Motley than Mackinaw,'" 304–26; Aron, *How the West*.

33. Jackson County Historical Society, *Jackson County, Illinois*, 60; Joseph Terry Williams, Revolutionary War Pension File, 1835, National Archives, Denver.

34. Jesse Gordon Revolutionary War Pension File, 1854, National Archives, Denver; Elinor Madison typescript of Tyner's memories, "Joshua Tinner" Tyner vf, JCHS.

35. Gordon, Revolutionary War Pension File.

36. Boon, "Sketches," 34–36; Henson vf, JCHS.

37. Larson, "Pigs in Space," 69–77; Etcheson, "Barbecued Kentuckians," 78–90; and Gray, "Stories," 123–39.

38. Calloway, *One Vast Winter Count*, 313–426; Calloway, *Shawnees*, 116–60; James Green Memoirs, Allen Papers, X; Ferguson, *Illinois*, 2–7, 188–89.

39. Ferguson, *Illinois*, 126–28; Boon, "Sketches," 53–55; *History of Jackson County*, 34; Moyers, "Story of Southern Illinois," 51–52.

40. Boon, "Sketches," 53–55, 70; Ferguson, *Illinois*, 32–36, 124, 180.

207

41. Boon, "Sketches," 67–68, 74.

42. Husband, *Old Brownsville Days*, 5–8; Livingston, *Pyle Family History*, 20–27; Wallace Heckman to Edward W. Ayer, December 7, 1915, Ayer Manuscript Collection.

43. Draper Manuscripts, S Series, XVIII, 120–23, 132. See also in S Series, IV, 44–45; XX, 109–23, 131, 144–49, 177; XXII, 116–26. Perkins, *Border Life*, 164–76.

44. Ford, *History of Illinois*, 136–65; Davis, *Frontier Illinois*, 193–98; Trask, *Black Hawk*.

45. Elliott, *Record*, 180–81; Jackson County Historical Society, *Jackson County, Illinois*, 88.

46. James Greene Memoirs, Allen Papers, X; Moyers, "Story of Southern Illinois," 52.

47. Perdu, *Cherokee Nation*.

48. "An Interesting Pioneer of Southern Illinois," Indians-Pioneers vf, JCHS.

49. Tyner Family vf, JCHS; Joshua Tyner, Revolution Pension Application.

50. Hinderaker, "Liberating Contrivances."

51. Newsome, *Historical Sketches*, 160–61.

52. Ibid., 142–45; Hall, *Seven Stories*, 34–46.

53. Allen, *Illinois Elections*, 97–98.

54. Michno, *Fate Worse Than Death*, 7–12.

55. Jackson County Historical Society, *Jackson County, Illinois*, 109–14.

56. Elliott, *Record*, 222–24; J. P. Jones, *"Black Jack,"* 5–10. Foos, *Short, Offhand, Killing Affair*; McCaffrey, *Army of Manifest Destiny*.

57. McCaffrey, *Army of Manifest Destiny*, 49–50; Allen, *Illinois Elections*, 113–14.

58. J. P. Jones, *"Black Jack,"* 5–10; Ozburn vf, JCHS.

59. The literature on violence continues to grow since the pioneer work of Hofstadter and Wallace, *American Violence*. For example, Smith-Rosenberg, *This Violent Empire*; Blackhawk, *Violence over the Land*; Slotkin, *Regeneration through Violence*.

60. Jefferson, *Notes on the State of Virginia*, in *Writings*, 288–89.

61. Foos, *Short, Offhand, Killing Affair*, 50; James Greene Memoirs, Allen Papers, X; *Chicago Press and Tribune*, 23 June 1860.

62. Jackson County map, vf JCHS; Moyers, "Story of Southern Illinois," 52.

63. Ezra Byars to John A. Logan, December 8, 1850, Logan, Papers, LM; Jackson County Historical Society, *Jackson County, Illinois*, 91–92, 113.

64. Jackson County Historical Society, *Jackson County, Illinois*, 91–92; Gildehaus, *Annotated 1850 U.S. Census*; Gildehaus, *Index to the 1870 U. S. Census*; *Eighth Census of the United States*.

65. Russo, *Keepers of Our Past*, 149–87; Kammen, *Mystic Chords*, 93–296.

66. Address to "Members of the Old Folks Association of Jackson County," September 10, 1880, Brush Papers.

67. Ibid.

4. Civil Wars and Silences

1. Wright, *History of Early Carbondale*, 41–44; John W. Allen and Leslie G. Kennen, "A Tribute to Bravery," Allen Papers, XXXVIII.

2. Logan, General Order no. 11, May 5, 1868, Allen Papers, XXXVI; Ecelbarger, *Black Jack Logan*, 251, 322; Logan Speech on Decoration Day, Logan, Papers, Library of Congress, LII.

3. Peter Bowers to "Dear Mother," January 8, 1863, County Archives vf, JCHS.

4. See Aley and Anderson, *Union Heartland*.

5. Carwardine, *Lincoln*, 144–51; Paludan, *"People's Contest."*

6. Daniel M. Davis to "Dear Uncle," July 12, 1860, Mayfield vf, JCHS.

7. Logan to Haynie, January 1, 1861, Logan Papers, Library of Congress, I. Also Ecelbarger, *Black Jack Logan*, 63–88.

8. Brush, *Growing Up*, 240–43; Brush, Regimental History, 200–201.

9. Brush, *Growing Up*, 243–49; Brush, Regimental History 1–3; Ecelbarger, *Black Jack Logan*, 70; "Secession Meeting at Carbondale," 3 April 1861, Brerer vf, JCHS; Weber, *Copperheads*.

10. Brush, Regimental History, 1–3; Ecelbarger, *Black Jack Logan*, 78–89.

11. Newsome, *Experience in the War; History of Jackson County*, 125–27.

12. Anonymous to Richard Yates, [spring 1861], Parker Earl and Charles Colby to Yates, April 21, 1861, B. Manes to Yates, April 30, 1861, Yates Papers, II; R. J. Wheatley to Yates, July 26, 1861, Yates Papers, III; I. M. Kelly to Yates, July 22, 1862, Yates Papers, VI; Charles Colby to Yates, September 7, 1863, Yates Papers, XIII. Towne, *Surveillance and Spies*, 14–16, 276–306.

13. Ecelbarger, *Black Jack Logan*, 123; "Wabash Notebook," T. W. Thompson vf, JCHS; I. M. Kelly to Yates, July 22, 1862, Yates Papers, VI; Emily Wiley to Benjamin Wiley, March 3, [1862], Wiley Papers.

14. Etherton family vf and Lee/Boon vf, JCHS; Brush, Regimental History, 27–28; Thomas Richards to Rachel Emeline Butcher, February 17, 1862, Richards Family Papers. I am indebted to Mike Jones for access to his invaluable compilation of data on deaths. The research done by Jones and associates at the John A. Logan Museum makes this information the most complete available. Helpful in this and later discussions is Jackson County Historical Society, *Military Census*. And, of course, the United States National Park Service, "Soldiers and Sailors" database is indispensable.

15. Lindorf Ozburn to Andrew Duff, July 6, 1862, Ozburn vf, JCHS; Ecelbarger, *Black Jack Logan*, 123; Benjamin Cummins to J. O. Cummins, March 30, 1863, Richards Family Papers.

16. Marshall, *American Bastille*, 155, 174–79; Ecelbarger, *Black Jack Logan*, 115–19; Allen and Lacey, *Illinois Elections*, 150–51; Allardice, "Illinois is Rotten with Traitors!"

17. Matthew Pate to brother, October 23, 1862, Pate vf, JCHS; Brush, Regimental History, 200–201. Manning, *What This Cruel War*.

18. People v. Chapman Ward, May 1863, Jackson County, Court Records, HSHS, F31.3359; People v. Isham Worthen, May 1863, Jackson County, Court Records, F31.3357; People v. William Parsons, Oct. 1863, Jackson County, Court Records F23, 2459; People v. Stephen Hall, Oct. 1863, Jackson County, Court Records, F14. 1469; People v. Benjamin Wiley, Oct. 1863, Jackson County, Court Records, F31.3358.

19. *Chicago Tribune*, December 11, 1862; Dexter, *Bondage in Egypt*, 399–402.

20. Ecelbarger, *Black Jack Logan*, 123; Special Order #6, April 10, 1863, United States, *Official Records of the War*, ser. I, XVII, pt. 2, 590–91.

21. Reese to Tisa [Altisadora], December 8, 1862; April 2, 6, 1863; July 18, 1863, Reese Papers.

22. Reese to Tisa, February 19, 1863, Reese Papers.

23. Reese to Tisa, 8December 8, 10, 1862; January 22, 1863, Reese Papers.

24. Foote, *Civil War*, 2:23–427.

25. Reese to Tisa, February 25, 28, March 2, 1863, Reese Papers.

26. Reese to Tisa, February 19, 25, 28, February 25, 28, March 2, 23, 1863, Reese Papers.

27. Reese to Tissa, February 19, 25, 28, March 2, 23,1863, Reese Papers.

28. Reese to Tissa, March 31, 1863, Reese Papers.

29. Reese to Tissa, April 2, 6, 17, 1863, Reese Papers.

30. Reese to Tissa, May 11, 25, 1863, Reese Papers. Also Arthur P. McCullough's diary, *For Honor and Union*, 29–36.

31. Reese to Tissa, May 11, 1863, Reese Papers.

32. Reese to Tissa, May 25, 1863, Reese Papers; McCullough, *For Honor and Union*, 38.

33. Reese to Tissa, May 25–26, 1863, Reese Papers. Bearss, *Campaign for Vicksburg*, 3:862–69.

34. Reese to Tissa, May 25–26, June 4, 1863, Reese Papers.

35. Reese to Tissa, June 7, 14, 1863, Reese Papers. Newsome, *Experience in the War*, 60–66.

36. Reese to Tissa, June 7, 14, 1863, Reese Papers.

37. McCullough, *For Honor and Union*, 155–61; Newsome, *Historical Sketches*, 206–8.

38. Jackson County Historical Society, *Military Census*.

39. Newsome, *Historical Sketches*, 207.

40. Purdy Family vf, JCHS; Etherton family vf, JCHS; Tope family vf, JCHS; Hagler family vf, JCHS.

41. Sinks, "List of Pensioners"; Worthen vf, JCHS; Whipkey vf, JCHS; Elmore vf, JCHS. For the following discussion, see: Marten, *Sing Not War*; Faust, *This Republic of Suffering*; Dean, *Shook over Hell*; Adams, *Living Hell*; Pizarro et al., "Physical and Mental Health Costs"; Blanchard, *Oscar Wilde's America*; Costa and Kahn, *Heroes and Cowards*; Gugliotta, "New Estimates."

42. Loosely to Ann Loosely, February 8 and June 1, 1863, Loosely Papers.

43. See especially Adams, *Living Hell*, 66–74. Doctorman, *Letters from Home*, x.

44. Brush, Regimental History, 96–99.

45. Faust, *This Republic of Suffering*, 33–100. McCullough, *For Honor and Union*, 52.

46. Loosely to "dear wife," July 22, 1863, and fragment to "dear wife," October 1863, Loosley Papers.

47. Reese to Tissa, June 4, 1863, January 20, 1864, Reese Papers; Loosely to "dear wife," July 22, 1863, Loosely Papers.

48. Reese to Tissa, December 15, 1863, January 4, 1864, Reese Papers.

49. Bearss, *Campaign for Vicksburg*, 2:604–5; Reese to Tissa, June 14, 1863, Reese Papers.

50. In Carbondale Township 23 percent of returning soldiers stayed for the 1870 census while 29 percent of their peers stayed. In Pomona Township the differences were extreme, with 19 percent of veterans staying until 1870 and 52 percent of their peers who did not serve remaining. In Kinkaid Township the veterans' persistence rate was 25 percent and nonveterans 50 percent; in Elk Township 6 percent and 33 percent; in Bradley Township 28 percent and 33 percent; in Murphysboro Township 43 percent and 50 percent.

51. McConnell, *Glorious Contentment*.

52. GAR muster rolls, LPL, Carbondale (box 22); Ava (box 28 and 45); Grand Tower (box 49); Murphysboro (box 12). Sinks, "List of Pensioners."

53. *Carbondale Daily Free Press*, December 18, 1905. Dean, *Shook over Hell*; Adams, *Living Hell*; Depastino, *Citizen Hobo*, 3–91; Kusmer, *Down and Out*, 35–40.

54. Newsome, *Experience in the War*, 214–17.

55. Reese to Tisa, April 17, 1863; March 4, 1863; July 25, 1863, Reese Papers; Loosely to "dear wife," May 6, 1863, Loosely Papers. Manning, *What This Cruel War*; Girardi, "I am for the President's."

56. Reese to Tisa, June 10, 1863, Reese Papers.

57. Reese to Tisa, December 27, 1864; February 22, 1865, Reese Papers.

58. Reese to Tisa, May 18, 1865, Reese Papers.

59. Wright, *History of Early Carbondale*, 39, 67; J. L. Jones, "Negroes in Jackson County," 19–55. For broader perspective, Davis, *"We Will Be Satisfied."*

60. GAR muster rolls, Murphysboro (Colored Post) (box 51). Tow, "Secrecy and Segregation."

61. *History of Jackson County*, 117; J. L. Jones, "Negroes in Jackson County," 35–59.

62. For national perspective, Blight, *Race and Reunion*; Blight, *Beyond the Battlefield*, 28–75, 93–120; Hahn, *Nation Under Our Feet*, 14–159; Calvin, *Toussaint Louverture*; Ward, *Slave's War*; Roediger, *Seizing Freedom*.

63. Ward, *Slaves' War*, 163–64; T. Jones, "Runaways and Resistance.

64. The term comes from Gilroy, *Black Atlantic*.

65. Dexter, "Southern Illinois Responds." Also for the following discussion see McConnell, *Glorious Contentment*, 213–18.

66. Newsome, *Experience in the War*, 214–17.

67. J. L. Jones, "Negroes in Jackson County," 54–59, 106–22; GAR muster rolls, Murphysboro (Colored) (box 51). Joens, *From Slave to State legislator.*

68. Dexter, "Southern Illinois Responds."

69. J. L. Jones, "Negroes in Jackson County," 110–17.

70. *Carbondale Daily Free Press*, August 5, 1905; August 6, 1917.

71. "Wendell Phillips," February 11, 1884, Allyn Papers, II. See Richard Hofstadter's chapter on Phillips in *American Political Tradition.*

72. Morris, *History 31st Regiment.*

73. *Carbondale Daily Free Press*, November 11, 1903; August 25, 1905; May 29, 1907; May 27, 1909.

74. *History 31st Regiment*, 23–27, 32, 36, 69–70.

75. *History 31st Regiment*, 74, 120–21, 153, 156–57, 168–69.

76. *History of Jackson County*, 20, 125–27; GAR Muster Rolls, Carbondale (box 22).

77. Allen and Lacey, *Illinois Elections*, 144–238; *History of Jackson County*, 96, 105.

78. Ingersoll address to "Comrades of the Grand Army," 1914, Ingersoll Papers, II. *Carbondale Daily Free Press*, November 5, 1906. A list of "Illinois Monuments" in Rose, *Blue Book*, 546–63, points to this silence. In contrast to the northernmost Illinois counties, none of the sixteen southernmost counties erected a monument. Also Volkmann, "Illinois Civil War Monuments."

79. For the process of forgetting and then remembering again, compare Buck's *Road to Reunion* with Blight's *Race and Reunion*. Also Blackmon, *Slavery by Another Name.*

80. *Carbondale Daily Free Press*, October 2, 25, 1906; Illinois-Vicksburg Military Park Commission, *Illinois at Vicksburg*. Waldrep, *Vicksburg's Long Shadow*, 194–234.

81. Illinois-Vicksburg Military Park Commission, *Illinois at Vicksburg*, 438–64. Also C. Vann Woodward's classic account of the postwar South and Governor Vardaman in *Origins of the New South*.

82. Illinois Central Railroad Company, *Vicksburg for the Tourist*; *Carbondale Daily Free Press*, February 2, 1907.

83. *Carbondale Daily Free Press*, November 7, 1906; Smith, *History of Southern Illinois*, 1:314–34; J. L. Jones, "Negroes in Jackson County," 98–99; Maycock, *Architectural History of Carbondale*, 99–100.

84. *Carbondale Daily Free Press*, August 25, 1905; Ingersoll notebook, Ingersoll Papers, I; Ingersoll address to "Comrades of the Grand Army," 1914, Ingersoll, II.

85. "Address Delivered by Daniel H. Brush at the Carbondale Cemetery in 1871," Allen Papers, XXXVI.

5. Gilding the Past

1. Brush, "A Memoir of the Commencement and Early History of Carbondale, Illinois," Brush vf, JCHS; Brush, *Growing Up*; Brush, "Members of the Old Folks Association of Jackson County," Brush Papers. Maycock, *Architectural History of Carbondale*, 3–11, 27–28, 38–39.

2. Kammen, *Mystic Chords of Memory*, 134–45; Ulrich, *Age of Homespun*, 26–27; Batinski, *Pastkeepers*, 121–93.

3. Brush, *Growing Up*, 22–24, 35, 47–48. Also Batinski's introduction to the 2016 (Carbondale) reprint edition of Brush's memoirs.

4. For perspective: Rugh, *Our Common Country*; Gray, *Yankee West*; Mahoney, *Provincial Lives*.

5. Brush, "Good Times Close at Hand" and "Early History of Carbondale, Illinois," Brush vf, JCHS.

6. Brush, regimental history, typescript, Brush vf, 31, 46, 67; Brush, "Members of the Old Folks Association of Jackson County," 6; Brush, "Early History of Carbondale"; Brush, *Growing Up*, 55–57.

7. For broader context, Green, *Death in the Haymarket*.

8. Brush, Regimental History, 241.

9. Brush, *Growing Up*, 241.

10. Newsome, *Historical Sketches*, 172–73. Fishback, *History of Murphysboro*, 177–78. Maycock, *Architectural History*, 11–26.

11. In addition to Kammen's *Mystic Chords of Memory* and Ulrich's *Age of Homespun*, see Seelye, *Memory's Nation*.

12. Allyn, *Worth of Human Life*. And Allyn, "Genuine Greatness: Its Conditions and Value," Allyn Papers, I; Allyn, "Wendell Phillips," February 11, 1884, and "Progress," 1884, Allyn Papers, II.

13. Wright, *Laws and Ordinances*, 96–99, 125–26, 141.

14. Ibid., 118–23; Brush, *Growing Up*, 179.

15. Wright, *Laws and Ordinances*, 87, 101–7, 159–60.

16. Brush, "Good Times Close at Hand."

17. Brush, *Growing Up*, 239–43.

18. Still relevant is Richard Hofstadter's sketch of Wendell Phillips, "Patrician as Agitator," in *American Political Tradition*.

19. Brush, *Growing Up*, 185–86.

20. W. K. Ackerman to L. Randolph, July 13, 1877, President's Letterbook, Illinois Central Archives, 261–63. Also Ackerman to Randolph, July 10, 1877, President's Letterbook, Illinois Central Archives, 255.

21. Wiebe, *Search for Order*, 44–75.

22. T. Morris Chester to James C. Clark, April 23, 1886, Illinois Central Archives, ser. 1, C 5.5, box 30. Also Lightner, "Construction Labor."

23. Russo, *Keepers of Our Past*, 80, 149–64.

24. *How 'Tis Done*; Spahn and Spahn, "Wesley Raymond Brink."

25. Ibid., 120–21.

26. French, *Life Retrospect*, 38–40; Wright, *History of Early Carbondale*, 81, 250–51.

27. Maycock, *Architectural History*, 20–21; *History of Jackson County*, 79–82.

28. *History of Jackson County*, 79–82, 130; Wright, *Early Carbondale*, 263, 271–72.

29. *History of Jackson County*, 68–78, 124, 128; Fishbank, *History of Murphysboro*, 55–56; Ecelberger, *Black Jack Logan*, 266–67.

30. *History of Jackson County*, 68–70, 93–98, 114–16.

31. Russo, *Keepers of Our Past*, 149–64; Batinski, *Pastkeepers*, 140–44.

32. *History of Jackson County*, introduction, 11; *History of Macoupin County*, introduction; *History of Washington County*.

33. *History of Jackson County*, 11, 17–18, 28.

34. Ibid., 17–18.

35. Ibid., 11, 26–27.

36. Ibid., 37–41.

37. Ibid., 41–43; Thomas, "Sixth Report."

38. *Carbondale New Era*, December 7, 1866. For town boosterism, Doyle, *Social Order*, 62–91, and the variation in Boorstin, *Americans*, 113–68.

39. *History of Jackson County*, 108–9.

40. Ibid., facing 68.

41. Ibid., facing 68, 72.

42. Allyn, *Scholar's Duties*, 7; "Obedience to Law," sermon delivered at Carbondale, 1876, Allyn Papers, I; "Progress," lecture delivered at Edwardsville, Illinois, 1874, "Progress—Whither," 1885c, "The Scholar's Inheritance and His Duties," June 8, 1884, Allyn Papers, II.

43. Jones, "Negroes in Jackson County," 14–59.

44. *History of Jackson County*, 117; Jones, "Negroes in Jackson County," 23, 44–48, 84–90; *Debates and Proceedings of the Constitutional Convention*, 1:679–80, 2:1297; Tow, "Secrecy and Segregation."

45. Allyn, "Garfield's Death," 1881, Allyn Papers, I; "Wendell Phillips," February 11, 1884, Allyn Papers, II.

46. Allyn, "Progress," Allyn Papers, II.

47. Jones, "Negroes in Jackson County," 107–13.

48. "Jackson County Hangings," vf, JCHS. Lears, *Rebirth of a Nation*, 12–50.

49. *History of Jackson County*, 27–28, following 72.

50. For elaboration on this counternarrative, see Lears, *Rebirth of a Nation*, 51–133. Also Adams, "1870s Agrarian Activism."

51. Kusmer, *Down and Out*, 3–167; Higbie, *Indispensable Outcasts*; Depastino, *Citizen Hobo*, 3–91.

52. Sunset Haven (Poor Farm) vf, JCHS.

53. Aldrich, *Death Rode the Rails*; Lightner, *Labor*.

54. Ackerman, *Historical Sketch*; Ackerman to W. Osborn, July 27, 1877, President's Letterbook, Illinois Central Archive, 319.

55. Stowell, *Great Strikes of 1877*.

56. Ackerman to Osburn, July 26, 1877, President's Letterbook, Illinois Central Archive, 304; Ackerman to Governor Shelby McCollum, July 27, 1877, President's Letterbook, Illinois Central Archive, 315; Ackerman to Douglass Galston, August 20, 1877, President's Letterbook, Illinois Central Archive, 381; telegrams attached to Ackerman to Osburn, July 26 and 27, 1877, Illinois Central Archives, ser. 3.4, box 4; Ackerman, *Historical Sketch*, 108–11.

57. Carbondale Council Minutes, July 27, 1877, book B, 290; Jackson County Jail Records, September 22, 1877; *Cairo Bulletin*, July 27, 1877; *Jonesboro Gazette*, August 4, 1877; *Chicago Inter Ocean*, July 27, 1877; People v. John Morgan and David Clark, September 1877, Jackson County Circuit Court, JCHS, F21.2150. Dacus, *Annals*.

58. Ackerman, *Historical Sketch*, 108–11; George Kennedy Jr., "History of Murphysboro," in *History of Jackson County*, 70. Also Wright, *Early Carbondale*, and Fishback, *History of Murphysboro*.

59. See Judt, *Ill Fares the Land*, on Goldsmith's poem.

60. Newsome, *Historical Sketches*, 1–3.

61. Ibid., 4–22.

62. Ibid., 14–24.

63. Ibid., 2–3, 153–61.

64. Ibid., 78–94.

65. Ibid., 95, 109–11, 97–98.

66. Ibid., 105–7.

67. Ibid., 118–21.

68. Ibid., 102–5, 126–40, 184.

69. Ibid., 212.

70. Ibid., 100–101, 121–26.

71. Ibid., 141–53.

72. Ibid., 152.

73. Ibid., 107–9.

74. Ibid., 105–9, 123, 126.

75. Newsome, *Experience in the War*, 11–12, 37–38, 170–71; Newsome, *Historical Sketches*, 229.

76. Newsome, *Historical Sketches*, 184–89.

77. Ibid., 200, 203–6, 213–15. And, Carbondale City Council Minutes, August 1, 1877, book B, 291; Carbondale City Council Minutes, July 14, 1885, book C, 108; Carbondale City Council Minutes, book C, June 1, 1886, 129; Carbondale City Council Minutes, book C, June 7, 1887, 156.

78. Newsome, *Historical Sketches*, 225–33.

79. Allyn, "Progress," 1884, Allyn Papers, II.

80. Smith, *History of Southern Illinois*.

81. Ibid., 1:336–43.

82. Ibid., 1:2–21.

83. Ibid., 1:23–29, 57, 119–23.

84. Ibid., 1:12–16, 484.

85. Ibid., 1:10–12, 419–22.

86. Ibid., 1:iii–iv, 158, 317. Jones, "Negroes in Jackson County," 98; Smith, "American Citizenship," Smith Papers, IV.

87. Smith, *History of Southern Illinois*, 1:481–85.

88. Smith, *History of Southern Illinois*, 2:643, 744–45, 3:1395–99.

6. Passersby, Rich and Penniless

1. Illinois Central Railroad Company v. Rosario Panebiango, April 18, 1907, in Illinois Supreme Court, *Reports of Cases at Law*, 170–77.

2. *Carbondale Daily Free Press*, March 18, 1903; July 1, 1905.

3. Ackerman to L. Randolph, July 10, 1877; Ackerman to N. Osborn, July 21, 1877, Illinois Central Railroad Archives, Letterbook.

4. *Daily Free Press*, April 22, 1903; December 20, 1906; May 1, 1918.

5. McIntyre, *Light of Persia*; Nelson, *Revolutionary Memory*, 1–85. Also Gutman's classic *Work, Culture and Society*, 3–117.

6. Smith, *History of Southern Illinois*, 2:672–73, 707–8, 737–39, 966–66; Wright, *History of Early Carbondale*, 153–54, 185, 190–91.

7. Newsome, *Historical Sketches*, 102–3, 128–29. Also Wiebe, *Search for Order*, 44–75.

8. For another town, Lansden, *History of the City of Cairo*.

9. Jackson County Deeds, book D, 488–96, book E, 456, book 5, 456–57, book H, 304–5. This wonderful source was found by Mike Jones, who generously, as always, shared his discovery.

10. *Chicago Tribune*, January 26, 1892; October 26, 1898; September 22, 1919; *Wall Street Journal*, November 1, 1906; *St. Louis Post-Dispatch*, January 6, 1891; April 22, 1900; *New York Times*, April 4, 1891; August 14, 1900; Coyle, *Report*; William Ackerman to Douglas Galston, August 20, 1877, Illinois Central Railroad Archives, President's Letterbook.

11. Wright, *Early Carbondale*, 150–51, 153–54, 257; Minutes and Board Minutes, Illinois Central Archive; *Daily Free Press*, February 19, 1920.

12. Gildehaus, *Annotated 1850 U.S. Census*, 206–7.

13. Willis vf, JCHS; People v. James Willis, January 1844, Jackson County, Court Records, F31. 3282 and 3288.

14. Materials for this and later sections on workers were discovered in ancestry .com.

15. Maycock, *Architectural History of Carbondale*, 106–9, 134–36.

16. Wright, *Early Carbondale*, 153, 257, 312; Time Books, Illinois Central Archives, Minutes and Board Records.

17. *Daily Free Press*, April 22, 1946.

18. *Daily Free Press*, June 2, 1900; April 2, 1902; June 26, 1912.

19. *Daily Free Press*, June 13, 1906.

20. *Daily Free Press*, February 5 and 8, 1901; February 5; 1902; February 3, 1910.

21. Mitchell, *100 Years*.

22. Jackson County Coroner's Record; *Daily Free Press*, January 28 and February 18, 1903.

23. *Daily Free Press*, March 18, 1899; Austin Bolin v. Illinois Central Railroad, September 1901, Jackson County Court Records, 1055.

24. Lightner, *Labor*, 356–73; Aldrich, *Death Rode the Rails*.

25. Bessie Baldwin v. Illinois Central Railroad, April 1903, Jackson County Court Records, 1067; Illinois Railroad and Warehouse Commission, *Thirty-Third Annual Report*, 192–97.

26. Lightner, *Labor*, 372–73; for local cases, see Illinois Central Railroad v. Frank Harris, in Illinois Appellate Courts, *Reports of Cases Decided*, LXIII, 172–77; Illinois Central Railroad v. Trustees of Schools, Illinois Appellate Courts, *Reports of Cases Decided*, XXVIII, 111–16; Illinois Central Railroad v. Mary Eicher, Illinois Supreme Court, *Reports of Cases at Law*, 202:556–75.

27. Illinois Central Railroad Company v. Rosario Panebiango, gen. no. 4, 639, Court of Appeals of Illinois, Second District, 129 Ill. App. 1; 1906, *Reports of Cases Determined in the Appellate Courts of Illinois*, CXXIX, 2–7; Illinois Central Railroad Company v. Rosario Panebiango, in *Reports of Cases at Law*, 227:170–77.

28. *Carbondale Daily Free Press*, November 24, 1903; Jackson County Coroner's Record, November 19, 1903.

29. *Daily Free Press*, February 8, 1901; Illinois Central Railroad v. Laura Atwell, Illinois Appellate Courts, *Reports of Cases*, vol. C, 513–19.

30. *Carbondale Daily Free Press*, April 22, 1903; Jackson County Coroner's Record, April 19, 1903.

31. *Carbondale Daily Free Press*, January 28, 1903.

32. Green, *Death in the Haymarket*; Stowell, *Streets, Railroads*.

33. Illinois Central Railroad Archives, Group 1, 2.91; George, *Forty Years on the Rail*; French, *Railroadman*.

34. *St. Louis Post Dispatch*, April 1 and 8, 1886; *Chicago Tribune*, April 13, 1886; May 4, 14, 26, 1886; Ingersoll Diary, May 23, 1886, Ingersoll Papers, box I. For memories of 1886, see *Carbondale Daily Free Press*, November 3, 1910.

35. Angle, *Bloody Williamson*, 3–133.

36. Illinois Bureau of Labor Statistics, *Seventeenth Annual Report*, 230, 236; Illinois Bureau of Labor Statistics, *Annual Coal Report, 1907*, 149, 161; Angle, *Bloody Williamson*, 89–91.

37. Smith, *History of Southern Illinois*, 3:1395–98; Wright, *Early Carbondale*, 173–74.

38. Maycock, *Architectural History of Carbondale*, 134–35.

39. Angle, *Bloody Williamson*, 89–116; *New York Times*, September 28, 1899.

40. Illinois Board of Arbitration, *Fifth Annual Report*, 73–77.

41. *Chicago Inter Ocean*, 1 June 1899.

42. *Chicago Inter Ocean*, August 13 and 14, 1899; *Carbondale Daily Free Press*, August 19, 1899.

43. Wright, *Early Carbondale*, 158.

44. Angle, *Bloody Williamson*, 116.

45. *Chicago Inter Ocean*, September 6, 1899; March 13, 1900.

46. At midcentury, this history was being sketched by Mills in *Power Elite*, 30–46. Also Russo, *American Towns*, 117–75.

47. [Carbondale] *Daily Free Press*, 25 Dec. 1901, 13 Aug. 1902, 10 Jan. 1919, 18 Oct. 1920.

48. Woodruff, *American Congo*, 16–18.

49. *Carbondale Daily Free Press*, December 25, 1901, and August 13, 1902.

50. *Carbondale Daily Free Press*, January 10, 1919.

51. *Carbondale Daily Free Press*, November 12, 1902.

52. *Carbondale Daily Free Press*, August 14, 1925; Jones, "Negroes in Jackson County," 75–77; Maycock, *Architectural History of Carbondale*, 121–22, 156.

53. *Carbondale Daily Free Press*, July 29, 1903; August 17, 1917; August 31, 1929; February 25, 1946; July 31, 1947.

54. *Carbondale Daily Free Press*, January 10, 1919; January 30, 1930.

55. *Carbondale Daily Free Press*, January 8, 1931; November 14, 1931; June 5, 1935; July 8, 1936; Seana Coulson, "The Hobo Community," Research Papers vf, JCHS.

56. *Carbondale Daily Free Press*, June 5, 1935. Also, DePastino, *Citizen Hobo*, 195–220.

7. Reconstruction and Race

1. Hahn, *Nation Under Our Feet*, 13–313; Blight, *Race and Reunion*; Ward, *The Slaves' War*; Levine, *Black Culture*, 3–154; Roediger, *Seizing Freedom*, 1–103. For Illinois, Joens, *From Slave to State Legislator*.

2. J. L. Jones, "Negroes in Jackson County," 54–59, 106–22.

3. J. L. Jones, "Negroes in Jackson County"; Tow, "Secrecy and Segregation"; T. Jones, "Runaways and Resistance"; *Chicago Daily Tribune*, June 1, 1874, April 4, 1876; P. M. Jones et al., "Forgotten Soldiers: Murphysboro's African-American Civil War Veterans" (Murphysboro, 1994); Guardman vf, JCHS.

4. *History of Jackson County*, 117.

5. *History of Jackson County*, 117.

6. Ward, *Slaves' War*, 163–64; T. Jones, "Runaways and Resistance."

7. *Chicago Daily Tribune*, February 6 and 8, 1874; *New York Times*, February 12, 1874.

8. For a report in detail, see *Chicago Daily Tribune*, August 13, 1875. Also, Angle, *Bloody Williamson*, 72–88.

9. The following discussion is aided by Patterson, *Rituals of Blood*; Pfeifer, *Lynching beyond Dixie*; Jaspin, *Buried*; Williams, *They Left Great Marks*.

10. Letter to the editor of the *Murphysboro Independent* reprinted in the *Chicago Daily Tribune*, June 1, 1874.

11. Brown, "Legal and Behavioral Perspectives."

12. Hubbs Papers, III; Jackson County Hangings vf, JCHS; J. L. Jones, "Negroes in Jackson County," 128; People v. Tom Moberly, January 1902, Jackson County Court, JCHS, F 21.2207.

13. For example: People v. Francis M Wheeler, May 1864, JCHS, F31.3370.

14. Angle, *Bloody Williamson*, 86–87.

15. Jackson County Hangings vf, JCHS.

16. This self-consciousness appears in the letter to the editor of the *Murphysboro Independent*, reprinted in the *Chicago Daily Tribune*, June 1, 1874. Also *Chicago Daily Tribune*, August 21, 1875.

17. *Murphysboro Daily Independent*, February 4, 1950; Tarpley vf, JCHS.

18. *Chicago Tribune*, August 30 and 31, 1915; *Chicago Defender*, October 23 and 30, November 6, 1915; Dolinar, *Negro in Illinois*, 122.

19. *Carbondale Daily Free Press*, August 30 and 31, September 15 and 12, and October 16, 1915; Photographs, JCHS, 30.3.

20. *Carbondale Daily Free Press*, October 23 and 30, November 15, 1915; *Chicago Defender*, November 6 and 9, 1915.

21. *Standard Atlas of Jackson County*, 73.

22. Macklin, *Generations*, 217.

23. T. Morris Chester to James C. Clark, April 23, 1886, Illinois Central Railroad Archives, 1C5.5, box 30; J. L. Jones, "Negroes in Jackson County," 47–54; Angle, *Bloody Williamson*, 96–104; Interview with Frank Caliper, 1941, Illinois Writers Project, box XLIII, 27.

24. J. L. Jones, "Negroes in Jackson County," 87–88, 129.

25. *Carbondale Free Press*, March 27, 1917.

26. *Chicago Defender*, July 14, 1917.

27. *Chicago Defender*, September 5, 1914, August 2 and 30, 1919.

28. A. W. White et al. to O. G. Villard, July 23, 1917, NAACP.

29. C. A. Woods to [Director of Branches], July 13, 1926, and Director of Branches to C. A. Woods, July 15, 1926, NAACP; *Chicago Defender*, September 5, 1914.

30. A survey of the *Defender* in the mid-1920s, in which local celebrations of emancipation were reported, documents preference for observing January 1.

31. Macklin, *Traces in the Dust*, 89.

32. *Chicago Defender*, September 5, 1936.

33. *Carbondale Daily Free Press*, August 3, 1936.

34. *Carbondale Daily Free Press*, August 4 and 5, 1936.

35. *Chicago Defender*, August 22, 1936. For the following, see Illinois Writers Project, X; Otterson, "Growing Up Black in Carbondale," ML, 64; Macklin, *Generations*, 217; Macklin, *Legacy of Attucks*, 322–23; Macklin, *Traces in the Dust*, 327–28, 335–36.

36. *Obelisk* (1927), 124; (1929), 126; (1930), 44; Stalls, "History of African Americans."

37. Emma Lewis to NAACP, July 31, 1939, NAACP; Department of Branches NAACP to W. J. Anderson, January 25, 1934, NAACP.

38. Southern Illinois Normal University, *Catalogue, 1894–95*, 83; *Catalogue, 1936*, xx; Southern Illinois University, Admissions and Records; *Carbondale Southern Illinoisan*, December 20, 1951; *Chicago Defender*, December 6, 1930, May 20, 1939.

39. Anderson to NAACP, September 18, 1933, NAACP; Lewis to NAACP, July 31, October 3 and 27, 1939, NAACP.

40. Macklin, *Traces in the Dust*, 64–71; Application for Charter, October 2, 1939, NAACP Records.

41. Department of Branches NAACP to W. J. Anderson, January 25, 1934, NAACP; William Perkins to Lewis, October 27, 1939, NAACP; Lewis to NAACP, October 27, 1939, May 10, 1940, May 4, 1943, NAACP.

42. Application for Charter, October 2, 1939, NAACP; *Obelisk* (1930), 130; (1938), 125; *Carbondale Daily Free Press*, January 18, 1936.

43. *Chicago Defender*, July 4, 1942. Also, *Chicago Defender*, October 31, 1942, December 9, 1944. See Sugrue, *Sweet Land of Liberty*, 32–58.

44. *Obelisk* (1942).

45. Julia Mae Thompson, "Hard Times," in Macklin, *Legacy of Attucks*, 322–23; Sugrue, *Sweet Land of Liberty*, 87–162

46. *Carbondale Free Press*, August 9, 1946.

47. *Egyptian*, February 13 and 22, May 10, July 19, October 4 and 11, 1946, February 7, 14, 21, 1947.

48. *Obelisk* (1948), 117, 130–31; phone conversation with Algee's widow, April 2002.

49. The following discussion depends on: author's memorandum of phone conversation with Franklin Hamilton, October 1, 2004; Franklin Hamilton to author, October 18, 29, November 4, 2004; author's memorandum of phone conversation with Helen Mataya Graves, October 22, 2004; author's memorandum of phone conversation with Richard Hayes, June 8, 2004; author's interview with Mary Sasse, October 26, 2004.

50. *Egyptian*, November 26, 1946, February 7, March 24, 1947.

51. *Egyptian*, October 4 and 11, 1946, February 7 and 21, 1947.

52. Carter Cafe vf, ML.

53. *Carbondale Free Press*, March 24 and 25, 1947.

54. *Egyptian*, April 11, 1947.

55. *Egyptian*, April 4, 1947.

56. Ibid.

57. Ibid.

58. Ibid., April 18, 1947.

59. Macklin, *Legacy of Attucks*, 312; Macklin, *Traces in the Dust*, 275; Carbondale High School Board Records, August 27, 1947, August 15, 1949.

60. Gregory, *Callus on My Soul*, 20–24; *Southern Illinoisan*, August 21, 1955.

61. *Defender*, September 10, 1955.

62. *Defender*, May 29, 1954, September 10, 1955.

63. *Southern Illinoisan*, September 16, 21, 23, 1955.

64. *Southern Illinoisan*, May 29 and 31, 1952; Archibald McLeod "Century of Progress, 1852–1952," McLeod vf, ML.

65. Griffith, *Century of Progress*.

66. Macklin, *Legacy of Attucks*, 309–46.

67. Prince Hall Grand Lodge, *Proceedings*, 12–14, 76, 107–8.

68. Woman's Club of Carbondale, *Carbondale Remembered*; Macklin, *Legacy of Attucks*, 310, 322–23; Macklin, *Traces in the Dust*, 338–40. For similar practices, Batinski, *Pastkeepers*, 81–119.

69. See Illinois Commission on Human Relations, Papers, box V, especially: Wendell O'Neal to William K. Williams, January 10, 1963; memorandum of interview with Robert Taylor, January 29, [1964], and attached documents; Annual Report Carbondale Human Relations Commission [1963]; Carbondale Human Relations Commission to Blaney Miller, August 1964; Conference on Freedom of Residence in Carbondale, January 19, 1961; *Southern Illinoisan*, October 21, 1955, June 15, 1965; *Chicago Defender*, October 2, 1965; author's email correspondence with Bradley Skelcher, February 2, 2016; Michael Batinski and Larry Hickman interview with Don Boydston, January 18, 2005, Center for Dewy Studies, Southern Illinois University Carbondale. Loewen, *Sundown Towns*, 276–79, 380–81.

70. Report on Freedom of Residence in Carbondale, January 19, 1961, Illinois Commission on Human Relations, V.

71. FitzGerald, *America Revised*, 7–145.

72. Muzzey, *History of Our Country*, 322–28.

73. McCoo, *Ethiopia at the Bar of Justice*, 345–73; Macklin, *Legacy of Attucks*, 145; Photos, JCHS, album 36.1, Carbondale.

74. *Obelisk* (1942), 148; Notice of Termination of Tenancy, May 3, 1947, Carter's Café vf, ML.

75. *Southern Illinoisan*, May 6, 1954.

76. Boydston interview.

77. *Southern Illinoisan*, February 19, 1960; *Egyptian*, May 5, 1960.

78. *Chicago Defender*, March 28, April 16, 1960; Student Action Committee to State Commission on Civil Liberties, [April 1960] and Attorney General Grenville Beardsley to Illinois Commission on Human Relations, March 2, 1960, Illinois Commission on Human Relations, V. Sugrue, *Sweet Land of Liberty*, 253–85.

79. Newspaper clipping from *Centralia Sentinel* in Illinois Commission on Human Rights, Papers, V.

Conclusion

1. Sandburg, *Complete Poems*, 12.

2. Allen, *Legends and Lore*; Allen, *It Happened*; *Southern Illinoisan*, August 29, 1969.

3. *Journal of the Southern Illinois Historical Society*.

4. Smith, "Negro Lore."

5. Becker, *Everyman His Own Historian*.

BIBLIOGRAPHY

Manuscript Sources

Allen, John W. Papers. Special Collections, Morris Library, Southern Illinois University.

Allyn, Robert. Papers. University Archives. Morris Library, Southern Illinois University.

Ayer Manuscript Collection, Newberry Library, Chicago.

Boydston, Don. Interview transcript. Center for Dewy Studies, Southern Illinois University Carbondale.

Brush, Daniel Harmon. Papers. LPL.

——. Regimental History, transcript, Brush vf, Jackson County Historical Society.

Carbondale Council. Minutes, Carbondale City Hall.

Carbondale High School Board Records.

Draper, Lyman. Manuscripts, State Historical Society of Wisconsin.

Grand Army of the Republic (GAR). Muster Rolls. LPL.

Hubbs, Barbara Burr. Papers, ML.

Illinois Central Archives. Newberry Library, Chicago.

Illinois Commission on Human Relations. Papers. LPL.

Illinois Survey Field Notes (1849). [Springfield: s.n., 1965].

Illinois Writers Project. Chicago Public Library Woodson Branch.

Ingersoll, Ezekiel. Papers, ML.

Jackson County Coroner's Record, Illinois Regional Archives Depository, Carbondale.

Jackson County. Court Records. Jackson County Historical Society.

——. Deeds. Jackson County Courthouse.

——. Jail Records, Jackson County Historical Society.

Jackson County Historical Society. Vertical Files (vf).

Logan, John A. Papers. John A. Logan Museum, Murphysboro, IL.
———. Papers. Library of Congress, Manuscript Division.
Loosely, Edwin. Papers. ML.
National Association for the Advancement of Colored People (NAACP). Records, Carbondale Chapter, Library of Congress.
Reese, John. Papers. ML.
Revolutionary War Pension File. National Archives, Denver.
Richards Family. Papers, John A. Logan Museum, Murphysboro, IL.
Southern Illinois University Carbondale. Admissions and Records, University Archives, Morris Library.
Wiley, Benjamin. Papers, ML.
Yates, Richard. Papers, LPL.

Newspapers

Cairo JC;JCHSBulletin.
Carbondale Daily Free Press.
Carbondale New Era.
Carbondale Southern Illinoisan.
Chicago Defender.
Chicago Inter Ocean.
Chicago Press and Tribune.
Chicago Tribune.
Jonesboro Gazette.
Murphysboro Daily Independent.
New York Times.
Southern Illinoisan.
Southern Illinois University Carbondale. *Egyptian.*
St. Louis Post-Dispatch.
Wall Street Journal.

Print Sources

Ackerman, William K. *Historical Sketch of the Illinois Central Railroad.* Chicago: Fergus Press, 1890.
Adams, Jane. "1870s Agrarian Activism in Southern Illinois: Mediator between Two Eras." *Social Science History* 16 (Autumn 1992): 365–400.
Adams, Michael C. *Living Hell: The Dark Side of the Civil War.* Baltimore: Johns Hopkins University Press, 2014.
Afro-American Genealogical Society. *In Unity There Is Strength: A Pictorial History of the African American Community of Carbondale, Illinois.* Paducah, KY: Turner, 1999.

Aldrich, Mark. *Death Rode the Rails: American Railroad Accidents and Safety, 1828–1965*. Baltimore: Johns Hopkins University Press, 2006.

Aley, Ginette, and J. L. Anderson, eds. *Union Heartland: The Midwestern Home Front During the Civil War*. Carbondale: Southern Illinois University Press, 2013.

Allardice, Bruce S. "'Illinois is Rotten with Traitors!' The Republican Defeat in the 1862 State Election." *Journal of the Illinois State Historical Society* 104 (Spring–Summer 2011): 97–114.

Allen, Howard W., and Vincent A. Lacey, eds. *Illinois Elections, 1818–1990: Candidates and County Returns for President, Governor, Senate, and House of Representatives*. Carbondale: Southern Illinois University Press, 1992.

Allen, John W. *Legends and Lore of Southern Illinois*. Carbondale: Southern Illinois University Press, 1963.

Allyn, Robert. *The Scholar's Duties*. St. Louis: R. P. Studley, 1874.

———. *The Worth of Human Life*. Cincinnati: n.p., 1865.

Angle, Paul M. *Bloody Williamson: A Chapter in American Lawlessness*. New York: Knopf, 1952.

Aron, Stephen. *How the West Was Lost: The Transformation of Kentucky from Daniel Boone to Henry Clary*. Baltimore: Johns Hopkins University Press, 1996.

Baring-Gould, William S., and Ceil Baring-Gould. *The Annotated Mother-Goose*. New York: Clarkson N. Potter, 1962.

Barnhart, Terry A. "'A Common Feeling': Regional Identity and Historical Consciousness in the Old Northwest, 1820–1860." *Michigan Historical Review* 29 (Spring 2003): 39–70.

———. "'Elegant and Useful Learning': The Antiquarian and Historical Society of Illinois." *Journal of the Illinois State Historical Society* 95 (Spring 2002): 7–32.

Barr, Daniel P., ed. *The Boundaries between Us: Natives and Newcomers along the Frontiers of the Old Northwest Territory, 1750–1789*. Kent, OH: Kent State University Press, 2006.

Batinski, Michael C. *Pastkeepers in a Small Place: Five Centuries in Deerfield, Massachusetts*. Amherst: University of Massachusetts Press, 2004.

Bearss, Edwin Cole. *The Campaign for Vicksburg*. 3 vols. Dayton, OH: Morningside, 1986.

Becker, Carl Lotus, *Everyman His Own Historian: Essays on History and Politics*. New York: F. S. Crofts, 1935.

Beres, Thomas E. *Power and Gender in Oneota Culture: A Study of a Late Prehistoric People*. DeKalb: Northern Illinois University Press, 2001.

Bieder, Robert E. *Science Encounters the Indian, 1820–1880: The Early Years of American Ethnology*. Norman: University of Oklahoma Press, 1986.

Billington, Ray A. *America's Frontier Heritage*. New York: Holt, Rinehart, and Winston, 1966.

Blackhawk, Ned. *Violence over the Land: Indians and Empires in the Early American West.* Cambridge, MA: Harvard University Press, 2006.

Blackmon, Douglas A. *Slavery by Another Name: The Re-Enslavement of Black Americans from the Civil War to World War II.* New York: Doubleday, 2008.

Blanchard, Mary Warner. *Oscar Wilde's America: Counterculture in the Gilded Age.* New Haven, CT: Yale University Press, 1998.

Blight, David W. *Beyond the Battlefield: Race, Memory, and the American Civil War.* Amherst: University of Massachusetts Press, 2012.

———. *Race and Reunion: The Civil War in American Memory.* Cambridge: Harvard University Press, 2001.

Boon, Benningsen. "Sketches of the Early Settlement of Jackson County, Ill." In Edmund Newsome, *Historical Sketches of Jackson County,* 25–75. Carbondale: Newsome Publisher, 1894.

Boorstin, Daniel J. *The Americans: The National Experience.* New York: Random House, 1965.

Bowes, John P. *Land Too Good for Indians: Northern Indian Removal.* Norman: University of Oklahoma Press, 2016.

Bradburn, Douglas. *The Citizenship Revolution: Politics and the Creation of the American Union.* Charlottesville: University of Virginia Press, 2009.

Brown, James A. "On the Identity of the Birdman within Mississippian Period Art and Iconography." In *Ancient Objects and Sacred Realms: Interpretations of Mississippian Iconography,* edited by Kent Reilly III and James F. Garber, 56–106. Austin: University of Texas Press, 2007.

———. "The Regional Culture Signature of the Braden Art Style." In *Visualizing the Sacred: Cosmic Visions, Regionalism, and the Art of the Mississippi World,* edited by George E. Lankford et al., 37–63. Austin: University of Texas Press, 2011.

Brown, Richard Maxwell. "Legal and Behavioral Perspectives on American Vigilantism," *Perspectives in American History* 5 (1971): 95–144.

Brush, Daniel Harmon. *Growing Up with Southern Illinois, 1820 to 1861.* Edited by Milo Milton Quaife. Chicago: Lakeside Press, 1944.

Bruckner, Martin. *The Geographic Revolution in Early America: Maps, Literacy, and National Identity.* Chapel Hill: University of North Carolina Press, 2006.

Buck, Paul H. *The Road to Reunion, 1865–1900.* Boston: Little Brown, 1937.

Calloway, Colin G. *One Vast Winter Count: The Native American West before Lewis and Clark.* Lincoln: University of Nebraska Press, 2003.

———. *The Shawnees and the War for America.* New York: Viking, 2007.

Calvin, Matthew J. *Toussaint Louverture and the American Civil War: The Promise and Peril of a Second Haitian Revolution.* Philadelphia: University of Pennsylvania Press, 2010.

Carwardine, Richard. *Lincoln: A Life of Purpose and Power.* New York: Vintage, 2003.

Cayton, Andrew R. L., and Susan E. Gray, eds. *The American Midwest: Essays on Regional History*. Bloomington: Indiana University Press, 2001.

Combined History of Randolph, Monroe, and Perry Counties, Illinois. Philadelphia: J. L. McDonough, 1883.

Combined History of Shelby and Moultrie Counties, Illinois. Philadelphia: J. L. McDonough, 1881.

Costa, David J. "Miami-Illinois and Shawnee: Culture-Hero and Trickster Stories." In *Algonquian Spirit: Contemporary Translations of the Algonquian Literatures of North America*, edited by Brian Swann, 292–319. Lincoln: University of Nebraska Press, 2005.

Costa, Dora L., and Matthew E. Kahn. *Heroes and Cowards: The Social Face of War*. Princeton, NJ: Princeton University Press, 2008.

Coyle, Randolph. *Report as to the Best and Cheapest Mode of Communication between the Coal Mines of the Mount Carbon Coal Company in Jackson County, Illinois, and the Mississippi River*. Washington, DC: J. T. Towers, 1851.

Dacus, J. A. *Annals of the Great Strikes in the United States*. St. Louis: Scammell, 1877.

Darby, William. *The Immigrant Guide to the Western and Southwestern States and Territories*. New York: Kirk and Mercein, 1818.

Davis, Hugh. *"We Will Be Satisfied with Nothing Less": The African American Struggle for Equal Rights in the North during Reconstruction*. Ithaca, NY: Cornell University Press, 2011.

Davis, James E. *Frontier Illinois*. Bloomington: Indiana University Press, 1998.

Dean, Eric T., Jr. *Shook over Hell: Post-traumatic Stress, Vietnam, and the Civil War*. Cambridge, MA: Harvard University Press, 1997.

Debates and Proceedings of the Constitutional Convention of the State of Illinois. 2 vols. Springfield, IL: E. El. Merritt, 1870.

Demos, John. *Circles and Lines: The Shape of Life in Early America*. Cambridge, MA: Harvard University Press, 2004.

DePastino, Todd. *Citizen Hobo: How a Century of Homelessness Shaped America*. Chicago: University of Chicago Press, 2003.

Dexter, Darrell. *Bondage in Egypt: Slavery in Southern Illinois*. Cape Girardeau, MO: Center for Regional History, 2011.

———. "Southern Illinois Responds to the Emancipation Proclamation: From Resistance to Celebration." Unpublished paper delivered at the Illinois History Symposium, Springfield, March 1, 2013.

Diaz-Granados, Carol, and James R. Duncan, eds. *The Rock-Art of Eastern North America: Capturing Images and Insight*. Tuscaloosa: University of Alabama Press, 2004.

Doctorman, Jo Ann Roberts, ed. *Letters from Home*. Carterville IL: Genealogical Society Southern Illinois, 1991.

Dolinar, Brian, ed. *The Negro in Illinois: The WPA Papers*. Urbana: University of Illinois Press, 2013.

Dorsey, J. Owen. "Osage Traditions." Smithsonian, *Annual Report Bureau of Ethnology (1888)*, 377–97.

Dowd, Gregory Evans. *War under Heaven: Pontiac, the Indian Nations, and the British Empire*. Baltimore: Johns Hopkins University Press, 2002.

Doyle, Don Harrison. *The Social Order of a Frontier Community: Jacksonville, Illinois, 1825–1870*. Urbana: University of Illinois Press, 1978.

Duncan, James R. "The Cosmology of the Osage: The Star People and their Universe." In *Visualizing the Sacred: Cosmic Visions, Regionalism, and the Art of the Mississippi World*, edited by George E. Lankford et al., 18–33. Austin: University of Texas Press, 2011.

DuVal, Kathleen. *The Native Ground: Indians and Colonists in the Heart of the Continent*. Philadelphia: University of Pennsylvania Press, 2006.

Ecelbarger, Gary. *Black Jack Logan: An Extraordinary Life in Peace and War*. Guilford, CT: Lyons, 2005.

Edmunds, R. David, ed. *Enduring Nations: Native Americans in the Midwest*. Urbana: University of Illinois Press, 2008.

Ekberg. Carl J. *French Roots in the Illinois Country: The Mississippi Frontier in Colonial Times*. Urbana: University of Illinois Press, 1998.

Eighth Census of the United States, 1860, Jackson County, Illinois. Murphysboro: Jackson County Historical Society, 1987.

Elliott, Isaac H., ed. *Record of the Services of Illinois Soldiers in the Black Hawk War, 1831–32, and in the Mexican War, 1846–48*. Springfield, IL: Journal Co., 1902.

Etcheson, Nicole. "Barbecued Kentuckians and Six-Foot Texas Rangers: The Construction of Midwestern Identity." In *The American Midwest: Essays on Regional History*, edited by Andrew R. L. Cayton and Susan E. Gray, 78–90. Bloomington: Indiana University Press, 2001.

Ethridge, Robbie. "Introduction: Mapping the Mississippi Shatter Zone." In *Mapping the Mississippi Shatter Zone: The Colonial Indian Slave Trade and Regional Instability in the American South*, edited by Robbie Ethridge and Sheri M. Shuck-Hall, 1–62. Lincoln: University of Nebraska Press, 2009.

Ethridge, Robbie, and Sheri M. Shuck-Hall, eds. *Mapping the Mississippi Shatter Zone: The Colonial Indian Slave Trade and Regional Instability in the American South*. Lincoln: University of Nebraska Press, 2009.

Faragher, John Mack. "'More Motley than Mackinaw': From Ethnic Mixing to Ethnic Cleansing on the Frontier of the Lower Mississippi, 1783–1833." In *Contact Points: American Frontiers from the Mohawk Valley to the Mississippi, 1750–1830*, edited by Andrew R. L. Cayton and Fredrika J. Teute, 304–26. Chapel Hill: University of North Carolina Press, 1998.

Faulkner, Charles H., ed. *Rock Art of the Eastern Woodlands*. American Rock Art Association, Occasional Papers (1996).

Faust, Drew Gilpin. *This Republic of Suffering: Death and the American Civil War*. New York: Knopf, 2008.

Feldman, Jay. *When the Mississippi Ran Backwards: Empire, Intrigue, Murder, and the New Madrid Earthquakes*. New York: Free Press, 2005.

Ferguson, Gillum. *Illinois in the War of 1812*. Urbana: University of Illinois Press, 2012.

Fishback, Woodson W. *A History of Murphysboro, Illinois, 1843–1982*. Murphysboro, IL: Jackson County Historical Society, 1982.

FitzGerald, Frances. *America Revised: History Schoolbooks in the Twentieth Century*. Boston: Little, Brown, 1979.

Fitzpatrick, Ellen. *History's Memory: Writing America's Past, 1880–1980*. Cambridge, MA: Harvard University Press, 2002.

Foos, Paul. *A Short, Offhand, Killing Affair: Soldiers and Social Conflict during the Mexican-American War*. Chapel Hill: University of North Carolina Press, 2002.

Foote, Shelby. *The Civil War: A Narrative*. 3 vols. New York: Random House, 1958–74.

Ford, Thomas. *History of Illinois*. Chicago: S. C. Griggs, 1854.

Fredrickson, George M. *White Supremacy: A Comparative Study of American and South African History*. New York: Oxford University Press, 1981.

French, George Hazen. *Life Retrospect of George Hazen French*. Rangoon: American Baptist Mission Press, 1936.

French, Chauncey Del. *Railroadman*. New York: Macmillan, 1938.

George, Charles B. *Forty Years on the Rail*. Chicago: R. R. Donnelley, 1887.

Gildehaus, Valerie Phillips, ed. *The Annotated 1850 U.S. Census of Jackson County, Illinois*. Murphysboro, IL: Murphysboro, 1998.

———. *Index to the 1870 U. S. Census, Jackson County, Illinois*. Murphysboro, IL: Jackson County Historical Society, 1996.

Gilroy, Paul. *The Black Atlantic: Modernity and Double Consciousness*. Cambridge: Harvard University Press, 1993.

Girardi, Robert I. "'I Am for the President's Proclamation Teeth and Toe Nails': Illinois Soldiers Respond to the Emancipation Proclamation." *Journal of the Illinois State Historical Society* 106 (Autumn–Winter 2013): 395–421.

Gray, Susan. *The Yankee West: Community Life on the Michigan Frontier*. Chapel Hill: University of North Carolina Press, 1996.

Gray, Susan E. "Stories Written in the Blood: Race and Midwestern History." In *The American Midwest: Essays on Regional History*, edited by Andrew R. L. Cayton and Susan E. Gray, 123–39. Bloomington: Indiana University Press, 2001.

Green, James. *Death in the Haymarket: A Story of Chicago, the First Labor Movement and the Bombing that Divided Gilded Age America.* New York: Pantheon, 2006.

Gregory, Dick, with Sheila P. Moses. *Callus on My Soul: A Memoir.* Atlanta: Longstreet Press, 2000.

Griffith, Mrs. Will. *Century of Progress, Carbondale, 1852–1952.* Carbondale, IL: Century of Progress Committee, [1952].

Gross, Jan T. *Neighbors: The Destruction of the Jewish Community in Jedwabne, Poland.* Princeton, NJ: Princeton University Press, 2001.

Gugliotta, Guy. "New Estimates Raise Civil War Death Toll." *New York Times,* April 2, 2012.

Gutman, Herbert G. *Work, Culture and Society in Industrializing America: Essays in American Working-Class and Social History.* New York: Knopf, 1976.

Hahn. Steven. *A Nation under Our Feet: Black Political Struggles in the Rural South from Slavery to the Great Migration.* Cambridge, MA: Harvard University Press, 2003.

Hall, James. *Legends of the West.* New York: G. P. Putnam, 1853.

———. *Letters from the West.* London: H. Colburn, 1828.

———. *Seven Stories.* Edited by Mary Burtschi. Vandalia, IL: Fayette County Bicentennial Commission, 1975.

———. *The Western Monthly Magazine.* Cincinnati: Taylor and Tracy, 1833.

Higbie, Frank Tobias. *Indispensable Outcasts: Hobo Workers and Community in the American Midwest, 1880–1930.* Urbana: University of Illinois Press, 2003.

Hinderaker, Eric. *Elusive Empires: Constructing Colonialism in the Ohio Valley, 1673–1800.* New York: Cambridge University Press, 1997.

———. "Liberating Contrivances: Narrative and Identity in Midwestern Histories." In *The American Midwest: Essays on Regional History,* edited by Andrew R. L. Cayton and Susan E. Gray, 46–68. Bloomington: Indiana University Press, 2001.

History and Memory.

History of Fayette County, Illinois. Philadelphia: J. L. McDonough, 1878.

History of Jackson County, Illinois. Philadelphia: J. L. McDonough, 1878.

History of Macoupin County, Illinois. Philadelphia: J. L. McDonough, 1879.

History of Marion and Clinton Counties, Illinois. Philadelphia: J. L. McDonough, 1881.

History of Washington County, Illinois. Philadelphia: J. L. McDonough, 1879.

Hobsbawm, Eric, and Terence Ranger, eds. *The Invention of Tradition.* Cambridge: Cambridge University Press, 1983.

Hofstadter, Richard. *The American Political Tradition and the Men Who Made It.* New York: Knopf, 1948.

Hofstadter, Richard, and Michael David Wallace, eds. *American Violence: A Documentary History.* New York: Knopf, 1970.

Horsman, Reginald. *Race and Manifest Destiny: The Origins of American Racial Anglo-Saxonism.* Cambridge, MA: Harvard University Press, 1981.

How 'Tis Done: A Thorough Ventilation of the Numerous Schemes Conducted by Wandering Canvassers Together with the Various Advertising Dodges for the Swindling of the Public. Chicago: n.p., 1879.

Husband, Will W. *Old Brownsville Days: An Historical Sketch of Early Times in Jackson County.* Murphysboro, IL: Jackson County Historical Society, 1973.

Hulbert, Matthew Christopher. *The Ghosts of Guerrilla Memory: How Civil War Bushwhackers Became Gunslingers in the American West.* Athens: University of Georgia Press, 2016.

Illinois Appellate Courts. *Reports of Cases Decided in the Appellate Courts.* Chicago: Callaghan, 1896–1907.

Illinois Board of Arbitration. *Fifth Annual Report.* Springfield: State Printer, 1900.

Illinois Bureau of Labor Statistics. *Seventeenth Annual Report of the State Bureau of Labor Statistics Concerning Coal in Illinois.* Springfield: The Bureau, 1899.

———. *Annual Coal Report of the State Illinois, 1907.* Springfield: State Printers, 1908.

Illinois Central Railroad Company. *Vicksburg for the Tourist.* [Chicago]: n.p., 1913.

Illinois Railroad and Warehouse Commission. *Thirty-Third Annual Report.* Springfield: State Printers, 1904.

Illinois Supreme Court. *Reports of Cases at Law and in Chancery argued and determined in the Supreme Court of Illinois.* Bloomington: Pentagraph Printing, 1903–7.

Illinois-Vicksburg Military Park Commission. *Illinois at Vicksburg.* Chicago: Illinois-Vicksburg Military Park Commission, 1907.

Jackson County Historical Society. *Jackson County, Illinois: Formation and Early Settlement.* Murphysboro, IL: Jackson County Historical Society, 1983.

———. *Military Census and Military Rolls, 1862–1863, Jackson County Illinois.* Murphysboro, IL: Jackson County Historical Society, 1990.

———. *Eighth Census of the United States.* Murphysboro, IL: Jackson County Historical Society, 1987.

Jaspin, Elliott. *Buried in the Bitter Waters: The Hidden History of Racial Cleansing in America.* New York: Basic Books, 2007.

Jefferson, Thomas. *Papers of Thomas Jefferson.* Edited by Julian P. Boyd. Princeton, NJ: Princeton University Press, 1950–.

———. *Writings.* Edited by Merrill D. Peterson. New York: Library of America, 1984.

Jennings, Francis. *The Creation of America: Through Revolution to Empire.* New York: Cambridge University Press, 2000.

Joens, David A. *From Slave to State legislator: John W. E. Thomas, Illinois' First African American Lawmaker.* Carbondale: Southern Illinois University Press, 2012.

Jones, James P. *"Black Jack": John A. Logan and Southern Illinois in the Civil War Era*. Tallahassee: University Press of Florida, 1967.

———. *John A. Logan: Stalwart Republican from Illinois*. Tallahassee: University Press of Florida, 1982.

Jones, Johnetta L. "Negroes in Jackson County, 1850–1910." MA thesis, Southern Illinois University Carbondale, 1971.

Jones, P. M., et al. "Forgotten Soldiers: Murphysboro's African-American Civil War Veterans" Murphysboro, IL: The Class, 1994.

Jones, Tina Cahalan. "Runaways and Resistance against Slavery in Williamson County." From Slaves to Soldiers and Beyond—Williamson County, Tennessee's African American History, May 2, 2018, http://usctwillcotn.blogspot .com/2018/05/runaways-and-resistance-against-slavery.html.

Jordan, Winthrop D. *White over Black: American Attitudes toward the Negro, 1550–1812*. Chapel Hill: University of North Carolina Press, 1968.

Journal of the Southern Illinois Historical Society, 1944–1951.

Judt, Tony. *Ill Fares the Land*. New York: Penguin, 2010.

Kammen, Michael. *Mystic Chords of Memory: The Transformation of Tradition in American Culture*. New York: Knopf, 1991.

Kapller, Charles J., ed. *Indian Affairs: Laws and Treaties*. 7 vols. Washington, DC: Government Printing Office, 1904.

Kukla, Jon. *A Wilderness so Immense: The Louisiana Purchase and the Destiny of America*. New York: Anchor Books, 2003.

Kusmer, Kenneth L. *Down and Out, On the Road*. New York: Oxford University Press, 2002.

La Flesche, Francis. "The Osage Tribe: Rite of the Chiefs; Sayings of the Ancient Men." Smithsonian, *Annual Report Bureau of Ethnology* (1921), 157–85.

Lankford, George E. "The Great Serpent in Eastern North America." In *Ancient Objects and Sacred Realms: Interpretations of Mississippian Iconography*, edited by Kent Reilly III and James F. Garber, 107–35. Austin: University of Texas Press, 2007.

———. "The 'Path of Souls': Some Death Imagery in the Southeastern Ceremonial Complex." In *Ancient Objects and Sacred Realms: Interpretations of Mississippian Iconography*, edited by Kent Reilly III and James F. Garber, 174–212. Austin: University of Texas Press, 2007.

Lankford, George E., et al., eds. *Visualizing the Sacred: Cosmic Visions, Regionalism, and the Art of the Mississippi World*. Austin: University of Texas Press, 2011.

Lansden, John M. *A History of the City of Cairo, Illinois*. Chicago: R. R. Donnelly, 1910.

Larson, Lauritz. "Pigs in Space; or, What Shapes America's Regional Cultures?" In *The American Midwest: Essays on Regional History*, edited by Andrew R. L. Cayton and Susan E. Gray, 69–77. Bloomington: Indiana University Press, 2001.

Lears, Jackson. *Rebirth of a Nation: The Making of Modern America, 1877–1920.* New York: HarperCollins, 2009.

Leichtle, Kurt E., and Bruce G. Carveth. *Crusade against Slavery: Edward Coles, Pioneer of Freedom.* Carbondale: Southern Illinois University Press, 2011.

Levine, Lawrence W. *Black Culture and Black Consciousness: Afro-American Folk Thought from Slavery to Freedom.* New York: Oxford University Press, 1977.

Lewis, Malcom G., ed. *Cartographic Encounters: Perspectives on Native American Mapmaking and Map Use.* Chicago: University of Chicago Press, 1998.

Lightner, David L. "Construction Labor on the Illinois Central Railroad." *Journal of the Illinois State Historical Society* 66 (Spring 1973): 285–301.

———. *Labor on the Illinois Central Railroad, 1852–1900.* New York: Arno Press, 1977.

Linklater, Andro. *Measuring America: How an Untamed Wilderness Shaped the United States and Fulfilled the Promise of Democracy.* New York: Walker and Co., 2002.

Livingston, Leva, and Florence Tait et al. *Pyle Family History, 1594–1954.* N.p.: H. Pyle, [1955].

Loewen, James W. *Sundown Towns: A Hidden Dimension of American Racism.* New York: New Press, 2005.

Lowenthal, David, *The Past Is a Foreign Country.* Cambridge: Cambridge University Press, 1985.

Macklin, Melvin LeRoy Green. *Generations: A Pictorial Review of African Americans in Carbondale, Illinois.* Dallas: Ingenuity Press, [2004].

———. *The Legacy of Attucks and Black Institutions in the Northeast Carbondale Community.* Dallas: Ingenuity Press, 2004.

———. *Traces in the Dust: Carbondale's Black Heritage, 1852–1964.* Magnolia, TX: Ingenuity Press, 2001.

Mahoney, Timothy R. *Provincial Lives: Middle-Class Experience in the Antebellum Middle West.* New York: Cambridge University Press, 1999.

Manning, Chandra. *What This Cruel War Was Over: Soldiers, Slavery, and the Civil War.* New York: Knopf, 2007.

Map of Jackson County, Illinois. Olney, IL: J. B. Westbrook, 1874.

Marshall, John A. *American Bastille: A History of the Illegal Arrests and Imprisonment of American Citizens in the Northern and Border States on Account of Their Political Opinions during the Late Civil War.* Philadelphia: Thomas W. Hartley, 1882.

Marten, James. *Sing Not War: The Lives of Union and Confederate Veterans in Gilded Age America.* Chapel Hill: University of North Carolina Press, 2011.

Masthay, Carl, ed. *Kaskaskia Illinois-to-French Dictionary.* St. Louis: C. Masthay, 2002.

Maycock, Susan E. *An Architectural History of Carbondale, Illinois.* Carbondale: Southern Illinois University Press, 1983.

Mazrim, Robert. *The Sangamo Frontier: History and Archaeology in the Shadow of Lincoln.* Chicago: University of Chicago Press, 2007.

McAdams, William. *Records of Ancient Races in the Mississippi Valley.* St. Louis: C. R. Barns, 1887.

McCorvie, Mary R. "Archaeological Griots: An Environmental History Program at Miller Grove, a Free Ante-Bellum African American Community in Southern Illinois." *African Diaspora Archaeology Newsletter,* December 2005.

McCaffrey, James M. *Army of Manifest Destiny: The American Soldier in the Mexican War, 1846–1848.* New York: New York University Press, 1992.

McConnell, Stuart. *Glorious Contentment: The Grand Army of the Republic, 1865–1900.* Chapel Hill: University of North Carolina Press, 1992.

McCoo, Edward J. *Ethiopia at the Bar of Justice.* In *Plays and Pageants from the Life of the Negro,* edited by Willis Richardson. Washington, DC: Associated Publishers, 1930.

McCullough, Arthur P. *For Honor and Union.* Edited by George Thomas McCullough. N.p.: Private press, 2012.

McIntyre, George P. *The Light of Persia or the Death of Mammon and Other Poems of Prophecy, Profit, and Peace.* Chicago: Wage Workers' Press, 1890.

Michno, Gregory, and Susan Michno. *A Fate Worse Than Death: Indian Captivities in the West, 1830–1885.* Caldwell, ID: Caxton Press, 2007.

Mills, C. Wright. *The Power Elite.* New York: Oxford University Press, 1956.

Mitchell, Betty, ed. *100 Years: The Woman's Club of Carbondale, 1896–1996.* Carbondale, IL: [The Club], 1996.

Morgan, M. J. *Land of Big Rivers: French and Indian Illinois, 1699–1778.* Carbondale: Southern Illinois University Press, 2010.

Morris, W. S., et al. *History: 31st Regiment Illinois Volunteers; Organized by John A. Logan.* [Evansville, IN: Keller Printing and Publishing Co.], 1902.

Morrissey, Robert Michael. *Empire by Collaboration: Indians, Colonists, and Governments in Colonial Illinois Country.* Philadelphia: University of Pennsylvania Press, 2015.

Moyers, William Nelson. "A Story of Southern Illinois, the Soldiers' Reservation, Including the Indians, French Traders, and Some Early Americans." *Journal of the Illinois State Historical Society* 24 (April 1931): 26–104.

Muzzey, David Saville. *A History of Our Country.* Boston: Ginn, 1955.

Nabokov, Peter. *A Forest of Time: American Indian Ways of History.* New York: Cambridge University Press, 2002.

Nelson, Cary. *Revolutionary Memory: Recovering the Poetry of the American Left.* New York: Routledge, 2001.

Newsome, Edmund. *Experience in the War of the Great Rebellion by a Soldier of the Eighty First Regiment Illinois Volunteer Infantry.* Carbondale, IL: Newsome Publisher, 1880.

———. *Historical Sketches of Jackson County. . . .* Carbondale, IL: Newsome Publisher, 1894.

Nora, Pierre, ed. *Realms of Memory: Rethinking the French Past.* Translated by Arthur Goldhammer. New York: Columbia University Press, 1996.

Obelisk. Southern Illinois University Carbondale, 1930–48.

Onuf, Peter S. *Jefferson's Empire: The Language of American Nationhood.* Charlottesville: University of Virginia Press, 2000.

———. *Statehood and Union: A History of the Northwest Ordinance.* Bloomington: University of Indiana Press, 1987.

Owens, Robert M. "Jean Baptiste Ducoigne, the Kaskaskia, and the Limits of Thomas Jefferson's Friendship." *Journal of Illinois History* 3 (Summer, 2002): 109–36.

———. *Mr. Jefferson's Hammer: William Henry Harrison and the Origins of American Indian Policy.* Norman: University of Oklahoma Press, 2007.

Paludan, Phillip Shaw. *"A People's Contest": The Union and the Civil War, 1861–1865.* New York: Harper & Row, 1988.

Patterson, Orlando. *Rituals of Blood: Consequences of Slavery in Two American Centuries.* New York: Civitas, 1986.

Patterson Robert W. *Early Society in Southern Illinois.* Chicago: Fergus, 1881.

Pauketat, Timothy R. *The Ascent of Chiefs: Cahokia and Mississippian Politics in Native North America.* Tuscaloosa: University of Alabama Press, 1994.

Perdu, Theda, and Michael D. Green. *The Cherokee Nation and the Trail of Tears.* New York: Viking, 2007.

Perkins, Elizabeth A. *Border Life: Experience and Memory in the Revolutionary Ohio Valley.* Chapel Hill: University of North Carolina Press, 1998.

Pfeifer, Michael J. ed. *Lynching beyond Dixie: American Mob Violence Outside the South.* Urbana: University of Illinois Press, 2013.

Phillips, Christopher. *The Rivers Ran Backward: The Civil War and the Remaking of the American Middle Border.* New York: Oxford University Press, 2016.

Pizarro, Judith, Roxanne Cohen, and JoAnn Prause. "Physical and Mental Health Costs of Traumatic War Experiences among Civil War Veterans." *JAMA Psychiatry* 63 (February 2006): 193–200.

Pocock, J. G. A. *The Machiavellian Moment: Florentine Political Thought and the Atlantic Republican Tradition.* Princeton, NJ: Princeton University Press, 1975.

Prince Hall Grand Lodge. *Proceedings of the Forty-Third Annual Communications of the Most Worshipful Prince Hall Grand Lodge.* Chicago: n.p., 1909.

Radin, Paul. "Winnebago Hero Cycles: A Study in Aboriginal Literature." *International Journal of American Linguistics* 14 (July 1948): 123–32.

Reilly, Kent, III. "The Petaloid Motif: A Celestial Symbolic Locative in the Shell Art of Spiro." In *Ancient Objects and Sacred Realms: Interpretations of Mississippian Iconography*, edited by Kent Reilly III and James F. Garber, 39–55. Austin: University of Texas Press, 2007.

Reilly, Kent, III, and James F. Garber, eds. *Ancient Objects and Sacred Realms: Interpretations of Mississippian Iconography*. Austin: University of Texas Press, 2007.

Ress, David. *Governor Edward Coles and the Vote to Forbid Slavery in Illinois, 1823–1824*. Jefferson, NC: McFarland, 2006.

Reynolds, John. *The Pioneer History of Illinois: Containing the Discovery, in 1673, and the History of the Country to the Year Eighteen Hundred and Eighteen, When the State Government Was Organized*. Chicago: Fergus, 1887 [1852].

Rice, Alan. *Creating Memorials, Building Identities: The Politics of Memory in the Black Atlantic*. Liverpool: Liverpool University Press, 2010.

Roediger, David. *Seizing Freedom: Slave Emancipation and Liberty for All*. London: Verso, 2015.

Rose, James A., ed. *Blue Book of the State of Illinois, 1905–1906*. Springfield, IL: Secretary of State, 1906.

Rugh, Susan Sessions. *Our Common Country: Family Farming, Culture, and Community in the Nineteenth-Century Midwest*. Bloomington: Indiana University Press, 2001.

Russo, David J. *American Towns: An Interpretive History*. Chicago: Ivan R. Dee, 2001.

———. *Keepers of Our Past: Local Historical Writing in the United States, 1820s–1930s*. New York: Greenwood, 1988.

Salafia, Matthew. *Slavery's Borderland: Freedom and Bondage along the Ohio River*. Philadelphia: University of Pennsylvania Press, 2013.

Samuel, Raphael. *Theatres of Memory*. Vol 1: *Past and Present in Contemporary Culture*. London: Verso, 1994.

Sandburg, Carl. *Complete Poems*. New York: Harcourt, Brace, 1950.

Sayre, Gordon. "The Mound Builders and the Imagination of American Antiquity in Jefferson, Bartram, and Chateaubriand." *Early American Literature* 33 (Winter 1998): 225–49.

Schoolcraft, Henry. *Travels in the Central Portions of the Mississippi Valley*. New York: Collins and Hannay, 1825.

Seelye, John. *Memory's Nation: The Place of Plymouth Rock*. Chapel Hill: University of North Carolina Press, 1998.

Shackelford, Alan G. "The Frontier in Pre-Columbian Illinois." *Journal of the Illinois State Historical Society* 100 (Fall 2007): 182–206.

———. "The Illinois Indians in the Confluence Region: Adaptation in a Changing World." In *Enduring Nations: Native Americans in the Midwest*, edited by David R. Edmunds, 15–35. Urbana: University of Illinois Press, 2008.

———. "On a Crossroads: American Indian Prehistory and History in the Confluence Region." PhD diss., Indiana University, 2004.

Sheehan, Bernard W. *Seeds of Extinction: Jeffersonian Philanthropy and the American Indian.* Chapel Hill: University of North Carolina Press, 1973.

Silver, Peter. *Our Savage Neighbors: How Indian War Transformed Early America.* New York: Norton, 2008.

Silverberg, Robert. *Mound Builders of Ancient America: The Archaeology of a Myth.* Greenwich, CT: New York Graphic Society, 1968.

Simeone, James. *Democracy and Slavery in Frontier Illinois.* DeKalb: Northern Illinois University Press, 2000.

Sinks, John D., ed. "List of Pensioners on the Roll, January 1, 1883." *Saga of Southern Illinois* 4 (Fall 1977): 46–51.

Slaughter, Thomas P. *The Whiskey Rebellion: Frontier Epilogue to the American Revolution.* New York: Oxford University Press, 1986.

Slotkin, Richard. *Regeneration through Violence: The Mythology of the American Frontier.* Middleton, CT: Wesleyan University Press, 1973.

Slyomovics, Susan. *The Object of Memory: Arab and Jew Narrate the Palestinian Village.* Philadelphia: University of Pennsylvania Press, 1998.

Smith, George Washington. *A History of Southern Illinois.* 3 vols. Chicago: Lewis Publishing, 1912.

Smith, Grace Partridge. "Negro Lore in Southern Illinois." *Midwest Folklore* 2 (Fall 1952): 159–62.

Smith-Rosenberg, Carrol. *This Violent Empire: The Birth of an American National Identity.* Chapel Hill: University of North Carolina Press, 2010.

Smithsonian Institution. *Annual Report of the Board of Regents of the Smithsonian Institution.* Washington, DC: Government Printing Office, 1883.

———. *Annual Report Bureau of Ethnology.* Washington, DC: Government Printing Office, 1888–1921.

Sneed, Glenn J. *Ghost Towns of Southern Illinois.* Royalton, IL: Glenn J. Sneed, 1977.

Southern Illinois Normal University. *Catalogue.* Carbondale: Southern Illinoisan, 1894–1936.

Spahn, Betty, and Raymond Spahn. "Wesley Raymond Brink, History Huckster." *Journal of the Illinois State Historical Society* 58 (Summer 1965): 117–38.

Stalls, Madlyn. "A History of African Americans at Southern Illinois University at Carbondale, 1915–1987." PhD diss., Southern Illinois University Carbondale, 1990.

Standard Atlas of Jackson County. Chicago: G. A. Ogle, 1907.

Stowell, David O., ed. *The Great Strikes of 1877.* Urbana: University of Illinois Press, 2008.

———. *Streets, Railroads, and the Great Strike of 1877.* Chicago: University of Chicago Press, 1992.

Sugrue, Thomas J. *Sweet Land of Liberty: The Forgotten Struggle of Civil Rights in the North*. New York: Random House, 2008.

Swann, Brian, ed. *Algonquian Spirit: Contemporary Translations of the Algonquian Literatures of North America*. Lincoln: University of Nebraska Press, 2005.

Thernstrom, Stephen. *The Other Bostonians: Poverty and Progress in the American Metropolis, 1880–1970*. Cambridge: Harvard University Press, 1973.

Thomas, Cyrus. *Catalogue of Prehistoric Works East of the Rocky Mountains*. Washington, DC: Government Printing Office, 1891.

———. "Report on the Mound Explorations of the Bureau of Ethnology." In *Twelfth Annual Report of the Bureau of Ethnology to the Secretary of the Smithsonian Institution*. Washington, DC: Government Printing Office, 1894.

———. "Sixth Report of the State Entomologist . . . on the Noxious and Beneficial Insects of the State of Illinois." In *Transactions of the Department of Agriculture of the State of Illinois*, 4–15. Springfield: s.n., 1878.

Tow, Michael. "Secrecy and Segregation: Murphysboro's Black Social Organizations, 1865–1925." *Journal of the Illinois State Historical Society* 97 (Spring 2004): 27–40.

Towne, Stephen E. *Surveillance and Spies in the Civil War: Exposing Confederate Conspiracies in America's Heartland*. Athens: Ohio University Press, 2015.

Townsend, Richard F., ed. *Hero, Hawk, and Open Hand: American Indian Art of the Ancient Midwest and South*. New Haven, CT: Yale University Press, 2004.

Trask, Kerry A. *Black Hawk: The Battle for the Heart of America*. New York: Henry Holt, 2006.

Trouillot, Michel-Rolph. *Silencing the Past: Power and the Production of History*. Boston: Beacon Press, 1995.

Ulrich, Laurel Thacher. *The Age of Homespun: Objects and Stories in the Creation of an American Myth*. New York: Knopf, 2001.

United States. *Official Records of the War of the Rebellion*. Ser. I. Washington, DC: Government Printing Office, 1880–1901.

US House of Representatives, *Journal* 15. Washington, DC: Duff Green, 1830.

Usner, David H., Jr., *Indians, Settlers, and Slaves in a Frontier Exchange Economy: The Lower Mississippi Valley before 1783*. Chapel Hill: University of North Carolina Press, 1992.

Volkmann, Carl. "Illinois Civil War Monuments and Memorials." *Illinois Heritage* 15 (November–December 2011): 18–21.

Wagner, Mark J. *The Archaeology and Rock Art of the Piney Creek Ravine, Jackson and Randolph Counties, Illinois*. Champaign: Illinois Transportation Archaeological Research Program, 2002.

———. *An Archaeological Survey of Fountain Bluff, Jackson County, Illinois*. Carbondale, IL: American Resources Group, 1990.

———. "Written in Stone: An Overview of the Rock Art of Illinois." In *Rock Art of the Eastern Woodlands*, edited by Charles H. Faulkner, 47–79. American Rock Art Association, Occasional Papers (1996).

Wagner, Mark J., Mary R. McCorvie, and Charles A Swedlund. "Mississippian Cosmology and Rock-Art at the Millstone Bluff Site, Illinois." In *The Rock-Art of Eastern North America: Capturing Images and Insight*, edited by Carol Diaz-Granados and James R. Duncan, 40–64. Tuscaloosa, University of Alabama Press, 2004.

Waldrep, Christopher. *Vicksburg's Long Shadow: The Civil War Legacy of Race and Remembrance*. Lanham, MD: Roman & Littlefield, 2005.

Ward, Andrew. *The Slaves' War: The Civil War in the Words of Former Slaves.* New York: Houghton Mifflin, 2009.

Warhus, Mark. *Another America: Native American Maps and the History of Our Land*. New York: St. Martins, 1997.

Watts, Edward. *An American Colony: Regionalism and the Roots of Midwestern Culture*. Athens: Ohio University Press, 2002.

Weber, Jennifer L. *Copperheads: The Rise and Fall of Lincoln's Opponents in the North*. New York: Oxford University Press, 2006.

Whitney, Ellen M., ed. *The Black Hawk War, 1831–32, Collections of the Illinois State Historical Library* 35 (1970).

Wiebe, Robert H. *The Search for Order, 1877–1920*. New York: Hill and Wang, 1967.

Williams, Kidada E. *They Left Great Marks on Me: African American Testimonies of Racial Violence from Emancipation to World War I*. New York: New York University Press, 2012.

Woodruff, Nan Elizabeth. *American Congo: The African-American Freedom Struggle in the Delta*. Cambridge, MA: Harvard University Press, 2003.

Woman's Club of Carbondale. *Carbondale Remembered*. Carbondale: Woman's Club, 1975.

Woodward, C. Vann. *Origins of the New South, 1877–1913*. Baton Rouge: Louisiana State University Press, 1951.

Wright, Henry T., ed. *Laws and Ordinances Governing the City of Carbondale*. Carbondale: Observer Printing, 1874.

Wright, John W. D. *A History of Early Carbondale, Illinois, 1852–1905*. Carbondale: Southern Illinois University Press, 1977.

Theses and Dissertations

Jones, Johnetta L. "Negroes in Jackson County, 1850–1910." MA thesis, Southern Illinois University Carbondale, 1971.

Shackelford, Alan G. "On a Crossroads: American Indian Prehistory and History in the Confluence Region." PhD diss., Indiana University, 2004.

Stalls, Madlyn. "A History of African Americans at Southern Illinois University at Carbondale, 1915–1987." PhD diss., Southern Illinois University Carbondale, 1990.

Weight, Donovan Stoddard. "'Come Recently from Guinea': Control and Power in the African-Descended Illinois Country, 1719–1848." PhD diss., Southern Illinois University Carbondale, 2010.

Internet Sources

Jones, Tina Cahalan. "Runaways and Resistance against Slavery in Williamson County." From Slaves to Soldiers and Beyond—Williamson County, Tennessee's African American History, May 2, 2018, http://usctwillcotn.blogspot.com/2018/05/runaways-and-resistance-against-slavery.html.

United States National Park Service. "Soldiers and Sailors Database." http://www.nps.gov/civilwar/soldiers-and-sailors-database.

INDEX

railroads, 111, 120, 122, 123, 126–27, 138, 144–45, 148, 149. *See also* Illinois Central Railroad
Randolph, A. Philip, 177
Red Corn, 13
Reed's Creek, 51
Reese, Altisadora, 81
Reese, John, 81, 86; on black Americans, 82, 93, 94, 97; Civil War, 83, 84–86; Civil War trauma, 90–91; family, 82–84
Reynolds, John, 48, 65
Richards, Thomas, 79
Roberts Hotel, 175
Robertson, Joe, 143
Rogers, William, 114
Roosevelt, Eleanor, 178, 179
Roosevelt, Franklin D., 178, 192
Ross, Martin, 113

Sandburg, Carl, 197
Sand Ridge, Illinois, 25, 26, 27, 28, 35, 56, 61
Schmidgall, John L., 132
Schoolcraft, Henry, 11
Schwartz, William, 154
"Scotchtown," 60
Sczerkowsky, Charles, 55
Sczerkowsky, Gottwald, 55
Shawnee Indians, 33, 34, 35, 63
Shepherd, Forrest, 140
Shryock, Jessie, 144
Silas, Eura, 155
Silas, John, 155
Simon, Jeanether, 184–85
Simon, Lit, 185
Sims, Henry, 171
Sisney, George, 164
slavery, 56; attitudes, 46–47, 69–70, 80. *See also* Boon, William; Brush, Daniel; Coles, Edward; Jefferson,

Thomas; Logan, John, Dr.; Logan, John A.
Smith, Bessie, 144
Smith, George Washington, 102; on American Indians, 22, 130; on black Americans, 102, 130; on labor, 131; on race, 131; on resources, 131–32; pastkeeper, 130–33, 136, 139, 140
Smith, Grace Partridge, 198
Smith, Lamar, 186
Smith, William, 171
Southern Illinois University, 22–23, 102, 129, 133, 175, 178, 179, 181–83, 188, 197, 198
Springfield, Illinois, race riot, 171
Squier, Ephraim, 11
St. James, Warren, 179, 181, 182–83, 184
St. Louis Iron Mountain and Southern Railway Company, 140
St. Louis Ore and Steel Company, 140
Stoddard, James, 141
Stoddard, Violet, 141
Stone, Joe, 83
Stratton, Samuel, 92

Tappan, John, 140
Tecumseh, 34, 35
Tenney, Charles, 184, 192
Thomas, Cyrus, 8, 11, 13, 113
Thompson, James B., 140
Thornton, Elnora, 155
Thornton, Robert, 155
Till, Emmett, 185–87
Till, Mamie, 186–87
Trail of Tears, 66–67
Truman, Harry, 178
Turley, Lenus, 194
Tuscan Lodge (African American Masons), 187

Tyner, Ann Eliza, 61, 66
Tyner, Joshua, 61, 66
Tyner, Joshua, Jr., 61, 66–67
Tyner family, 66–67

United Mine Workers, 149, 150

Vardaman, James, 102, 171
Varsity Theater (Carbondale, Illinois), 178, 181
Vergennes, Illinois, 164
Vicksburg campaign, 83, 84–86, 160; pastkeeping, 101–3
Villard, O. G., 173
violence, 53, 60–65, 69, 164–69, 172, 175. *See also* lynching
Vogel, Henry, 7

Walker, Benjamin, 54
Walkup, Harry, 138, 155
Ward, Chapman, 80
Wa-tse-mon-be, 23
Weaver, William, 165
Weingarner, Robert, 180, 181
White, Alexander, 172, 173
white pastkeeping, 133, 136, 137, 159, 199; on American Indians, 9–10, 12, 22–23, 26, 27, 38–39, 65–66, 70; on black Americans, 94–96, 99, 121–22, 171, 175, 179–80, 182, 183–84, 186–89, 192, 195, 198;

on business, 123, 139; Civil War, 74–75, 78, 80, 91–92, 99–100, 103; on labor, 122–23; post-Civil War, 108–13, 139–41, 153–54, 156–58, 163, 165–69, 171, 187–88; pre-Civil War, Illinois, 42–46, 52–53, 60–65. *See also* forgetting
Wiley, Benjamin, 79, 81
Wiley, Emily, 79
Will, Conrad, 45–46, 55–56, 59, 65, 68
Williams, Jeremiah ("Jerry the Bootblack"), 92
Williams, Jerry, 161
Williams, John, 161
Williams, Joseph, 61
Williams, Nathaniel, 161
Williams, Reuben, 161
Williams family, 162
Willis, Susannah, 141
Willoughby, John, 155
Winnebago Indians, 12–13, 18, 65
Woodlawn Cemetery, 73, 188
Woods, Edward, 92
Woods, Jerry, 92
Worthen, Elias, 88
Worthen, Isham, 81
Worthen, Richard, 59
Worthen, William, 59

Yates, Richard, 78

MICHAEL C. BATINSKI taught history at Southern Illinois University Carbondale. After writing two books on early American politics, he turned to local historical consciousness. That project led to the writing of a first book on pastkeeping in Deerfield, Massachusetts, covering five centuries, which in turn drew him to Illinois and Jackson County. He is beginning a study of radical consciousness in American history.

 *A Shawnee Book*

Also available in this series . . .